Praise for Jaiya John's
Black Baby White Hands

"I had to remind myself that this was life itself, and not a novel. This is a story for every family."

—Virgil H. Adams, III, PhD, Professor of Psychology
University of Kansas

"Nearly a century after DuBois' *The Souls of Black Folk,* and fifty years after Ellison's *Invisible Man,* this book takes us a similar leap forward. John poignantly elucidates the significance of race and culture in transracial adoptions."

—Leonard G. Dunston, MSW, President Emeritus
National Association of Black Social Workers, Inc.

"One of the few books to examine transracial adoption from a balanced perspective and to make a strong case for considering culture in placement decisions. It should be read by all adoptive parents, caseworkers, agency heads, policymakers, and groups concerned about the best interests of children of color in foster care."

—Robert B. Hill, PhD, sociologist and author
of *The Strengths of Black Families*

"One senses that writing this book was both a painful and empowering experience for Dr. Jaiya John, and one he could not avoid. We are all richer for his willingness to confront this major American dilemma. He has given us a truly beautiful account that is must reading for social scientists, parents, and caring people everywhere."

—Camara Jules P. Harrell, PhD
author of *Manichean Psychology*

"*Riveting.* John has given all of us a gift that will grow through the years. Read this book."

—Sharon L. McDaniel, EdD, Founder, President & CEO
A Second Chance, Inc.

"**Ingenious**. This experienced voice from the cradle can't be ignored. A must read for professionals in adoption and foster care. A challenging yet affirming voice for children who are placed transracially."

—Gloria King, MS, Executive Director
Black Adoption Placement and Research Center

"This is where theory meets practice. Our clients deserve the benefit of this enlightened perspective. Experience it and be moved."

—Yakiciwey Washington, MSW, Executive Director
YIP Family Services

"A moving and emotional journey of love, truth, confrontation, and respect—a must read for social workers, adoptive parents, adoptees, and anyone who thinks they have an opinion about transracial adoption."

—Toni Oliver, MSW, Founder & Executive Director
ROOTS Adoption Agency

"Race, culture, identity, family—the full spectrum of the human social rainbow is written here in words that will be among those taking our society to its next necessary evolution."

—Zena Oglesby, Jr., MSW, Founder & Executive Director
Institute for Black Parenting

"Countless books have been written about this nation's black-white relations. But few touch the truly human side of the "American dilemma"—especially the emerging issues of identity in cross-racial families. Here is a beautifully written and disarmingly honest account of this unexplored territory by a man who has lived it. Highly recommended for those who wish to look to a better racial future for our country."

—Thomas F. Pettigrew, PhD, race relations expert and author
of over 300 publications and 10 books spanning 44 years

Black Baby
White Hands

A View from the Crib

Jaiya John

Soul Water Rising

SILVER SPRING, MARYLAND

Printed in the United States of America

Soul Water Rising
Silver Spring, Maryland
http://www.soulwaterrising.com

Library of Congress Control Number: 2005903107
ISBN 978-0-9713308-1-8

Second Edition, May 2005
FIRST SOUL WATER RISING EDITION: 2002

Memoir—African American—Adoption

Silent Reunion reprinted with permission of Mary E. Woods
Copyright © 1983 by Mary E. Woods.

Co-Chief Editor: Charlene R. Maxwell
Co-Chief Editor: Jacqueline V. Richmond
Cover design: Eric Gann & Niambi Jaha
Interior art design: R. Eric Stone
Soul Water logo: R. Eric Stone

Not to know is bad.
Not to wish to know is worse.

—Nigerian Proverb

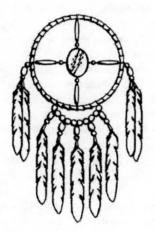

Honor & Gratitude

This is who I am . . .

My Great Spirit God and Creator•Jordan Jhala•Rudolf & Betty Danz•Harold Potter & Marie Koss Potter Warsaw•Boss Jenkins & Rose Lee Adams•Alberta & Joseph Woods•Mary & Willie Hyatt•Mom & Dad•Mary•Whitfield & Loretta•Kristin•Greg •Anna"Lou"•Rudy•Allan•Arnold•Patrice•Clarissa•Sharon•Diane•Lorraine•Elaine •Tijuana•Rose•Ali•Edgar ReVay•Jordan•Ben•Michelle•Ross•Reggie•Neal• Jeremy •Papa Jack & Peachie•Big Ma & Big Daddy•all my broader family•the Mortensens• Father Frank•Keesha• the Aviñas•Roberta Cocking•R. Eric Stone•Char Maxwell•Brother Virgil & family•Michael H & family•Danny G & Lynette•Beckie & family•Barbara, Mike & family•Sherrilyn & family•Tawna & Damon•Sydney Duncan•Leonard Dunston•Tom Pettigrew•Julie Sherman & family •Helena Carlson•Lee D'Anna•Maiesha & family•all the B-ball Pios•Nepal crew •Marci• Dom•Jean & Dave•Donnie G.•Jumain & Charmaine•Jules & Zabra Harrell & family•Ava G.•Mike Heffner•Laura House•Rob Hall•the McNeeses• Nate & Carlos•Anna Santa Cruz•Lily & family•Ometha & family• Barbara Grimes & family• Marcia•Mike B.•Cre•Addie•Frances•the Heenans•John & Katy• Askhari•Kia•Niambi•the Katkos•Fran & De'Andre •Obafemi•Kent Kuo• the Lama family•Natasha•Yves & Nanci•David & Mary Susan•Gary & Judi•Matt W.•Henry W.•Nancy F.•Luis•Loren•Zola•Ray Warren•Octavia & Auntie•Denise Toussaint•Kewanee•Merlene•Dahlia•Shani• Shiretta•Leora Berry•Butch Brown•all my true HU students•Tara•Delmar•T & the Lawerys •Beth Mac•Daniel Begay•E. Cammack•Dr. Jean•Ka'ren•Dwight & Evelyn•Serge•Sherry M.•Ethelbert & family•Jamila•Gwen, Darnell & family•Rachel N.•Chuck & Carol•Patty & Vince•Cesarine•Lillie•Meredith Njeri•Laura Siemon•Dean & Madge•Purnima & Tara•M.B.•Dave & Alison•Saidat & the Molake family•Dr. Pinder•Tori & family•Walter•Zena•Toni• Sharon McDaniel•Robert Hill•James Jones• Terrie Williams•Pearle & Mary Anne•D. Nielah•Sharon D.•Al Roberts•Fran Caldwell•Harriet D.•James Collins•Gloria J.C.•Renee Dalene•Steve Reder•Janaé• Kat Pratt•Erik Sillen & Momma Miriam•Jacqueline Richmond•Sally File•Shireen F. •Yakiciwey & family•Jermaine R.•Eric Gann•Tonjua•E. Faison•Julie Schimshock•Loren P. Shaw• Peter Christenson•Shereen Reaney•BZ, Tay Tay & family•Oronde, Amina & family• Bekki & family•Kevin S.•Matt Roth & family•Filly & family•Sadara•Adeola•Ona• Esther & family•Jackie•Angela A.•Dita & family•the Emerys•all of you who have touched my life•all the true prophets•the unknown warriors•my ancestors•my descendants•my humanity•Sky•Wind•Earth •Water•Fire•my dreams• my fears•my past•my future . . . my Love.

There are no human words for what you mean to me. May the passion with which I live, if not the abundance of my imperfections, serve for you as my everlasting gratitude.

CONTENTS

GJP . . . We are loving you

Lizard wept though
lizards have few tears
green stalk whimpered
at its coming death though
green stalks have no fears
fright was a blaze and blaze
crept . . . coming, coming. . . .

THE FIRE

FOR a deceitful moment, I believe the world has not been destroyed. That moment ends. My mind awakes. I am surrounded by National Guardsmen with weapons. We are on a yellow school bus. The bus crawls slowly down deserted streets on a charred mountaintop in New Mexico. My family is with me. Other families fill this bus, too. All of us wear the pale, slack faces of ghosts. We are stunned. It is as though we are peering through the walls of our dimension out into something unreal and possibly a trick of nature. Tricksters inhabit the desert, especially coyotes, creating treacherous illusions.

Outside of the windows pulled closed to keep away the stench, we see black ground on smoldering hillsides, gray ash a heavy blanket on the things that used to be. Cars seem to have actually dissolved. Their frames, windows, and tires are melted. They have become shrunken, torched beetles that never made it underground. Nearly gone are the proud pine trees that made this place a fantasy forest to my young mind. The few that remain smolder, cold dark remnants of life.

Houses stood here once: structures where lives unfolded; love was made; domestic friction was audibly on neighborhood display. These were the homes I delivered newspapers to at an age when fences were head-high to me, and my only salvation against the raging canine beasts those fences restrained was a container of mace and my long legs. Now all the familiar landmarks are gone and I cannot even tell which block we are driving through. We are ghosts on a yellow bus, staring at the black and gray of what used to be.

The fire was already being called *the Cerro Grande Fire*. Only days old, it was legend. The National Park Service at Bandelier National Monument enacted what now seemed surrealistically termed a *controlled burn,* as a fire prevention measure. The burn itself turned out to be the one in control. Summer rains had not yet come. The moisture-scorned land was parched and combustible. The man-made burn chose to leap from its bed and sleepwalk through canyons until it crawled over arroyo lips and came creeping, with destruction on its mind and consumption pangs in its gut, into *our town.*

Its heat was enormous. In a sweeping lick from God, it had blackened the giant mountains towering over the community, leaving licorice stain on what had been a sea of green pines and aspens at up to 9,000 feet in elevation. Then the fire trespassed upon the homes of people used to calamities more along the lines of summer hailstorms and ducks from Ashley Pond crossing a street into traffic. This was a catastrophe upgrade.

It is May of 2000. Folks in Los Alamos, like the rest of the country, had been worrying about our great technological web crashing in the wake of the exiting millennium. Nature took that as a slight to her majesty. Here was her response. The flames leapt 50-foot pine trees like sugar-charged 7-year-olds playing hopscotch. The air was heated into an invisible conduit, the fire raced across it into yards and onto rooftops. Entire neighborhoods were incinerated. We are staring now at what looks like the after-effects of an atomic bomb detonation. The irony of our town's history as the development site of the Fat Man and Little Boy that blackened Hiroshima and Nagasaki has not yet occurred to us.

Somebody hold Mom. The bus has rolled up, in front of our house. I mean, to where our house used to be. The humble dark chocolate-colored abode no longer fills that space. *Mom is falling . . .* into some unimaginable abyss where mothers go whose *space* is suddenly lost forever. That space where Mom raised five children and stood watch over the flow of blood, tears, anger, love, Kool-Aid, and dreams. *Somebody hold Mom.* We all do—hold her. We hold her tight, hands on her shoulders as she slumps crying in a seat sized for children. We are a father, a mother, and their five offspring, resorting back to the comfort of communion in the face of fear and agony.

The air outside stinks, inside it is rank with sorrow. *This bus was made for children. We shouldn't be here. We've already gone to school, Mom. We shouldn't be here.* But we are. And it is true. Our home is gone. An endless settlement of fingerprints, scents, rituals, and daily routines that left their impressions in wood and walls gathered themselves into a crackling cadenza. They curled on thermal currents up into the sky, vaporizing into carbon on their way.

As the seven stunned souls of my family surrender to a great loss, one of those souls realizes another consequence. A possibility that only he could have come across among this family: *Family . . .*

Here I am with my family. We have lost our home and all that it contained. The trigger for our memories is vanished, if not the memories themselves. But what if what also went up in those flames was the space in which I suffered alone with my private circumstance? That awful, tendril-laden knot of discord that balled up in my chest and throat all those years was tied to a life I led in a particular place. That place is gone. What if that whole season has now evaporated, as if my Great Spirit has said to me, "You may go forward now, my son?"

My mind works over a dawning thought. My spirit works more nimbly through the truth of it. A long season has ended for my family. In this new one thousand years, this time after our home, it will be a time for new truths, a new season. I imagine that for the rest of my family that house also was the sight of secret wounds, and of the deep joys accumulated by the stability and love we shared over time. For me, the emotions and thoughts that I bred in my bedroom, in that home, became a wall between my family and me. Though they likely do not realize the full height and thickness of that wall, it was central to my being. And now the spawning pool for that barrier has been dismissed by a Spirit eager to see me walk farther down the road.

This home—where I was loved and raised—was also where I battled against my demons and never felt quite *a part of.* But now the house is gone. So too, perhaps, should my ghosts be gone. Revelation fills me. This fire has left behind more than embers and awe. I am not the only one in the community who feels humbled and spoken to by this act of nature. But in a most blatant and symbolic way, I have received both clenching loss and Divine opportunity in one great moment of destruction. Now I have no choice but to complete my healing, resurrect my infant heart, and go forward.

Los Alamos was scorched, stripped of its security. Beauty blossomed already in the cracks left behind. What sprouts in me is a resolve to take advantage of this opportunity to let my family know the adult me, the true nature that had been there in spirit before birth—the person that I am determined to achieve reunion with in days ahead. My parents would resolve to rebuild their house on that same property. I would commit to revealing myself to them. I must leave my former pain under the bed in that old, frigid room where I slept those long youthful nights—the same room that has now taken to flames and disappeared into the sky.

But for now, we are on the bus. Mom's sense of being is flickering weakly, tottering between composure and utter dissolution. Besides the spirit of the place, she has also lost material things. Things laden with value like her wedding ring and her antique pianos. All those black and white keys she oiled and polished like stones on river's bottom with the natural substance of her fingertips, singing those soulful songs.

The 'she' of her identity hadn't been 'career' or 'social life'. She was composed of less glamorous things. Band-Aids on small knees and elbows, laundry stained with life, child laughter, and a husband's never-ending support system. So many of the physical locations of her identity had now disappeared. Who would she be now? She could not have imagined how cold it could feel to be torn in one moment from a kind of gestation space, only to be told by life to *start over.* Twice—at birth and again in my infancy—life had asked me to do the same. Here now in the midst of a great burning was a bridge, however subtle, between mother and son.

I shall make for me
a consequence
bend sky
split water
I shall take from the corners
of the universe and make for me
a consequence

CONVERGENCE

THE dark-haired airplane passenger was from Peoria, population 100,000 strong. Her name was Darlene Danz. She was on her way to visit her fiancé. It was July of 1964. Darlene had just turned 22 and was on a journey of great magnitude for both her and her tightly connected family. She had helped her mother raise her two younger sisters and a cousin, now her presence would be sorely missed back in the Danz family home. "You're going where, Mexico?" her family had asked, incredulous of the distance and confused by the foreign-sounding name.

In addition, Darlene and her mother, Betty, were best friends. She could not leave her best friend and travel across the west's expansive states to a strange place where long distance phone calls would be expensive and rare, and not suffer the pangs of loss. But now she was in the sky and headed toward the man she would soon vow to stand by for the long haul. That's what her people did, whether marrying a man, farming the land, working the rails, or raising their children. They stood by for the long haul.

The couple met in November of 1963 on a blind date, arranged by a mutual friend, while her betrothed was on Thanksgiving break from college. Either the college student knew just what he wanted in a woman, and had amazing insight and intuition about people he had just met, or he was a victim/beneficiary of love at first sight. He asked this dark-haired beauty to marry him after only seven dates—on St. Patrick's Day. Fortune followed them thenceforth in four-leaf clovers. They would be together—this odd coupling of introverted scientist and extroverted songbird—forever after. She recounted the brief stretch of days over which their relationship had flowered as the plane carried her forward. The engines spoke brutishly as she drew near to her new homeland.

As she flew, a fire blazed in her chest. The miles stacked up between what she knew and the life destination she didn't— between a well-worn sense of past and an unknown future, between family and isolation, incinerating her sense of connection. Separation swallowed her. This adoption of a new life would not be easy.

Jim Potter drove west from his hometown of East Peoria—a small town of 20,000 located about a three-hour drive southwest of Chicago, along the Illinois River. He was 22 years of age and 1964 stretched out before him, a bonfire of promise and opportunity. He would marry Darlene Danz on August 29th, two weeks after his 23rd birthday. He had graduated from the University of Illinois with a degree in engineering physics months before, in January. His destination was a place called Los Alamos where the Los Alamos Scientific Laboratory, 'the Lab', was the centerpiece of the community. He had not heard of Los Alamos before his February interview there, even though the Laboratory was the sight of the World War II Manhattan Project, the top-secret missive that spawned the great beast that growled and leveled Hiroshima and Nagasaki—introducing the world to atomic rage.

During that first trip in February, he was overtaken with the clear New Mexico skies and the crisp high-altitude air. No one had rolled out the red carpet for his arrival, but Nature obliged him with three feet of snow as its way of saying, "Bien Venidos." *Welcome.*

Now it was April and Jim was driving west in his 1964 Nash Rambler station wagon. He made the $2,800 purchase with a hefty contribution from his grandparents, who were persuaded by his father, and a loan from the local bank based on his new job. He would arrive in Los Alamos on the 18th, eager to begin work as a staff member at the Lab for $700 per month. This was the West—Jim was young, anxious, and adventurous. He could have no inkling of just how daring he was about to be.

A young man his own age, named Cassius Clay, had taken the world heavyweight boxing title from Sonny Liston in February of that year down in Miami Beach. Only vaguely aware of this, the product of Peoria drove on toward his own ambitions. From within his White, Midwestern, decidedly non-athletic life, Jim could not know that in training for the Liston fight, Clay had briefly encountered a certain man down on that peninsula. A man who would, not too far into future's reach, play a central role in Jim's pioneering family endeavor.

That mystery man and Clay had come to blows. Their conflict was friendly, inspired by Clay's need for a sparring partner. In the bruised after-mood of President Kennedy's assassination, Clay had been training. He pondered his humble origins in a Black Louisville community, sweating himself into shape, chasing his greatest dream through hot months. These were days of uncertain emotional pitch following that late summer's March on Washington, where a 34-year-old minister described his own distant freedom dream. Clay's ambitions drove his 6'3" chassis, toned and strong, into winter. He sparred on a Saturday, December 7th, 1963, at the famous Fifth Street Gym in Miami Beach with a young Black offensive lineman from legendary coach Jake Gaither's Florida A&M football team.

Florida A&M would battle Jackson State on grass the next day in the Orange Blossom Classic; but on this day, two heavyweights traded shots, framed by turnbuckles and ropes, their feet pounding the canvas like it was a drum. They threw their manhood through fists at each other, their joust friendly but testing. As they circled, jabbed, and feinted, their movement told the tale. One heavyweight, Whitfield Jenkins, was obviously a football player. The other was obviously the next heavyweight champion of the world. Days later, Clay went on to fell Liston, become Muhammad Ali, proclaim his faith, and become legend. Whitfield Jenkins' next journey would take him into Uncle Sam's Army, the New Mexico desert, and war.

The long, imposing body of the nearly 25-year-old raw buck private from the deep woods of Bethlehem, an old Black north Florida community, was stuffed into the train seat. Sitting next to him was another soldier, with whom the man was fast developing a friendship. "Jenkins, we're pulling into Mississippi."

Whitfield Jenkins stirred from his sleep. This was his first train ride and only his second time headed this far into the West. But all the newness and the strange side-to-side rocking and clattering mechanics of the train couldn't keep sleep away. This 14-hour trip was the culmination of a whirlwind induction into the United States Army.

Jenkins had been drafted from out of Ocala, Florida, that year on February 17, 1965, just four days before a tall slender Muslim leader newly renamed El-Hajj Malik El-Shabazz would be sprayed with 16 shotgun pellets on the stage of Harlem's Audubon Ballroom. With shouts of, "They killed Malcolm!" still ringing in his ears, Jenkins traveled by Greyhound bus to Jacksonville, Florida, and then to Fort Jackson, South Carolina, for processing. Next, it was on to Fort Gordon, Georgia, for eight weeks of basic training in the Military Police MOS (Military Occupational Specialties). Now it was early September and the country boy was riding on steel tracks through a changing landscape toward a place that sounded foreign from the name alone: Albuquerque, New Mexico. Vietnam was on in the Far East and he was headed into the desert. Assassinations and war—the world, cleft and perforated, was breaching.

Jenkins' seatmate, John Kroll, was a White man from Pittsburgh, Pennsylvania. Together, they had endured basic and artillery infantry training. Kroll had played professional baseball with the Boston Red Sox. Uncle Sam had just plucked Jenkins, a promising offensive lineman, from the previous fall's training camp with the AFL's Denver Broncos. The two elite-level athletes struck up an easy banter.

For Jenkins, basic training had been much like the Broncos' training camp. "No fear" and "no pain" were the mottoes that carried him through the tortuous strain of both passages. His thoughts returned for a moment back to that camp: it was his first real experience—in a life of one-quarter of a century—with race equity. He was also left wondering about the 'what ifs' of this change he was making. This trip to the West, and eventually the Far East, was a movement in a direct line away from his dreams for a long and successful football career. War changes the direction of uncelebrated lives in ways final and without notice.

He received the draft letter in the spring of 1964 while still a student at Florida A&M University in Tallahassee. A government intent on pulling more lives into the war had caught him up in a dragnet of 50,000. Having completed training, Jenkins was now only months shy of the government age cutoff of 26 for draftees. Like many African Americans, he was not privy to a social network of connections and relationships that might lead to draft deferment. It was rare for someone so near to the age exclusion mark to be drafted. But he was Black and this was the U.S.—he knew well how the dice rolled and so often came up 'unbiased and coincidental' on the side of young White men and unfavorably for those 'like' him. Spades in gambling and in the draft lottery are not nearly so equal a coincidence. Even so, he was resigned to the course of such things, and besides, next to him was a White example that proved there are no absolutes in the world of men.

The two rolled on through the thick woods of the South, the widening and flattening stretches of the Oklahoma/Texas plains, and into the sparse whispering-wind land that was New Mexico. Outside of the windows in the night darkness and shadows, woodland trees morphed into low-lying shrubs and strange-looking plants. Jenkins and Kroll speculated on what lay ahead. They were grateful they hadn't been shipped out directly to Vietnam, as had some of their partners in basic and artillery infantry training (AIT). They could not know that fate would soon return from Vietnam to clutch them too in its talons. This trip, on rails through the night, was the first uninterrupted stretch of time following nearly six months of grueling physical training. Jenkins was dog tired, in mind and body. Sleep would carry him to the desert.

When he awoke, the flatland, green space, lakes, ponds, and rivers of his lifetime thus far had been stolen and replaced by mountains, tumbleweeds, and alien-looking cacti and yucca. *Is this a dream? What world is this?* The train groaned and whined to a stop. Jenkins stepped off, and onto the ground of an entirely new world of cultural diversity—something vaguely reminiscent of Old West television shows. Albuquerque was a flat valley, sloping up its eastern side into the foothills of the towering Sandia Mountains. The air was dry and the scent of food coming from homes and restaurants was a spicy aroma he had never known.

His military barrack at Sandia Base in Albuquerque was a mansion compared to his previous assignments, which eased the transition. He sought out the familiar. Future Indiana Pacers star Mel Daniels and some of his University of New Mexico teammates would come by the base gym to play pick-up basketball games with Jenkins and the other soldiers. The ball moving from his hand to the floor and back was a familiar predictability that eased his nerves. The basket was still 10 feet high, just like before. *This is more like it, some rhythm, soul, and sweat.* Bolstered by battles on the court, he began to enjoy the level of racial tolerance he noticed in this part of the country. A drastic improvement compared to the South he knew.

Then, just when the cacti began to seem not so threatening, and the Sandia Mountains looming overhead took on a familiar rather than menacing mien, Fate came calling, demanding that he pack his bags for Vietnam. He was assigned to Military Police Company—USA Element Fld. Comd. DASA (5805). That unit was now being deployed to helicopter into combat areas and transport Americans who had committed crimes to Danang Prison. Then to stockades in the Philippines; from there to military trial locations in the States, and if convicted, finally to Ft. Hood, Texas. It was March of 1966.

The war was escalating into a daily bloodbath as U.S. involvement sped past 'advisement' and straight into full-fledged intrusion. Several men from Jenkins' company at Sandia Base had already found their mortal fate. Fear was a formidable psychological block for these stateside soldiers. They holstered an absolute, chilled horror over the way soldiers 'in country' were suffering their demise: grisly, gaping wounds from Viet Cong booby traps. The soldiers vented their fears to each other, expressing their preference for being shot to death rather than being maimed by stakes covered with feces.

May 23, 1966. Danang, Vietnam. The air was heavy with moisture and clean other than for the greasy exhaust of the noisome Black Hawk helicopter. Inside its belly, 45-caliber machine guns mounted on gun ramps racketed to the air turbulence, anxious. Corporal Whitfield Jenkins rode in that Black Hawk over a dense jungle area near the city. The 'copter was a plump target over a fierce battle zone where Death was running around, gleefully tagging young men, and whispering: *You're it.* On these missions, Jenkins' unit had to land and pick up the detainees and prisoners right out in the open fields of rich green elephant grass too often stained scarlet red.

Green foliage blurred by them below, a menacing carpet. The gunner's door of the helicopter was open. Jenkins stood, gripping the doorframe to get a better view of the area below. He heard the sound of silence that precedes a storm. Hell broke. The sky spat ammunitions like sand in a windstorm. He suddenly experienced excruciating pain in his arm and hand. Blood flowed heavily, releasing itself from the pressured confinements of his body, seeming to exhale as it spilled out into the air above Danang. Projectile rounds pierced the helicopter, sparking against the metal hull, singing shrill notes as they bedded down or deflected.

"Jenkins is hit!" The pilot slammed the controls and quickly maneuvered the helicopter out of the area, while the medics administered treatment. One soldier, Jenkins, was down, but at least not on the ground.

The wounded corporal was transported to the Danang hospital for surgery on a shattered navicular bone and shredded nerves and vessels in his left wrist. He was then reassigned back to Sandia Base in Albuquerque for additional surgery and recovery. In that faraway place, thick with vegetation like back in Bethlehem, he had seen horror that men were not made to see. That hell lodged somewhere in his lower throat and would never make it past his lips once he was finally back home in the States for good. The bullet that violated Jenkins had providence written on it. It altered the course of his life, and would soon bring him into an ordained convergence with a White family that his most bizarre thoughts would not have conceived.

Back in Los Alamos and now married, Darlene Potter was exercising her theatrical talents in the Los Alamos Light Opera. James Potter, holder of a draft deferment due to his work at the Laboratory, was growing accustomed to the fiery taste of huevos rancheros for lunch and the howling whine of coyotes at night. The two Peoria-bred pioneers were making their young home and navigating the headwaters of an emerging desire for children.

Her name was Mary and she was separated from her identical twin sister, Martha. She was born in Bagdad, Florida, a small town of 1,000 in Santa Rosa County, in the Pensacola watershed area of the state's northern panhandle. Raised in Birmingham, Alabama, by her adoptive kin, Mary Woods had known only the South. Now all that would change. It was June of 1966 and her twin sister's husband, James, had come to Birmingham to transport Mary and her sons, Allan and Arnold, to Albuquerque, New Mexico.

In April and May of 1963, in response to history-making protests by African Americans, Birmingham Commissioner of Public Safety, Eugene "Bull" Connor, had unleashed insecurity's spite. He expressed his fear in the form of German Shepherd police dogs, fire hoses, and pure hatred. Black skin burnt on the streets from things that were not the sun. *I cannot raise my boys in this. Lord, take me to somewhere they will be treated as human.* Mary was working for the Social Security Administration at the time. She transferred to the Atomic Energy Commission in Albuquerque. She was 31 years of age and on the anxious cusp of a new life.

The trip to Albuquerque took nearly two days, with an overnight stay at Shepherd Air Force Base in Wichita Falls, Texas. They arrived June 8. The weather was cool—though it was early summer—so they slept under blankets. *Lord, this got to be the strangest place I've ever seen.* New Mexico abounded with adobe structures, Hispanics, Mexican nationals, and American Indians. Not the kind of American Indians found around much of the nation, whose physical appearance was hardly distinguishable from White persons. These people were brown-skinned, jet black-haired Indians, with facial structures and features distinctly other than Caucasian. Shock gave way to fascination as this unfamiliar cultural extravaganza greeted her.

After eating some good Mexican food and realizing how friendly the people were, the state began to grow on her. In contrast to the racial hostility that she had known, this southwestern hospitality was an offsetting but relieving splash in the face.

She planned to live in New Mexico one year and then return to Alabama. But by the time Allan and Arnold had experienced one year of life there, it was clear that her children could not go back to such a racially tempestuous, socially static place. And by June of 1967—that one-year mark—she would have already been carrying in her womb another reason to stay away from Birmingham. For certain transgressions, such as an out-of-wedlock birth, brought their own special backlash in Alabama's social sanction pool.

The tall soldier wore charm on his face and walked with an athlete's sure gait. The woman fresh from Birmingham was wit, intelligence, and southern manner. The two young Black southern transplants, far away from their homes, region, and culture, struck up easy conversation. Friendship came to Whitfield and Mary with a grace brought on only by a higher plan in the making. Their knowing of each other was kind, sincere, and brief. The corporal was honorably discharged from the military in February of 1967. He left Albuquerque not knowing that Mary was carrying a child conceived only weeks before. He would not know he had a son until 16 years had passed.

Bethlehem had met Birmingham on the road of circumstance. The stars had aligned and the universe was an architect pleased with itself. A Black baby carrying southern heritage was to be loosed forth into a place of mesas and arroyos, Hispanic tradition, and ancient Anasazi and Pueblo Indian legacy. It was a mystical land and the road ahead would be wondrous, played out on an arid stretch defined by the cross-shaped overlap of I-40 and I-25, and the communities that ran alongside the life-giving waters of the Rio Grande.

Mary Woods suffered severely from ill health while she carried her child. She was not young as mothers went in those days; her two sons, Allan and Arnold, were already going on 11 and 10. The medical specialists could not gain a clear handle on what ailed her. Their diagnoses veered from diabetes to brucellosis, to the rare blood disease, porphyriah. Whatever the source, her condition was weakening and unstable. Mentally, she was showing the strain that often comes with the kind of clairvoyance and extreme sensitivity she and her family line were known to have. Her health and life transitions were tantamount to a trauma that sent her cascading into nervous overload and depression.

Mary was now living with, and largely in the care of, her identical twin, Martha, and Martha's husband, James Bruno, along with the Brunos' three children, James, Greg, and Faye. Mary's health crisis and pregnancy was a great concern. Mary was seriously ill, with a condition that still had not been diagnosed. Could she survive giving birth again in her condition? Would this baby survive? The doctors had their doubts. Martha and James carried the load with their children and Mary's boys, while Mary pondered the gravity of the moment. *If only I could clear my mind. I'm frightened, dear Lord. Please, show me the way.*

This child's father was not a ready option for Mary. She could not bear to shift such weight onto a man she hardly knew, even if she could somehow locate him in the world. She knew only that he had been discharged from the Army, but had no idea beyond that where he was. Guilt and fear of the idea of informing him of her pregnancy coagulated into an emotional barricade past which she would not venture. *This is a challenge God has brought me,* she reasoned in a mood of self-flagellation. *I have to see this out on my own.*

The social workers thought nothing of the idea that this baby's father might provide a resolution to the crisis. They gave no thought to the possibility that the father's family might also be willing and able to raise or support the child. Perhaps a gender or racial bias against this child's father halted the social work planning process before it began to venture down Whitfield Jenkins' road. Whatever the reason, the entire sphere of planning remained constrained to a compromised mother and an uninspired if sincere system. Enduring family and community resources disappeared from consideration, if they were ever present.

These professionals were dealing with an overwhelmed, traumatized mother's crushing guilt and shame. Their assumptions and values likely played a role in not pursuing a resolution that would have kept the child at least in the broader family. Instead, they built a wall of shrunken possibilities. That wall effectively eradicated options involving the other, male half of the human equation that brought forth this soon-to-be *ward of the state*. For the first step in being a father is to be informed that you are one.

The word *adoption* stole into Mary's mind as a sleek feral menace, some time before it first became a spoken word. Once it was there, in that lonely mental darkness where Mary juggled her future, it grew in pace with the growing crisis. The fear, panic, love, and concern involved in this quandary coalesced into a desperation that ruled the moment. *Lord, what am I going to do with this baby?*

Already on AFDC (Aid to Families with Dependent Children) support, the young pregnant woman sought the advice of her social worker. "I just don't know what to do," Mary shared, frightened. "I feel like I've let everyone down. I'm worried about how another child would affect Arnold and Allan, and I just don't know if I'll be able to care for a child in my condition."

The caseworker now suspected that this woman was considering adoption. Her thought was immediately confirmed. "Is there any chance at all that a Negro child would be adopted in this state? By a strong, stable family?" Mary asked. "That's my greatest concern."

"Mary, there are many military Negro families here on the bases. I think the chances are excellent," the caseworker answered. With those words, the pendulum in the sky swung toward its chosen destination.

My dear child, you will never know how my heart is torn. I do this for you. May Dear God forgive me. Ma'Dear, I am sorry for this shame. One day, my child, may you find it in your soul to forgive me yourself. Mary experienced the rupture from her child before it happened. She had come to know this little soul, personalized it already. Earlier in the pregnancy, she had decided that if the baby were a boy, she would name him Austin, continuing the alphabetical trend of her sons' names. Austin would never reach the record books.

"Mother, please don't give him away! Please don't give my brother away!" Ten-year-old Arnold's shrieking, plaintive wail broke Mary's heart, and left her alone, screaming rivers of regret. How do you reason with a child about why his brother must leave him forever?

Split earth
rise waters
seed come come

dance sky
cry cloud
seed come come

go quick child
go get de drum

DAWN

I was born beside the big river. This was no Kamby Bolongo
(big river), like the River Gambia of Alex Haley's ancestral
locale. This was the Rio Grande. The New Mexican desert's
stunted idea of a large river flow—brown, mostly lazy, and
hardly difficult for a healthy adult to throw a rock across. I was
born to Mary Elizabeth Woods, then just four days past her
33rd birthday, in Albuquerque, New Mexico, on Thursday,
October the 26th of 1967.

Mary never laid her eyes on me—not immediately
following delivery, or thereafter. She was never told of my sex.
Fate allowed her a brief yet all-important glance at a sheet of
paper unintentionally left within her reach soon after the
delivery. On that sheet, she saw the words: *baby boy*. This
knowledge would become an immense truth years later as she
searched desperately to find her son.

I was born with a hole in my gut, near the place where the
umbilical cord begins its extension to connect a fetus to his
mother. *A hole near the place where I was connected to my mother.*
Described by the White social worker/doctor/experts as "not
unusual for his race," the medical term was *umbilical hernia*. In
the world of spirits such a hole is called foreshadow, or

reminder, depending upon the point in time of perspective. All babies are severed from their mothers at birth. For some, this act is more thorough. Certain American Indian cultures have a word—*Sipapu: the place of emergence*. Though this relates to the source and genesis of the world or universe, it can also be used to describe that place in the body representing the point of emergence of a new life from the predecessor life, of the baby from the mother. What happens when that place, whether as a physical location or moreover a holding point for a spiritual bond, is damaged or flawed? The answer would become the underground spring filtering through my life.

I was born in Bataan Memorial Hospital, a place named after the April 1942 World War II death march of American prisoners of war. The New Mexico National Guard was among the groups that surrendered to the Japanese. Eighteen hundred New Mexicans had been deployed there. Only 900 returned alive. I was born in Bataan, a place of memorial, for those who never made it home to family; Bataan, a no longer existing name for a place that swallowed many of the early facts of my life. I was born, and then I became a number/subject/case referred to in clinical passing on the pages of legal documents crowded by 'herebys' and 'aforesaids'.

Within days, I was placed in foster care with an African American woman in Albuquerque, who already had several foster children at the time. I do not know her name, or her essence, but I do know that the nine months I spent in her presence shaped me. I believe that she has passed away, but how I wish I could find her, wrap my arms tightly around her, and thank her for carrying me through my first nine months following birth, the second nine months of my existence. It was in her care that I became more than a pronoun. I acquired the name, 'Baby Boy Scott'.

Some time after I started college my parents shared with me what remained of the official story of my beginning. It was a case record. My relationship with my foster mother was only hinted at in the text. Beyond that, the details of my own life were whitened out from the only pages that could speak to me. My key truths were ghosts behind white clouds, torturing me with their almost-revelation. I held those clouds up to the light, determined to unleash something real and tangible, though I knew nothing could be seen. I was like a child who had never tasted candy swinging wildly at an empty piñata, hoping to beat those sweets into existence. The case record tells my story:

PARTIAL CASE RECORD: BABY BOY SCOTT

9/25/67: Information was received from Family Services caseworker ------- that one of her AFDC mothers was expecting a baby in October and planned to give it [up] for adoption through us. Mrs. ------- took necessary information from the woman and fully explained the adoption process to her.

NATURAL MOTHER: -------, born October 22, 1934 in -------. She is presently receiving AFDC for her first two children. She is full Negro and stands 5'5½" and weighs 115 lbs. Her build is slight and she is described as a very attractive person. Her eyes are brown, her hair black and her skin medium brown. She is a quiet, pleasant woman who is very tidy and who takes interest in her appearance.

TALENTS AND APTITUDES: ------- is interested in writing and public speaking and has won essay contests. She has also written some newspaper articles that were published.

NATURAL FATHER: Father of this baby is ------- for whom there is no address at this time. His weight is about 220 lbs. and his height is about 6 feet. He was built solidly, as he was a professional football player before going into the service. His eyes are brown, his hair brown and his skin is dark brown. ------- estimates he is about 28 years old and he is from -------. He is also full Negro. He is single and has never been married or divorced so far as she knows. She does not know what kind of student he is, but notes that he finished school at age 21, and has had additional training in the service which led him to become a military policeman. She stated that he excelled in any kind of athletic endeavor and that he was always a very neat careful dresser, and that he has a forceful personality. So far as she knows his health was excellent. He was quite concerned about his health and went out of his way to take excellent care of himself.

10/26/67, BIRTH OF BABY: Baby Boy Scott ------- was born on this date, weighing in at 7 lbs. 6 oz. His height was not given but he is a large healthy looking baby. He was placed in the foster home on 11/1/67. Scott is a rather light appearing Negro, although he has a flat nose and soft kinky hair, which was rather long for a Negro newborn. He appears that he might have a slight mixture of Anglo or Spanish, although this is not in the social history. His eyes are brown and features normal in all respects. Scott is to be bathed with dial [sic] soap and then rubbed with mineral oil. He is on a regular 3-hour schedule of evaporated milk formula.

11/22/67: A visit to the ------- home found Scotty sound asleep, looking very big and well cared for. Mrs. ------- reports he's a very good baby, who loves to be held.

1/11/68: A quick visit to the ------- home found Scotty doing fine and looking almost like a four or five month old baby. He's a big boy, who laughs at the other children in this foster home. He seems to enjoy attention from them and will attempt to talk ending up just making soft noises. As everything seems in order, I'm hopeful that we can find an adoptive family for Scotty in the near future.

2/9/68: I visited ------- in the ------- home on this date. Scott is a handsome, Negro baby boy, who has light chocolate skin and a nose that is slightly flat, but not extremely so. His lips too are slightly Negroid and he has soft, very curly hair. Scott is very chubby and is a large baby, partly due to the fact I suppose that his father was a football player. His food intake also is quite large.

Development: Scott is a very happy baby who will laugh and smile whenever shown any attention. He especially responds to the other foster children in this home who range in age from about four to seven. He is extremely strong, having a good, tight grip. Scott is very alert and gives me the impression that he will be quite intelligent. He likes to pull hair of anyone holding him and studies human faces very intently. Scott likes to talk, and the foster mother notes that Scott doesn't cry much.

Scott is probably the biggest three-month-old baby I have seen. He actually seems to be about six months and actually wears six-month old clothing according to the foster mother.

FEEDING: Scott is taking his original formula of evaporated milk and Karo syrup. He takes about four bottles daily. He is also eating all strained foods, including meat, vegetables, fruit and cereals. The foster mother swears its true that he will eat any place from three to four small jars of baby food per day.

4-5-68: I visited Scott ------- in the ------- foster home on this date for the last time. Scott was asleep, but I got one more good look at him. He is a very big boy. He is a sturdy, solid packed baby who looks as if he will follow in his father's footsteps as a football player.

This is an alert, bright, and healthy Negro baby boy with very light chocolate skin. I sincerely hope that he will be placed for adoption in the near future.

As I am now leaving the agency the case will be transferred to another worker.

4/?/68: [new case worker] I got my first look at this very handsome Negro boy on the marginal date, and although he was asleep, I was very impressed with his looks. At six months, his foster mother reports, Scotty is already moving about when placed in his walker and is eating regular table food that the rest of the family is eating. He eats everything. Loves ice cream and cake. His foster mother is very proud of him and refers to him as the "little man."

In reviewing his parental background, it would seem that Scotty has inherited their more positive qualities: his father was big, well-built and athletic; his mother was an honor student interested in writing and public speaking.

7/?/68: After having received the Potter Home Study as a possibility for Scotty on 7/10/68, and having determined it acceptable in conference, I informed Mrs. ------- of his impending placement and the necessity for arranging a pediatric examination.

This news came as a real blow to Mrs. ------- who had become very proud, attached and possessive of this child and she begged off taking him for this needed pediatric, so we agreed that I would take Scotty to the doctor myself.

Jim and Darlene Potter wanted a big family. Darlene had given birth to a daughter, Kristin, in July of 1967, but they were looking ahead. They thought that adopting children was a good way to have a large family without so much wear and tear on Darlene. Anticipating that the adoption would take a while, they did not expect that another child would be immediately brought into their home. In addition, the social workers desired to delay placing a baby in the Potter home until Kristin was at least one year old.

On the initial written questionnaire, the Potters were asked to list adjectives describing physical traits of the ideal baby from their perspective. They listed qualities like 'alert', 'healthy', 'intelligent', 'strong'. Realizing the couple hadn't specifically requested a baby with particular racial characteristics, the agency became very interested in the Potters' opinions about adopting a Black baby. The professionals took the couple's lack of racial reference as an indication of social liberalism. "How would you feel about adopting a Black child?" the caseworker asked, hesitantly.

The couple hadn't ever considered that the child they would adopt might be Black. This was New Mexico, and they had expected a Hispanic or Indian child, or a mixture of the two. Jim Potter had grown up in an all-White community in East Peoria, and had attended East Peoria Community High School, an all-White institution with about 1,200 students. His community and school were populated with blue-collar families. Most of the workforce was in the employ of Caterpillar Co., whose main plant was in Jim's school district.

His intimate exposure to Black folks was virtually nonexistent. They were the people across the street, on the other side of the tracks, in a realm separate from his own.

Darlene Potter had grown up in an old, working-class community in Peoria. She too had little exposure to Black people, as the Black community was concentrated mostly in the South End, where the more heavily integrated Manual High School was located. Darlene had attended Woodruff High School, where out of 1,000 students, less than 60 were Black. Only 14 of the students in Darlene's senior class were Black, and she rarely saw or interacted with those students during a school day. Located near Glen Oak Park, Woodruff High was host to many of the upper-class children from up on the Bluff. Among this progeny of lawyers and doctors, Darlene was a timid minority from the blue-collar world.

The one Black person Darlene was acquainted with in her entire childhood was a high school classmate she sat next to for an hour each day in choir practice, for two years. Most White students didn't favor sitting next to Black students. But the Black student, Leora Wilson, and Darlene were both Master Choir sopranos. For both it was the song that counted. Though not much conversation passed between the shy-as-a-mouse White schoolgirl and her fellow soprano, they shared adolescent laughter and the bond of singing side-by-side. Darlene polished her singing, drawing from the beautiful voice of the outgoing Leora. Those were their fleeting moments of contact. They lived in separate communities and socialized within the persistent boundaries of their respective races.

In another of life's curious twists, Leora Wilson had been a close friend of an elementary school classmate, Linda Brown, at McKinley Elementary in Topeka, Kansas. The same Linda Brown who was the daughter of Rev. Oliver Brown. *The* Linda Brown of the nation's landmark school desegregation case prosecuted by Thurgood Marshall: Brown v. Board of Education, in 1954. Leora Wilson had unwittingly walked through the life of a girl who would represent a historical social shift. Then, in high school, life laughed and gave it to her again. She would sit in choir rehearsal beside a White student, Darlene Danz, who would take part in her own historical first concerning racial integration.

How would you feel about adopting a Black child? The words did not reverberate in a vacuum but rather echoed off the walls of a great conflict of the times. Three months earlier, the Reverend Martin Luther King, Jr., had been murdered in the wake of national rumblings that 'the Negro' was pushing too hard, asking for too much, expecting change too soon. In three months, down to the south in Mexico City, U.S. track and field athletes Tommie Smith and John Carlos would shake their black-gloved fists from the medal stand—a beacon to the world of the human rights violations their own country was perpetrating on Black citizens. This was the season of Black power and social protest. Tense and taut, change was happening.

Jim Potter knew something of the dehumanizing sting of prejudice, although the magnitude of Black America's turmoil was beyond his grasp. He first encountered Black people while taking swimming lessons at a YMCA pool as a 10-year-old in 1951. The pool was in a Black neighborhood and was visited by a good number of Black children. Black and White folk swam at different times and could not be in the pool together, which mystified Jim.

As a high school student, he was at East Peoria's public outdoor pool in Fondulac Park when he saw a Black teenager riding his bicycle out in the pool's parking lot. The boy's White friends were inside swimming. The boy on the bicycle seemed resigned to his exclusion as he slowly circled the lot. Dejection and wanting faintly expressed themselves on his face as his friends splashed away. Jim watched this strange contradiction of friendship and segregation, and his heart told him then: *There is something wrong with this. Something is terribly wrong.*

As a young man, Jim was kicked out of the same pool in Fondulac Park, for wearing his hair too long. The '60s, with an escalating Vietnam, blooming liberalism, and threatened old-guard sensibilities, had turned its venom upon the White transgressor Jim had become. Castigation saturated in vitriol had been directed his way more than once: "Cut your hair, you damned Hippie!" Jim Potter wasn't a flower child, but neither was he marching in the mainstream, or close to it—so he had tasted a small portion of prejudice's fetid meal.

How would you feel about adopting a Black child? What the agency knew, but the Potters didn't at that moment, was that no Black child had ever been adopted by a White family in New Mexico. Anticipation was high and hopeful that this would be the first case. The family seemed right, in the adoption agency's way of looking at qualifications. The child's biological mother and the potential adoptive family were well matched in terms of education and apparent 'intelligence'.

The caseworkers nervously posed the question to the Potters. This was akin to the Brooklyn Dodgers' Branch Rickey asking Jackie Robinson to 'bite the bullet' and expose his soul to a nation's racist wrath. Black folk nationwide were burning for their true freedom. Jim and Darlene had respected Dr. King for the nonviolent manner in which he pushed for change, and were both stricken by the violent taking of King's life. Now they were a young White couple a long way from home being asked to place themselves in the firing line between two races presently engaged in a bitter standoff.

How would you feel about adopting a Black child? Is this something you would be willing to do? Darlene and James looked each other in the eyes. They knew each other's heart. In their young if somewhat naive tradition of simple and straightforward living, the answer was already waiting. They spoke it in concert, singular and understated: "Yes."

Once the Potters began the process of gaining legal custody of me, I became Los Alamos County case number 1908, Baby Boy Scott. One of the social workers, disregarding the race difference, commented to Mr. Potter that, "We consider this the best adoption match we've ever done." They also explained to Mr. Potter how they had inferred the potential of the baby from their interviews with and knowledge of the biological parents. This 'best match ever done' was presupposed as wonderful based upon Mary Woods' impressive intelligence for a Negro woman, the educational level of Ms. Woods and the unnamed father, and the intellectual personality of Mr. Potter. In this moment of child welfare, safety was a concept that drank from a rumor pond. Safety was a married couple, a steady job, a nice community, and a good value system. *Steady, nice, good.* Words that would come to mean something very different to me than they meant to the professionals sending me down a purposeful road.

In the heat-clench of the southwestern summer, Jim and Darlene went to the Health and Social Services offices in Albuquerque. There, they met me for the first time. "What a beautiful baby, Jim." Darlene sighed, her heart melting.

"Yes, honey, he's just what we asked for," Jim answered.

They took me home the same day. It was July 15, 1968, and Baby Boy Scott had been legally placed by the Department of Public Welfare with Mr. and Mrs. James Potter, with legal intent of adoption. It was one day before their daughter Kristin's first birthday. The nation was still burning. The flint and the stone were black and white to the bone.

It would take almost four years for the adoption to become legal. The original judge, who was reported to not look favorably upon the idea of adoption in general, much less transracial adoption, retired and a new judge took the case, facilitating its completion. The Potters used an attorney who worked on a fixed fee of fifty dollars. He was blind and for several years didn't even know that the adoption was transracial. Once he learned that the involved child was Black, he assumed either Mr. Potter or his wife was Black, and asked them so. The Hispanic judge in an American Indian land, who placed this Black baby with a White couple was blind and could not see . . . the color of my case. Amazing grace. Irony is a mischief caught persistently on the underside of our feet, while we walk on, greatly unaware.

In the meantime, I acquired the third generation of my names from my new adoptive parents:

NEW MEXICO DEPARTMENT OF PUBLIC WELFARE
FORM CWS#404

12. As further information for the Court, Petitioner(s) state that: they have had said child in their care, custody and control long enough to be convinced beyond a doubt that they would want said child as permanently theirs.

WHEREFORE, Petitioner(s) PRAY(s) that:

2. The Court grant that the name (s) of the aforesaid child(ren) be changed as follows: John Scott Potter

This 29th day of August, 1968.

"Go down to the potter's house,
and there I will give you my message."

Jeremiah 18:2

THE CHILD ADOPTS THE FAMILY

THAT first summer was a transition for all of us. I was unsettled. And, at only nine months, I was already indelibly Black. My first nine months, in the womb, had been a feast of gestation's generosity. Not only was I an immediate imprint of my mother Mary's diet, emotions, rhythms, dreams, and voice, and those of my brothers, cousins, aunt, and uncle; but in the succeeding nine months I had become shaped by my Black foster mother's mold. I absorbed her unique, intimate flavor, her own personal culture. I was immersed in her household rhythms, sounds, voices, words, emotions, energy, scents, routines, and the social influx into her home. I had become the okra and collard greens of her diet, and the vibration of conversations on race and social injustice that took on the particular tinge of Black folk speaking in the freedom of a private residence. That conversation reached me. These two nine-month periods made me a cultural artifact. An undeniable rendering of culture's magically transforming artistic skills.

In this new home, this Potter's house, I was at first unsteady. Though laid back, I was by nature highly sensitive to the rise and fall of voices, the rituals and habits that for the grown folk towering over me had receded into automated non-regard. But I was a child, and therefore a sponge. I soaked it all up. It was I, most of all, who was adopting. Adopting new ways into a young system not yet secured by years. It was I whose emotional comport and psychological compass were only beginning to develop, who was tested to accommodate myself to this new reality and find security within it. *It* was a home. *It* was a family, preexisting and settled into its patterns. I would have to leave much of my belongings behind.

My new mother, this strong-voiced woman who fixated her care on me, had to give me two or three bottles of milk before I was eased enough to fall into sleep at night. I drank milk constantly during the day. It was soothing and familiar at a time when not much was either. But nighttime was when the milk was a necessity. Dad often was the one doing his best to calm my nerves and send me to my sleep. In those tentative moments of early parenthood, he reached back to his own childhood for what he knew. He rocked me late into the night, singing one of the songs his father had sung to him. I could smell the coffee on his breath as he sang:

> "Old Hogan's goat was feeling fine,
> He just ate three red shirts right off the line.
> I took a stick and broke his back.
> I tied him to a railroad track.
> The fast express came whizzing by.
> Old Hogan's goat was doomed to die.
> He heaved a sigh as though in vain,
> Coughed up the shirts and flagged down the train!"

The transitions of that first year of my life, along with my pensive nature, left me restless. I was also under-stimulated when I arrived in my new home. The excessive stretches of lying still in my crib at the child-crowded foster home left a flat area on the back of my skull. My parents worked to stimulate my undeveloped muscles. I was chubby and could not even sit on my own when I first arrived. Infant calisthenics became my post-foster care rehabilitation. Dad, the big man with the beard that scratched my cheeks, bounced me up and down on his lap, pulling me up by my hands, forcing my legs to piston themselves into some degree of strength.

Her White Midwestern farm perspective is overcome by, or perhaps rather feeds, her spiritual understanding that this child needs to be connected with the rhythms and flavors of his early days. Down in the undercarriage of that consciousness, maybe she knows her child's needs surpass his early days and extend back all the way into that expansive and unknown-to-her forest of his heritage and ancestry. She wishes to bring him back to himself in some way. She has found this book of Negro spirituals, plantation songs. She is a singer. This is one thing she can do for him. She sings:

"Mama's little baby loves shortnin', shortnin',
Mama's little baby loves shortnin' bread,
Mama's little baby loves shortnin', shortnin',
Mama's little baby loves shortnin' bread."

Fall came. Time for our multi-race family to return to its White roots. My parents sold their antique Everett studio piano, crafted in 1895, which they had painstakingly refinished in white over its original black surface. *White over black.* Now it had to go. We crammed everything we owned into a homemade trailer and moved to the Orchard Street apartments in Champaign-Urbana, Illinois. This was during the academic years of 1968-69 and 1969-70, while Dad attended graduate school at the University of Illinois. That first fall, the National Guard was on the scene in Champaign-Urbana, martial law was in effect, and racial unrest was an understatement. It was not exactly the safest environment for a White couple with a Black child. Much of Mom's time was spent inside the apartment with Kristin and me.

The few times Mom bravely left the apartment was to shop for groceries. During one of those outings, she passed by an elderly White lady in a store. To Mom, the woman was the image of kindness. Until the woman's eyes caught the Black form in the stroller and old poison released itself from the breach in her soul. She shot hatred on a cold beam to Mom and veered her shopping cart almost into us. Mom was caught off guard by the rage from a White image she associated with safety. One more wound for her to lick.

There would be many more stares of hatred, some steely enough to leave Mom and Dad fearing for our family's safety. So much of America's racial hostility had always been cloaked: in the sweet, the elderly, the young, and in the educated and well mannered—the full rack of civilized appearance. Now it was rearing its ugliness up into Mom's face, coating her in bitter talc with which she was not familiar. She was drifting into the world Black folk inhabited. The world that her Black baby would inhabit: the windstorm of a thousand disdain-tipped needles. She was learning that to some, she and her husband had committed atrocity and become traitors. To some, her White family in effect had become Black.

The woman is scared. She is a new mother, now with two small children. She is under attack and her anxieties are rising. She knows comfort in song. She sings. As much to reestablish the thought within her in response to the battering social criticism as to baste her baby with self-worth, she sings:

> "Jesus loves the little children,
> All the children of the world;
> Red and yellow, black and white,
> They are precious in His sight,
> Jesus loves the little children of the world . . ."

We spent the summer of 1969 in Los Alamos, then moved to New Mexico permanently in the summer of 1970. For my parents these were days of exuberance and the kind of family life substance found in Norman Rockwell's inspiration. Dad indulged his piloting hobby, taking 5 a.m. flights with his friend, Ray Martin. My parents tore up trails and chassis in their Land Rover. They churned homemade ice cream in bright meadows of the Jemez. Grace was by their side.

During family trips to Santa Fe, Mom and Dad often pulled their children along the plaza in a red wagon. In contrast to our family's reception in Illinois, several times people came up to us and said to my parents, "What a beautiful family you have."

"Thank you," my parents responded, relieved that the comment was friendly and not critical. Comforted by this welcoming attitude, Mom and Dad knew they had made the right choice in settling down out here in the West. They told each other, "This is the place for us to be."

In the summer of 1969, my parents were ready to adopt another child. "Maybe if we adopt another Black child, John won't feel as alone," they reasoned. "It should be easier now to get them to place a Black child with us since we already have John."

News came of an available child, almost one year of age, down in Clovis, New Mexico. It was late summer when we all hit the road from Los Alamos, south to Clovis, five hours away. We checked into a hotel, then went over to the agency to see our soon-to-be addition to the family. Greg was small and desperate to be loved. It took him about two minutes to recognize that love had entered the room. Mom's strong waves of affection reached Greg and he jumped in. He clung tight to her and would not let go.

The social workers had expected us to bring baby Greg back to the hotel and keep him overnight with us to make sure everything was fine before heading back to Los Alamos. The workers were not warm to the idea of transracial adoption and slow to part with Greg. My parents had already proven— through their previous adoption and through their engagement and marriage—that they were not the types to wait. With Greg locked to Mom, the deal was sealed. We drove back that day. Kristin and I had a new brother. We were now, for the time being, a family of five, and two-fifths separated from all hopes of being seen by society as normal.

Greg took his transition into the family more easily than I did, perhaps in part because he had previously been in a White foster home. He spent the first few days with his face knotted up into a worrisome expression, but soon was in the flow of the family just as naturally as Kristin was. Greg and I were both, in our own individual ways, living, emoting examples of the fact that culture—more than just holidays and food—is a deeply subtle substance that is with us from birth. It resides in our spiritual inheritance, and is deepened further yet from the moment of conception as we absorb this new, dazzling world we have entered. By the end of our stays in foster care, culture composed enough of what Greg and I were as personalities that our abrupt dislocation into adoption created enduring shock waves within each of us.

Until kindergarten, Kristin, Greg, and I stayed together in one bedroom, on the second split-level of an apartment on 43rd Street. It was a room decorated with richly hued green and yellow jungle design curtains, with tigers prowling through its underbrush. The sunlight came through those curtains to create a child's wonderland in the room. And we lived just down the street from Urban Park, which to our young eyes seemed an endlessly ranging wilderness.

Most memorable to me about that apartment is the giant willow tree that stood in the front corner of the side yard, against the fence separating it from the front yard. It was magical. I waited every year for those first buds to show and transform into small furry blooms that looked like rabbit tails. Apricot and peach trees perfumed the backyard with their sweet scent. A sandbox was our main play area. The back two-thirds of the yard sloped down to the back fence and often was overgrown with weeds higher than my head. I pretended those weeds were safari land, feeding my love of transporting in spirit to distant places.

My spirit was highly permeable. The ancestors stayed loud in my head, early and forever. What felt good, or abrasive, up against my spirit was determined by a faraway source. In those early years, I was being spoken to in a way that caused me to experience things differently. Differently than what might have been expected by the adults caring for me. Even in the first days of my transition into the Potter family, I may have resisted aspects of what their love for me carried with it.

Those first three or four years of life were a rainbow of emotions, mostly happiness. I came into this world with a happy nature, a broad smile, brimming with love to give. The staggering fluctuation between attachment to others and withdrawal, and between peace and piercing pain was yet to emerge. It would do so in pace with the evolution of my peculiar awareness of my fascinating new family and community.

As early as pre-school I was conscious of the physical aspect of my race. One day I walked into the schoolroom, double-checking my skin and hair as I approached the other children. The children looked different from me, but similar to each other. I was more curious than anxious, but even in that moment, I extracted a divot of earth from the ground of my security. I didn't mention those thoughts or feelings to Mom or Dad, but my contemplation was underway.

I may not have comprehended the racial constructs of 'Black' and 'White', but I was able to discern differences. The tallies I took soon emerged along a color line. I recognized that my hair was shorter and more tightly curled than that of most other people and that my nose was broader. My lips were fuller, my skin darker. By five, I was self-conscious of my race to the point of withdrawing. The force of my discomfort overpowered any amount of positive reception I encountered from my young classmates. If popularity at that age had a great weight for my friends, it was barely a background hum for me. I needed it, but was blind to whatever acceptance I received.

Any affinity shown me was filtered through my quickly developing sense of being different, and was largely lost.

I contained a genetic and spiritual predisposition to feel my emotions very deeply. Those emotions would last for hours and days. This shaped my moods, sensitivities, and responses to life. I thrived on quiet and calm, and on large doses of reassurance and reflection. Our house was usually filled with noise, chaos, tough-skinned emotional flow, and little pause or allowance for pensive silence. The contrast affected my attachment in ways that would persist.

Finally, after nearly four years, the law caught up with our family reality. I was taken to the office of the new presiding judge for my adoption case. He wanted to clear out the old, unfinished business of the previous judge. The new judge asked me if I wanted to be 'adopted', a word beyond my full mental reach. I must have said yes. He signed the papers immediately. Formalities aside, I was now a 'valid' member of the family.

THE ADOPTION DECREE: [excerpted]

3. The child herein adopted was born on the 26th day of October, 1967 at Albuquerque, New Mexico, a male child whose name is shown on his birth certificate as "Unnamed."

WHEREFORE, IT IS ORDERED, ADJUDGED, AND DECREED, AND IT IS THE JUDGMENT OF THE COURT: That said unnamed male child be, and the same is hereby, declared to be adopted by Petitioners, James M. Potter and Darlene D. Potter, and henceforth be regarded in all respects as the child of said Petitioners; and that the name of said child be, and the same is hereby, changed as follows: John Scott Potter.

March 16, 1972

I was one warm season away from turning five years old.

Yellow light pours through the window into the dark room. Stillness except for dust particles rising and falling on air currents. She is a woman form in the shadows, with a mother's arms wrapped tight against a baby's shape. The two are one color in this light: the blended hue of calm and intimate solitude. Her movement in the rocking chair is the ocean's steady stroke upon a rocky shore: determined and persistent. She loves this child something painful. Enough to make promises. She sings:

"Hush little baby, don't say a word,
Mama's gonna buy you a mockin' bird.
If that mockin' bird don't sing,
Mama's gonna buy you a diamond ring . . ."

I grew older. The way in which, even at the age of five or six, I experienced being Black was far reaching, deep searching, and intense. It was not nearly all I thought about. I was as fascinated as any child by the simple beauty of life. But when those certain ideas reached me, my foundation shifted. Thoughts and fears were unformed and vague, but reached me through sharp emotions. All this remained floating in my head and heart, as I was starting to sense it was not to be placed on the table of family conversation and interaction. I couldn't have if I had tried. I didn't know the language for it.

As I started to pick up the messages from storybooks and the television about what was 'right' to have, I wanted it. What I saw were straight-haired, narrow-nosed, thin-lipped, fair-skinned children and people. Just as with the popular video game advertised in a commercial, I wanted one: one of those features. Not out of jealousy or greed, but because I didn't want to feel left out. I wanted to belong.

Being Black was a central and important part of my personality from the outset. I had no choice but to deal with it.

I couldn't ignore it. It wasn't my nature to stop thinking when thoughts came to me. I couldn't treat Blackness as a meaningless sidebar. Daily my race grew in stature, a miniature spirit sprouting from within. It grew as a matter of contrast: I didn't find my reflection anywhere I looked. Ghosts protested this fact in whispers like Saturn's rings around my heart. The ancestors would not let me rest.

I do not know what changes my family made to accommodate the fact that Greg and I were not only Black, but also that we came from real people, people with real personality, medical, and social legacies. They never told us these stories. Mom and Dad read to us at bedtime about all manners of imaginary characters and adventures and we lost ourselves in the tales. But the things before me that were not imaginary slowly became the things I wished Mom and Dad spoke about while tucking me in. *Do the creatures in Dr. Seuss' Whoville feel like I feel? Does the Cat in the Hat always feel like grinning like that? Am I still going to belong here when I wake up tomorrow?* Increasingly, I was concerned with how I should morph my personality in a way that would be both natural and would help me fit in.

In the end, these considerations became overwhelming. Mom and Dad must have been challenged as they tried to deal with the responses from others for adopting two Black children. But being limited, needy, and self-centered as a matter of my extreme youth, I needed these two grown people to somehow realize the turmoil I had already learned to keep from them, and to make our house my home.

As the years passed, I made ongoing deductions about how this adoptive family felt to me. I did not assume, even adopted at that early age, that I was naturally a part of these people. I tested them repeatedly in very small ways to see who they really were, and what was in their heart. At times I did not accept their love; hovering around it like a hummingbird, the wings of my heart blurred with the speed of readiness to fly away. *Come and get me if you can, or if you want. How far do I have to pull back before you won't come and get me anymore? Where is your limit, just what am I worth to you?*

So many interactions between family members and me became evidence to me that I didn't belong, or that they didn't really love me. I didn't care what the source of the conflict, or offense or slight was. Or even whether there was any actual friction in the interaction. My imagination ran all over the place, like a jackrabbit, darting and dashing, to find a rock to hide behind. That rock was the defensive thought that I wasn't a part of *this*, this family thing, so I better draw up into myself and hold on.

Before I even moved past elementary school, here was my mind, unleashed, decorated now in mature articulation:

Should I eat as they eat, talk as they talk, move as they move? Because after all, they are what I am supposed to be a part of. Why are they the Sun and I the shivering planet in orbit of their mass? Why must I dance to their rhythm, love the daylight like they do, when night is what I soothe to most?

My fears explode at night and fill my bedroom with red ribbons of blood and horror. I simply tread water to stay afloat 'til morning. They seem to sleep a better sleep, like this house was made for them. They only speak of certain things, but the truth that burns inside of me is lit aflame by stories filled with dark-skinned characters around the fringes of middle ground. The distant wails of brown-bodied blemishes to this white expanse curl nerves beneath my skin.

Should I give way and let myself forever fall into the personal volcano that is this community? Should I? And if I do, will what I was meant to be disappear? Should I speak more softly, speak with a higher pitch, not stand so tall, move more slowly, or speak only of nonracial things and the lighter beauty of the world? I know that without the presentation of my smile, these people, on their insides, suffer from a fear of me. Funny how when an animal shows its teeth in its world that is seen as a sign of aggression, but in this strange world when I bare mine that is the symbol for their White relief. I spend my life smiling so that I am not feared. I fear being feared and so I accommodate, but what changes, what distortions are made for me?

Each day I made decisions about how much I would open up myself, in a given moment, and act like a part of the family. It wasn't an absence of happiness but a recalcitrance to emerge. I was a turtle, holing up inside my protective shell, shy and hesitant as I stuck my head out, often grudgingly, to partake in what the family had to offer. More than just a metaphor, I truly acted out that turtle identity. At night, I pulled the covers over my head, pretending my blankets were my turtle shell, leaving only a small air hole for breathing. That was how I slept and constructed my sense of safety. My American Indian heritage might have spoken of this personality as my animal spirit. I knew it as the dam to withstand my flood of fears.

Then, my animal spirit came to me. As we drove home from the pool one summer day, in an afternoon downpour, I saw a box turtle, solitary and still, in the road not far from our house. I don't know how I noticed it in that heavy rain. "Mom, stop!" I yelled. "There's a turtle in the road!" Mom must have thought I was crazy, but she pulled the car over. We took the turtle home, where I found that it had a cracked shell. We nursed that turtle back to health over the next few months, but a private drama was playing out for me. I studied that turtle's personality closely. Noticed its reticence and shyness as it moved its head in and out from the haven of its shell. I could relate to its character. I didn't understand until years later why I felt so close to that small, silent creature. Never before, and not since, had I seen a box turtle in the wild in Los Alamos. Visions visit us of their own design.

After that experience, I had a recurring dream in which I walked into a large dark cave on the ocean side, and there were hundreds of turtles moving around in the sand. I sat down in the middle of those turtles and melted into happiness. That dream is the most reassuring one I can remember.

My nightmares were always of me being chased. The nightmare that left me screaming was of a witch on a broomstick, like from the Wizard of Oz, chasing me all over the Earth—through canyons and woods, over mountain tops, underwater, in the sky above from cloud to cloud. Another persistent nightmare found me chased across the world by a towering ape, huge as King Kong. I have a strong suspicion that it was the beast of rejection and heartbreak coming after me every time.

This was how my circumstance was born for me, and for my adoptive parents. A Black child in the care of White parents at a time when the nation was convulsing at its seams from a social straining based upon that very same Blackness and that Whiteness. I was apparently the first Black child adopted by a White couple in the state of New Mexico. In that sense, we lived our lives without the benefit of precedent. There were no support groups, talk shows, mentor families, books, articles, movies, or other resources to guide us through our journey. Mom and Dad read no literature in preparation; were offered no counsel. The absence of a guiding precedent would shape our relationship, and it would shape me.

She sings. Deep inside, her own soul is voicing its empathy for this baby. Or maybe she is imagining this child's future emotions. Perhaps she is spelling out her own alienation, born of this uncommon mother-child coupling, far from the home of her youth, in a world that seems angry at the choice she has made. Maybe all of this is true . . . as she sings:

> "Sometimes I feel like a motherless child,
> Sometimes I feel like a motherless child,
> Sometimes I feel like a motherless child,
> A mighty long way from home."

Given my circumstance and the identity I would soon develop, the fact that I was growing up in Los Alamos was sublime symbolism. I was living on soil that had been spat out from its womb, orphaned from its bed inside the Earth. The ground was a volcanic geology with an identity so turbulent that it grew volatile and sprouted up with strange things. Hordes of cholla and prickly pear cacti with coats of needles pockmarked the land. The ground must have grown these things in defense, to keep other living things away from its detachment wound.

Even the wider ground surrounding me was a mutant factory. It grew freakish things, like the limestone hollow of Carlsbad Caverns to the south—the largest underground chamber in the world. And White Sands desert: the world's largest deposit of gypsum—a 275-square-mile sea of white dunes stretching outward in waves. There was also a forest of ancient petrified trees, hard as stone. Medusa had caught them staring. And what kind of land is home to a bird that does not fly, but runs the road? Or an enormous creeping spider covered in fur? Where there are prehistoric leftovers, like a toad covered in horns and spikes like some shrunken dinosaur? Where the state flower is a shock of fearsome green blades, on guard to thrust and parry with the wind?

The land that cradled me was adorned with bold exaggerations. Brilliant stars at night suspended seemingly just above my face in the high altitude. Pollution-free air and the lack of 'civilized' lighting from the ground below made those stars and the planets and moon even more luminescent. The full moon hung so close and clear it was a tempting alabaster lollipop I swore I could lick. Rainstorms unloaded ponderous drops that hit the Earth like ripe melons, a barrage of transparent water balloons bursting on the pavement. Lightning serrated the sky in thick angry bolts forewarning of a thunder so loud it turned husky dogs into whimpering neurotics.

This land was fantastical. Sunset was a show-off, rainbows were saturated swaths of candy colors, and clouds built up a thousand stories high with billowing white possibilities. Snowstorms were more often measured in feet, not inches. The soil was either coffee brown, burnished red, or streaked with opaque, sun-glinted minerals. It was stacked in sedimentary layers that told great stories of the prehistoric ocean that had covered this land and the dinosaurs that had left behind their bones as symbols of their epoch.

To the northwest, near the only place in the country where the boundaries of four states meet, Ship Rock sailed, a 1,700 foot-high eroded volcanic core sacred to the Diné (Navajos). Battleship Rock was moored off to the side of State Road 4, on the way to Jemez Springs. It stood some 200-feet high. It took little imagination to believe you were staring at an actual ship. And there was Camel Rock, on US 285/84 leading up into Los Alamos, another slowly eroding monument to Nature's genius and whimsical creativity. Ancient Indian arrowheads, pottery shards, and petroglyphs were everywhere. Even the homes were rebels. Their walls were made of clay and straw—adobe—a feature that made them seem at once prehistoric and futuristic compared to the wood-sided homes of America's mainstream. Disney never had an imagination like this.

Northern New Mexico also harbors the communities of the Diné, and the Jicarilla Apache. And the people of the Pueblos, many of whose communities are located along the Rio Grande corridor running from the Carson National Forest near the Colorado border, down through Albuquerque around 100 miles to the south of Los Alamos. The 19 pueblos are the San Ildefonso, Taos, Picuris, Santa Clara, San Juan, Pojoaque, Cochiti, Jemez, Nambe, Tesuque, Santo Domingo, Zia, San Felipe, Santa Ana, Laguna, Sandia, Isleta, Acoma, and Zuni. This world fed me.

Mom took us to powwows, flea markets, and the old town squares in Santa Fe, Taos, and Albuquerque, where we were exposed to the Pueblo people selling their crafts and wares, and celebrating in dance worship. But it was within the boundaries of the pueblo where the people were most unfettered to mainstream ways. This was where they painted the sky with their texture, and it was a good thing.

Each pueblo had an annual feast day, days of celebration and prayer originally attached to their traditional indigenous calendar. But with the coming of the Spanish culture and Catholicism, the feast days became associated with the Catholic patron saint days.

Dancing, drumming, and sharing food defined the feast days. Dances were prayerful, spiritual, and an experience of generational bonding. From the littlest children, just past toddler-hood, to the grand elders, the whole pueblo danced. Dances were performed for good health, good harvest, and overall well-being of all people. Some were open to the public and some were private. Many of the songs and ceremonies were stories of their culture, existence, and history. They understood the importance of preserving a vivacious connection with their heritage as a means of ensuring and communing with the future. Among the dances were the green corn, the eagle, the buffalo, the deer, and the harvest dance.

Set to Earth-bound drumming, the dancers pounded dust up from the ground, their voices a chanting communiqué with the Great Spirit. For me, this was magic. The drumming rumbled through my chest, waking strong awestruck emotions. The togetherness they portrayed belonged to a past age.

During the feast days, a great tradition took place. Families opened up their homes to all other families in the pueblo— offering up a heaping bounty of food from the meagerness of their pantry. Groups of people came through in shifts, sitting at the long table, taking their meal. The hosts were generous in a way I have never seen elsewhere. To table after table of visitors, they urged on: "Eat plenty. Eat plenty." For the diners, this was an exercise in polite consumption that dwarfed the stuffed-belly legends of mainstream society's Thanksgivings. From home to home the people went, eating a full meal each time, lest the host be offended. Traditional feast day foods included blue corn, wild spinach, wild tea, tamales, corn, chilé, beans, tortillas, Pueblo bread, and fry bread.

The giving was not limited to meals served inside. During a particular feast celebration, a throng of Pueblo people moved down the corridors, gathering around one home at a time. From the rooftop of each house, family members happily grabbed at stores of nonperishable food and drink stacked beside them. They threw the goods down to the crowd below, a mass of extended hands excitedly reaching to catch the manna from these lesser rooftop heavens.

The families on the rooftops enthusiastically responded to the people below, like athletes to a hometown crowd. They threw their food and drink packages hard and far. Below, you had to stay alert or you could suffer a painful blow to the head or face . . . such wonderful, splendid chaos. It was feast day. In the midst of general poverty, here was a bountiful sharing, traditional to the communal values of the Pueblo. One I had never seen outside of the pueblos in communities of much greater affluence. These moments did not so much shape me as they highlighted my natural shape. *Eat plenty. Eat plenty.* I fed on this kind of affirmation wherever I found it.

There weren't many American Indian children in my classes at school. Most of those children's families lived down the hill in the valley—around Española, Pojoaque, and in the pueblos themselves. Still, I could feel their presence and my thoughts were of those children, those lives, every time we drove down to Santa Fe or Albuquerque. I stared out the car window toward the barren hills that I knew cradled Indian communities somewhere inside them. I identified with the brown skin and calm, understated demeanor of so many of the Indian people. My personality was often overmatched by the assertive, boisterous energies of many Los Alamos children. I was seeking cracks to hide in, stillness to stand beside. The brown skin of the Pueblo people was my drink of water in the desert. As I grew older, the Indian community became my surrogate Black presence, a private self-indulgence of which they were surely unaware.

The Pueblo people were daily a calm space that suited me. In the same way, it was good providence for me that the town I grew up in was also placid. Los Alamos was, to many of its residents, an idyllic community. It was the pinnacle of comfort and calm, overlooking the land of enchantment—a bubble on a hill, 7,200 feet above the level of the sea. The town is located on the eastern slope of the lower lap of the Jemez Mountain range, upon the afterbirth residue of the continent's largest extinct volcano. A photographer's dream abounded in the surrounding panorama. Great waves of the Earth's wooded splendor must have once built to fluid crescendo, cupping the community in majesty, and then froze. Now that wave of earth hung there at its tidal apex, a monument to how God's force makes men small.

Los Alamos had many of Small Town USA's requisite characters, cleanliness, and undercurrents. The public school system was strong and vibrant. There were two junior high schools and one high school. Children maintained the same friendships from kindergarten through senior graduation day. Stability was a local product.

Grievous violence, such as armed robbery, shootings, and murder, was virtually unheard of. One year, a high school student who lived on the block behind us was murdered. Although I hardly knew her, I was shaken by death so near to our home. It was the first instance of extreme violence I had been exposed to and it was difficult for my mind to embrace the event as real. Folks felt safe enough to leave their house doors unlocked, and frequently even their car doors. Children played freely on the street well into dusk and often past dark: double dutch, kick the can, spin the bottle, jacks, hide and seek, hop scotch. We had room to roam. Yards were large, bushes abounded for our cover, and cars yielded in the road as we tossed Nerf footballs and played out our stickball fantasies.

Los Alamos had one movie theatre, a bowling alley, and 'big time' restaurants like a McDonald's, a Sonic, and a Taco Bell. Twenty thousand residents ebbed through their days in this mountain enclave to a rhythm largely set by the 7,000 or so scientists, technicians, and support staff employed in the government-owned, Los Alamos Scientific Laboratory, later to be renamed the National Laboratory. This made for a unique population. In any restaurant over lunch you were just as likely to overhear patrons discussing quantum physics, ionic particle acceleration, or thermal dynamics as you were to hear sports talk. Napkins left over from meals in these establishments were often littered with formulas and equations beyond the reach of most reasonably intelligent people—the hieroglyphics of a rare and idiosyncratic clan. Here was the small town that large minds built.

Our town was clean air, clear, mountain tap water, and light traffic. We could ride our bicycles from one end of town to the other in less than half an hour. Nightlife was virtually nonexistent. The streets rolled up not too long after 5 p.m., when the crowd from the Lab returned to their homes. Living in the mountains encouraged a casual kind of attitude. People wore jeans and tennis shoes to work, and the pace on the streets was understated and unpretentious.

Los Alamos (Spanish for *the poplar trees*) was apple pie and ice cream. Families churning homemade ice cream on the Fourth of July. The kind of place where Shriners in their red bucket hats and tassels cruised proudly on their go-carts in parades and children sat perched on their fathers' shoulders screaming for a parade participant to shower them with candy. Piñatas and clowns starred in backyard birthday party scenes. The crime section of the town newspaper was filled mostly with stories of ducks straying from Ashley Pond and people pulled over for driving while intoxicated. No real hustle and bustle, a distinct slow or no-growth commercial attitude. Small, stable, rarely changing, predictable, nice Los Alamos. A great place to raise a family, I heard many residents say. But greatness is relative, and I'm not sure how many Black families would concur.

The presence of a significant number of Hispanic people in town became a saving grace for me. I held a private affiliation with them as kin in our departure from the standard. As I experienced it, Los Alamos was decisively White: numerically, but more importantly, culturally. The lifestyle, personalities, and overriding tone were the kind of Whiteness that stands on the opposite side of the perceptual Grand Canyon from Blackness. Lack of exposure sowed this seed. No appreciable Black community existed within 100 miles.

Those rare times when I experienced a 'Black sighting' in Los Alamos, a strange mix of emotions ran through me: excitement, like when you're in a place where no one speaks your language, and finally one person appears who can understand you. And shame, because seeing another Black child reminded me of that same Blackness in me that I was at odds with. A wall of fear would defeat my longing to connect with that other child. As though doing so would violate the cultural dictates of Los Alamos. I was thankful for the presence of other Black children, but it was an ambivalent gratitude. Just thinking about them called to my mind our extreme stranding upon this racial island.

The isolating geology of Los Alamos seemed to have served as a role model for its residents. As with many small towns, numerous people insulated themselves, seemingly from life itself. Change appeared to move in its steady way around the country whenever I traveled with my family outside of Los Alamos. But then, as we came back up that mountain road leading into town, Change would begin to flutter. Its wings crimped, it descended into a stillness on the ground. Los Alamos had technological richness and intellectual resources so great they were daunting to out-of-towners, but all the technology in the world cannot substitute for the capacity to relate to others—diverse others—in a comfortable and penetrating manner. Some people are made for places with a lack of social vibrancy. Struggling early and often with my race, I came to require a more varied infusion.

The lack of secure and meaningful attachments to other African American people was a vacuum that bore a hole into the bottom of my self-esteem reserve. Draining steadily out of me was the substance of my positive regard for the person I was. Meanwhile, my parents, teachers, and others would come to wonder why I was so shy and quiet, and why I receded into shadows like those dark places were my best friends.

My nesting place was a bittersweet beginning. It was a slow-paced, familiar, and predictable environment— characteristics I would grow to appreciate years later while soaking up the chaos and noise of larger cities. Some of the friends I would make there would be friends for life. Relationships were paramount, and family life was a dominant priority. Altitude, mountains, and silence mellow a person. I would encounter and be embraced by so many good souls and kind hearts.

I would return that embrace, loving the town and its people, because it was my entire world. Yet there were things in the air that did not feel like home to me. Things like a collective flirt with racial and ethnic tolerance that was rarely pushed to prove its mettle. It felt like a bubble, on a mountaintop, insulated. Sometimes it is good to bleed, to feel the sandpaper of cultural vibrancy against your skin. You may suffer a certain sting from the discomfort of unfamiliarity, but in the end the healing brings you a fruit that only the tree of social exposure may bear.

Even in the lap of beauty, nature grants us blemish. Los Alamos was no different than other communities in this regard. Los Alamos and New Mexico would grow their roots in me. This one-of-a-kind town, and this mystical land, would serve as my childhood cradle—leaving their marbled beauty as volcanic deposits that enriched me.

Who would step forward
and receive the honor
of my beloved children
need dare become a child again
dazzled at my knee
for these days surely will be
for learning

THE MOTHER TREE

HERITAGE shows up in a personality subtle as a rainstorm bull-rushing sun-baked ground. Mom was a blend of passion and hard-edged determination descended from generations of farmers who battled and coaxed the Earth for their survival. Her mother, Betty Danz, was of German and English descent. Grandma Danz's father, Grover Ball, had been a railroad engineer in Peoria, running locomotives to earn his keep. Like her mother before her, Grandma Danz was a homemaker who raised three daughters and a niece. Mom always thought Grandma Danz was the best mother in the world, a meticulous housecleaner, who kept her children tidy and presentable. Where her children went, there went Betty Danz's life investment: Midwestern simple, generations wise, and strapped down heavy with affection.

Grandma's world was defined by that house at 223 Rock Island Street, by the lives within it, and the yard surrounding it. This was where she made her keep. The house, located in an older, working-class community, was built around 1900 and her family purchased it in 1948. A modest country-style house set up off the street, it was surrounded by a wide green yard in the shadows of a huge oak tree. Squirrels ran wild all over that yard, scavenging for acorns, pitter-pattering across oak leaves, peeping the human activity as they paused, somehow in suspended crouch on the tree, perpendicular with the ground 10 feet below. They flew like circus performers from branch to branch in the canopy above, a constant scuffle of movement as background noise for our passing days.

The back of the yard held a shed in one corner with a garden in front of it. Tomatoes and snapping beans were the crowning crops. A concrete path meandered past the shed out the back fence toward the railroad track and the woods beyond. Those railroad tracks were our best entertainment. Against adult command, we children set out on those tracks, walking sticks in hands, daring ourselves farther down the way toward whatever grand adventure that day might hold. We were Tom Sawyer and Huckleberry Finn. We were young, and the tracks behind Grandma's house were our path to fantasy.

Pennies aren't for spending. They're for placing on railroad tracks, after which you squeal infantile delight like you're getting away with some great caper, then stand watch from a safe distance while the ground starts to shake, and the familiar rumble emerges from around the bend. The great freight train roars by, blowing back the skin on your face in its draft. Pennies are for picking up from railroad tracks, flattened into smooth oval amulets by an unimaginable force, so you can run back to the house showing off the magic you have wielded, turning copper into child's gold.

Grandma was the big-bosomed, short woman who drowned us children in cookies, cakes, candy, and everything sweet, whenever she could. Her kitchen was an authentic country knick-knack bonanza. From the flowered wallpaper to the decorated bread tin, the room was stuffed with colors, figurines, and wall hangings. It was a parade of stimulus Mom would replicate in our home back in New Mexico. Grandma's kitchen smelled of the promise of sugar. A door at the back wall led down into a dark, musty basement where jars of fruit preserves were stacked on shelves along the walls. Other things were stored down there, in that dark, but my mind has left those memories far behind in an act of fearful abandonment.

Grandma could be firm as she corralled her horde of grandchildren, including our cousins, Tonya and Laura, into a reasonable assembly of order. But mostly she soaked us in warmth and spoiled us way past rotten. "You kids want some ice cream?" Her words unleashed a stampede of grandchildren into the kitchen. I scanned Grandma's heart, worried about how two Black grandchildren played upon it. I could detect no flat or sharp notes. Only that ice cream sweetness. She was home to me. Grandma Danz is now 78 years old, and lives in Ottawa, Illinois, where I am sure she still keeps a cookie jar, stocked with love and confection.

Tonya and Laura were the daughters of Mom's youngest sister, my Aunt Donna. They were just about our age, so we quickly developed a bond in those early years that had us excited to get out to Illinois to see them again. Cousin love, forced to hold its breath most of the year across 1,300 miles for that once or twice a year release, can become a strong affection. Which was why it meant so much to me that whenever we all were together, it felt like a clean kind of interaction. Clean of racial ambivalence.

I don't remember a single Black person ever present in a family moment back there in Illinois, which was the status quo in the decisively segregated climate. But Tonya and Laura became familiar with Greg and me from an early age, allowing us all to fall into a regard for each other, and a comfort that might not have occurred at a later age. More than unconditional love, or bountiful love, it was clean love that made the world of difference for me. The vibes weren't polluted with a discomfort with my race, an avoidance of the idea of my race, or a strained tolerance or forgiveness for my race. Crisp and clean, that's how I needed it.

Though I have not been out that way in years, my heart still thinks of Tonya and Laura with a hopeful energy. Hoping that the way they thought of Greg and me when our days were young, sinking our bare feet into the sand at Twin Lakes, quarreling with the intensity only close love brings, is the way they feel for us now. Now that we have melded into our respective adult social value pools, pools likely circumscribed along the lines of race.

The middle daughter between Mom and Aunt Donna was my Aunt Sue, who was married to our Uncle Wayne. Donna, Sue, Wayne, Tonya, and Laura were the ones we spent most of our time with, beyond Grandma and Grandpa Danz. From these adults, Greg and I received the dependable and sincere affection a child would want from relatives. I cannot say the love I felt coming from the adult hearts was quite as clean as Tonya and Laura's. Though genuine, it was tempered somehow, as though they were reaching out to their Black nephews through more layers of social conditioning than Tonya and Laura. This is a peculiar jeopardy of aging. We can easily lose, if only in thin flakes, some volume from the unrestrained propensity of our child hearts.

These were our relatives—Mom's family, striving upstream against the current of their own community and culture to embrace two children that their own socialization told them they were not supposed to embrace. They succeeded in defeating the current; they reached us. My love for them today is true and sentimental. But the slight strain of their loving effort showed up in my deep down sense of belonging. It was subtle enough, a meek tremor, but it was enough to leave cracks in the place where belonging makes its name.

One of the cracks I would have to caulk originated from within the heart of a soldier. Mom's father, Rudolf Danz, was the son of an immigrant from the Bern Canton of Switzerland, a German-speaking area of the country. Grandpa Danz's father came to the U.S. as a young man, along with his twin brother, and worked as a farm hand until he saved enough money to buy his own farm. Grandpa's mother was an American, last name Miller, of German descent. An irony of Grandpa Danz's life is that he fought for this country against the coalition that included Hitler's Germany in World War II, serving in the 1943 Allied invasion of Italy's alluvial valleys. Generals George Patton and Omar Bradley, America's supreme commanders in that invasion, must have led many men in mortal conflict upon the land of the soldiers' own ancestors. Life's circles are stubborn about finding their way back to completion, even in the cruelest ways.

Mom remembers being about four years of age when a towering man in a brown uniform showed up at the family house in Peoria, splintering their all-female union. The soldier had been away for nearly four years and was a stranger to Mom. She noticed that his knee was wounded. Grandma Danz noticed that this man, her husband, had somehow changed. He would never revert to that smooth-surfaced soul he was when he left for war at age 19. This was his weight to carry. He did so admirably as he made what he could of the rest of his life.

Grandpa Danz made his living working on the railroad, and was as tough as the steel tracks he spilled his sweat over. He was a brakeman for the Peoria and Pekin Union Railroad, a small railroad running through East Peoria. His skin was thick like leather, his hair near black and feisty in texture. Friends described him as all grit, tough, and given to tormenting and teasing. He was meat and potatoes, tobacco and a pipe—dip in his cheek, and discipline on his mind. Grandpa Danz was a no-mess man, dripping vitriol as he walked, standing strong in denim overalls.

One time, when he was three, Greg lost hold of reality for a moment and dared to pour water into Grandpa's smoking pipe. You did not mess with the man's pipe. You couldn't really blame Greg; he was just matching ornery with ornery. In his typical gruff humor, Grandpa had teased Greg that he was going to cut off his ears. Greg did his thing, dousing the sacred pipe. Grandpa went to light his ritual into smoky effect. All of hell, and more than that, broke loose. "Dammit, you kids!" The walls shook, we shook, I think even Mom shook. We didn't come out of hiding from beneath beds and benches and from behind couches until hunger became the overpowering emotion. It took a lot of hunger.

Dating from when I was very young, as early as two or three years of age, I have strong recollections of being around Grandpa Danz, back in Peoria during one of our visits. I was truly afraid of the man. The images are clear: me as a little toddler, crawling and running around, looking way, way up at this huge grown person. *Grandpa doesn't like me.* Nor did I believe that he liked Greg. Perhaps it was not quite dislike, but it felt like some kind of aversion or displeasure somehow related to me. I had no idea why this would be, but I strongly sensed it, and I bore my child's intuition faithfully.

I remember Grandpa's generally scowling face, growling voice, and often grumpy presence. "You kids get in here and clean up this mess!" he boomed, sending our hearts into our throats.

Mom tried to explain and soothe: "Grandpa's just ornery. Just ignore his clowning. He's a little mean-spirited by nature, but in a loving kind of way." I wasn't convinced of that.

Grandpa was all kinds of ornery toward all of us. One of his gigs was to call one of us over to him. "Krissy, you want some tobaccy?" he asked with a devilish grin. He then took some of the dark brown stuff out of its pouch, coaxing us into placing a small amount in our lower lip, as though it were a secret treat just between him and his grandchildren. When we gagged and spit the stuff out on the floor, startled disgust registering on our face, the pleasure was all his. Yeah, he was that kind of ornery.

Still, I felt some different kind of energy from him, a clear vibration directed toward Greg and me. I knew even then that the vibe was a thing associated with a word that rhymes with *face,* and had to do with the color of mine. It wasn't spoken nor acted out, although there was little physical affection coming from him early on—but he was that way in general. It was an inaudible whisper I could detect from the space between and beneath his words. It was the hint of a glimmer of some tarnished light in the pupils of his eyes. It was not so strong as to be an announcement. But it was an ember with enough heat that it would have burned if I could have put my finger on it. I grew up gradually sensing Grandpa's love for Greg and me, but, as would be a theme of my life, I would have to settle for love with an undercurrent. All those undercurrents would leave me carved into a complexity far beneath my surface.

It wasn't until I was getting ready to go to college that I learned a piece of the truth about Grandpa that I had sensed even as a young child. Dad and me, and a classmate of mine named Nate, were driving back from a trip to visit Southern Colorado University to check out the campus and the basketball program as a potential place to enroll. It was night and I was asleep in the back seat. I woke up and heard Dad talking with Nate, who was in the front seat with him. I don't know if Dad knew I was awake or not, but he was sharing a story with Nate that I had never heard before. Nate was also Black, and I thought he must have asked Dad about my adoption. Maybe Dad was the one who struck up that particular conversation. Long hours on the road in the small space of a car, away from the rest of the world, can loosen the blockages that suppress old and boxed-in memories. Was Dad releasing pent-up energy, or was Nate braving to address a curiosity—a curiosity I shared but had failed to tend?

In the hum of the car on the road, in the night darkness, I heard Dad talk about Grandpa Danz. He shared with Nate, with candor and reflection in his voice: "Darlene's father carried some prejudiced attitudes about Black people years ago, okay? He was a product of his time and experiences. He spent so much of his life in the pre-civil rights era, and in the chilled racial climate of Peoria."

The next thing Dad said was something that both enlightened me and bore another measure of alienation into my breast. He said, "Darlene's father initially didn't take too well to the adoption. He had a hard time accepting it."

I transported myself back and envisioned that moment. "Darlene, what is this going to do to Kristin?" Grandpa had warned, concerned for my sister. "She's going to have to deal with this growing up. How are people going to treat her?" Grandpa was . . . *afraid.* He must have thought: *This is something I do not know crossing the line into my family.* His fears were born of real-life insight and imaginations fresh from a fable-based source: the lies of his own upbringing.

Mom's fears about what she was getting into must have been at least equaled by the clenching hurt of her father's disapproval. *Dad, this is my child. He's a beautiful baby boy, and I love him. Just give this a chance. I know you'll love him.*

Mom never spoke of that time or the specifics of what was said between a daughter and her family. She hoarded that to her, I assume as much out of a desire to suppress the emotions of that wound as out of a desire to protect me from a hurtful truth. But Mom's people were a close-knit family, and that significant flare-up must have been tremulous to all of them. That I heard of this first indirectly from the back seat of a car on the highway, on the breach of my adulthood, spoke volumes about my parents' enduring protective impulse, and to my exclusion from my own life story. That moment overhearing my father marked the beginning of my understanding that my parents were also victims of the ugly human response to their Black children.

What I had always sensed was true. Grandpa Danz had harbored some conflicting feelings toward my brother and me when we were young, and probably held some small portion of those feelings the rest of his life. But over the years, Grandpa steadily developed a strong love and acceptance of us. By the last decade of his life, he even developed a good friendship with Greg. Greg's magnetic and comic personality surely eased the way for Grandpa. Greg and Grandpa acted ornery together, and loved to buddy-up over any issue in arguments with Mom, Kristin, Grandma, or anyone else.

Greg and Grandpa were both die-hard Chicago Cubs baseball fans, and would watch games together on television all the time. Grandpa would come into the living room on visits out to New Mexico and bellow in his craggy voice, "Greggy! Cubs gonna win today?"

Greg would answer with the enthusiasm found in such male bonding moments, "Yeah! They're gonna blow them out!" They both glowed in the brief interchange. It was their personal ritual, worn to a polished gleam over the years as they reached across the canyons of generations, region, and race, to hold tight to the love a grandchild needs from a grandfather. A love the latter needed at least as much in reverse.

Whatever was true about my Grandpa's earlier attitudes, whether they may be labeled racist, prejudiced, bigoted, ignorant, or simply concerned, Grandpa was one of the greatest testaments I witnessed to the ability of human love to conquer the conflict of prejudice within its own heart. Grandpa willed himself toward transforming the substance of what was in his heart—despite the late stage of his life—once he realized that we, his Black grandchildren, were simply the children of his own daughter and therefore worthy of his love.

My grandfather was a big enough person to acknowledge this truth and then bend to it. My blue-collar, railroad-working, country farm-boy, simple man Grandpa, raised in an era and environment that said, "White folk belong over here, Negroes belong over there, and never the twain shall meet," was big enough to change his heart. He let the twain meet, in the most intimate of relationships—family and home. He saw that my brother and I were human, and he understood the humanity of our needs, so he gave us his love. His was a transformation I spent my childhood wishing the world would replicate.

I have a memory of Grandpa that draws for me an important and fundamental parallel between the two of us. Grandpa followed a particular ritual all his own when he and

Grandma visited Los Alamos. After a day or two, he grew restless, perhaps for the familiar or about the unfamiliar. But reliably, when he reached that point, he could be found downtown at the local VFW club, enacting that most private ritual of sharing, solace, remembering, and forgetting that only veterans of foreign wars may know. My grandfather, a full-grown adult, in these downtown jaunts of his, was exhibiting a very human need that people close to me often denied as my right to carry. We all gravitate toward those persons who can relate to our most personal, soul-shaping experiences. It is human to want to connect with that which speaks to us, and that which is able to relate when we speak.

Grandpa passed away in 1992, at age 72. The spitfire, tobacco-chewing hard case, with skin and emotions as steeled as the railroad tracks he worked, would always serve as a lantern light of hope and possibilities for me. He was a man for whom I have more respect than for the flocks of people of any race, who never find the reason or will to overcome their hurtful prejudgment of fellow human beings. Grandpa smelt love for his Black grandchildren from the stubborn furnace of his heart. The fabled John Henry may have been a Black man, but Rudy Danz was his kin.

This was the family ground that bore forth my mother. Like her father, she was expressive with her emotions, fiery, and unbridled. Physically, she was striking in our child eyes. Her dark brunette-to-black hair, eyes, and shapely figure brought to mind more than a hint of Elizabeth Taylor. The sharp, strong features of her face left more than a notion of Raquel Welch. Her theatrical persona was the embodiment of Dolly Parton: country flamboyance, warmth, and verve. Of average height for a woman, she was a lively and dominant spirit in the house. Her love for life and for her children and family were huge colorful blossoms like the ones she nurtured in her garden.

Even with her first three children up under her, clamoring for her attention every moment, Mom was a creative geyser: macramé, crochet, quilting, knitting, sewing, stitching, piano, singing, acting, dancing, arts and crafts. I learned how to do much of that needlecraft from her, sitting by her side as she pulled yarn and thread through impossible holes, her fingers all rhythm—threading, looping, pulling. Quilts, plant hangers, potholders, and aprons sprang forth from the summoning of her hands. It was silent singing. Private contemplation and peace, a way of being I could relate to. Every winter she made decorative holiday Christmas trees, about 18 inches high, and gave them out as gifts to neighbors and friends. The trees were made of Brazil nuts, almonds, walnuts, acorns, buckeyes, moss she imported from her friend in Oregon, seeds, pinecones, and whatever else inspired her.

Mom also had a vivacious spirit in the way she dressed, decorated her home, or celebrated a holiday. She later came to be known all over town as the 'Granny' who decorates the outside of her house and her yard with elaborate themes for Christmas, Halloween, and any other reason to celebrate. She was full force, river rush, and life lust. She was raised Catholic, but kept her religious thoughts, feelings, and inspiration mostly to herself. I don't remember many conversations that directly touched on religion. Most of her spiritual current was lived, daily, rather than spoken.

I think the kitchen was one of her temples. By clinging to her side, the kitchen also became a temple of mine. First it was Mom doing dishes after every meal. That kept her in the kitchen much of the day—we were always eating. Later, in our new home on 47th Street, I was assigned to clean the kitchen. Each child had a responsibility for cleaning daily one room of the house, along with his or her bedroom. I suspect I was stuck with the kitchen because it was the hardest to clean and I most reliably performed my chores. *Got to be a good little boy.* My cleaning the kitchen often coincided with Mom's preparation of the next meal.

We learned to move in syncopation past each other in the small space lined by counters, refrigerator, sink, and dishwasher. I brought dishes from the table to the sink; she peeled the potatoes and carrots on the counter and placed them in the pot on the stove. I rinsed the dishes off and filled up the dishwasher, while she buttered the baking tins for the dinner rolls. I sidestepped her to the refrigerator to put away the butter, ketchup, mustard, milk, and lemonade. She reached down below to pull pots from the lower cupboard. The years passed. I grew bigger and the space grew smaller. Then I was the one reaching for the ingredients and dishes in the high cabinets and handing them to her.

While cooking she seemed focused and in a different kind of space, not the unsettled, overloaded one she was often in as she rushed around doing errands, taking children to music and athletic practices, and cleaning the house. Maybe as she cooked, she was back in Peoria, a little girl with her mother preparing the evening meal. *Mama's gonna bake you shortnin' bread.* Wherever she was, it was peaceful, and it felt good being next to her during those times. At the base of my being, next to Mom was the place I wished to belong and be accepted.

I watched her shred cheddar cheese, chop onions, and fill pans with blue corn tortillas and red chilé sauce. In a flash, enchiladas were going into the oven and that wonderful baking chilé scent came up through the spaces between oven and stove. She made sopaipilla dough from scratch, flouring the counter, rolling out the dough, balling it up, coating it with vegetable oil, and letting it rise in a dish towel-covered bowl. I watched, intently, as she dropped the square sopaipilla dough pieces into the pot of boiling oil and tapped the pieces with steel salad tongs as they puffed up into their pillow shapes. I paid rapt attention to her rhythm and timing as she pulled out the sopaipillas and laid them on paper towels to drain. The best part was opening a hole in those light brown pillows, and filling the inside with honey or honey butter. We ate the heaven she made, in batches piled high to our delight.

Through the years, I watched, helped when I could, and learned, as Mom made an endless array of dishes. She faithfully worked, mostly from scratch, to feed her family tacos, burritos, green chilé hamburgers, pizza, green chilé chicken enchiladas, au gratin potatoes, chilé rellénos; her native sauerkraut, sausage and dumplings; and Dad's favorite: beef stroganoff. *This feels good, I can be a part of this.* She made chili, barbecued spare ribs, lasagna, pork chops, shish kebobs, sloppy joes, spaghetti, soups, baked beans, and potato salad. *I can feel your love, Ma.* Banana nut bread, coffee cake, Dutch baby pancakes, apple crisp, mocha cake, peach cobbler, hot fudge sauce, and Dad's favorite: German chocolate cake. *Fill me up some more, Ma. Fill me up.* During Christmas she baked buckeyes, Santa Claus sugar cookies, English toffee, fudge, peanut brittle, and Russian teacakes. *Sing, Ma, sing.*

Mom's whole world was her children and family. She put everything she had into us. It was her identity, her reason for being, although I am sure she had other life desires that she subdued over time. Managing what would eventually be five children far away from her family and hometown community would not be easy. Mom was instinctively aware of the importance of rearing us into a strong obedience, so she pushed herself past her limits to keep us corralled, disciplined, and on point. In the process, much of her personality evolved into a firm resolve to *get the job done.*

Much of my relationship with Mom was forged through the sparks of our conflicting personalities. She was an early riser. I yearned to sleep till noon. She loved the sunlight. I loved the moon. My body rhythm took me to dinnertime hunger around six. She liked to eat dinner at four, like her farming relatives; folks like Uncle Jim back in Canton, Illinois. Those people ate four heaping meals a day to fuel their hard labor. Every time we visited, they stuffed us with food at the table until I was ready to burst. 'Near to bursting' was also a good description for my overall emotional state.

Because I felt things so deeply, Mom's emotional fire ran through me in a way that perhaps it did not for her other children. Her temper mellowed through the years, but when it rose, it was not shy. It came at you. She moved on quickly from her moods and emotional states, and expected her children to do the same. She was raised to be tough and thick-skinned. She was taught to take it on the chin and then get on with things. But I rarely could. I walked slowly, begrudgingly away from my emotions, especially the solemn, sullen ones. Those feelings were like tar-soaked snakeskin. I could not shake them off so easily, and they left behind their stains long after their initial coating.

"Quit hanging your lip!" she would snap at me, fatigued by the Scorpio mood I dragged around the house. And whatever the cause of that initial mood, her stern admonishment usually only drove me further into that cloud. *Hold up, Ma. Give me some more time with this. I'm not ready to smile again yet. I gotta work through this. Leave me alone.* I held onto my emotions like a bag lady hordes her stash. Sadness, hurt, fear, self-punishment—they were all marbles in my jar. I couldn't throw them back into the world without spending time with them according to my rhythm. My body language and facial expression affected the mood in the house considerably. For someone like Mom, most comfortable with a space where clouds blew in quickly and left just the same, I must have been a tremendous challenge.

Over time, the angst I churned up over being Black mixed in my mind with the oil-and-water friction between Mom's nature and mine. I could not discern between her emotions that came from the pressures of maintaining a household, raising children, and the discomfort she seemed to have specific to my growing racial unrest. It did not help Mom that I could not articulate exactly what was troubling me. All I expressed were banners of distress in the form of gloom, mope, and increasingly angry tones. *What darkness had descended upon my child?*

As I moved from infancy, to toddler, to child, to pre-adolescence, I was growing both closer to and further from the simple comfort I had found in Mom at our beginning. I was growing to need her more in certain ways that she could not fulfill. She was the center of my life, and as my life evolved into a processing of constant racial messages and interactions, I needed her to play the role of conductor, explainer, and the one who made the bad things go away. She neither understood the totality of what I was beginning to choke upon nor was composed of personality to pull free what was choking me.

I was plagued with a fear that Mom didn't really like me, not deep down. I felt nearly everything about me, including race, was at odds with her. I wondered constantly, especially whenever my feelings were hurt, which was often: *Why did she adopt us in the first place?* Although many children endure the insecurity of doubting their parents' love, mine was magnified by an absence of biological connection between the two of us.

Adoption and race were detachment points of mine from Mom that made everything else more uncertain. Everything about me she seemed to either not agree with or wasn't able to relate to. "You're such a serious child," she intoned, as though it was an unfortunate thing. The sense of humor I did have was different than hers. I had a strong sense of humor and loved to play the clown, but by the time I was in high school, I didn't feel safe showing that side of myself to family because it made me vulnerable to the unpredictable moments of disharmony between us. Humor became the pulse I showed only to friends, only within those relationships where I was not so deathly afraid of rejection.

When it came to Mom and me I could not see the separation between personality conflict and race conflict. They became one. When she was frustrated with me, then grew even more aggravated over my hurt feelings, moping, or self-pity as a response, a hot flame of hurt cut through me—a powerful sense of rejection. A few of those times I stormed out of the house, intending to run away, yet frightened of the absolute aloneness that that would bring.

A flood of thoughts went through my mind as I ran or walked away from that house, trying to find somewhere that I could go and just . . . be. I thought of all the sights, sounds, and smells in that house that I would never experience again. I thought of my brothers and sisters: *I wonder how they would feel if I never come back.* I imagined my parents being brokenhearted because they realized they had done their child wrong and now they would never see him again—the age-old and shortsighted perspective of a child who thought he saw the whole picture.

Wandering around in the dark of Los Alamos, not knowing which direction I could walk toward to find release from the struggle, I thought of Mom. *She got herself into something she regretted by adopting me. Now she's just playing out the string.* Dad usually drove around in the station wagon looking for me after I ran out of the house. I half desired that he would find me. I didn't make it too hard for him. But when he found me, I said to him, washed hot with tears, "She doesn't love me," or, "Why did she adopt us?" I was confused and young. All my pain ran together like watercolors on a warped page.

Our family spent many Saturdays in Old Town, Santa Fe, walking the plaza, where Mom's highly developed bartering expertise was released into full flush. The plaza was a square, center-pieced with a small, lightly wooded park. The storefronts that formed the four walls of the plaza were mostly tourist haunts stockpiled with jewelry, clothing, artwork, and other Indian/Spanish artifacts. The broad sidewalks along these four streets allowed for a healthy push of tourists up and down the way.

The real stars of this Old Town scenario were the Pueblo and Diné craftspeople positioned on plastic food and milk crates or woven blankets alongside the shops' outer walls. They sat, their artistic pride laid out on blankets on the sidewalk for the tourists to descend upon like birds of prey. Necklaces, bracelets, earrings, broaches, hairpins, and bolo ties competed for attention, flashing tropic-blue turquoise, jet-black onyx, rustic red coral, burnished copper, and sterling silver in the sunlight. The Pueblo people were descendants of those who inhabited this Northern New Mexico land since 10,000 years before Christ. They had claim to much more than narrow plots on concrete sidewalks in a tourist plaza.

The artists wore eyes like sepia moons, and facial skin like leather, worn by many winds. Their cheekbones were wide prairie plains that caught the sun. Hair of Samson, onyx-black like the jewels they sold, and nurtured to great length. Some wore an imbricate of their own wares, layered in beautiful stones and silver.

This was a unique and strange ritual: The brown people sitting low as the mass of tourists, mostly White, flowed and ebbed, a sea of humans entranced as much by the site of these 'authentic Indians' as by the crafts displayed on the ground before them. Even as a child, holding the hand of Mom or Dad, I thought the scene should have been reversed. These brown-skinned people seemed much too dignified to be looked down upon. They should have been up on platforms, somehow elevated above the crowd. It should have been a pilgrimage, an honoring of these still, stoic redwoods representing a time since passed and life's urge for what should be again.

Strange glances passed between tourist and artist. The artists simply wished to make a sale. Their eyes were hopeful, in their own subdued way. Sometimes a shy smile breached the stoicism. The tourists appeared caught somewhere between buying mode and anthropological curiosity. They searched the faces of the artists in stolen glimpses for something beneath the brown skin surface. *Are they looking for approval, forgiveness, or for signs of resentment, or recognition of friendliness?* Cultures wrestled silently in the air between the seated and those towering over them.

Sometimes the tourists were deferential and inquisitive. Mom was one of those. She spoke to them as people: "How much are these here?" and "How did you make these?" and, "I like that one you're wearing, do you have one like that?" Her banter was easy and grown to natural through years of repetition. Others were not so engaging. An awkward, "How much?" sufficed for the transaction. In such cases the tourist's eyes drifted barely or not at all to meet those of the artist. An attitude of superior civility or expectation of subservience cascaded down more than a few times as I beheld the scene, small and unnoticed.

Many of the tourists clearly regarded the artists as slightly dignified beggars, strewing out their belongings desperately hoping that the good people would throw some money into the pot. Charity . . . that's what some of the purchases amounted to in spirit. Those same people would go into the Anglo-owned shops adjacent to the outside market—fancy, frilled stores selling 'authentic Indian crafts', where they paid handsomely for the same jewelry and pottery being sold outside. But these purchases were made from White faces that somehow made the transaction less charity and more high-toned cultural acquisition. Never mind that very little of the money spent here would trickle down to the actual artists. No, like a boxer to a promoter, a writer to a publisher, a singer to a record company, within many of these stores, Pueblo, Diné, and Hopi artists were being taken. Maybe not criminally or immorally, but certainly they were being taken in a business sense—in a good old American business sense.

Standing before the artists, holding onto Mom or Dad, I searched the sepia moons on the other side of the displaying blankets for a different kind of truth. *Do you see me as these people who condescend to you? Can you tell the difference at least in my spirit? That I do not fear you or look down on you? That I love you? Who am I to you? Because I do not fit here, on this side of the blanket, and I need you to love my skin in the way that I love yours.* They sometimes looked back at me. Maybe they were curious about this Black child with his White mother. Maybe they were instinctively worried for me. But maybe they saw me seeing them, and cherished it.

While Mom negotiated prices for turquoise stones that to her were as valuable as any diamond, I peered at faces. Brown faces that held for me my own priceless value, as I hoped to take home with me my own jewels in the form of a look or nod that said, "I see you, child. I see you."

Those trips to the plaza were a regular joy for Mom. She was big on rituals when it came to family. Housecleaning on the weekends; yard sales on Saturday morning; television off at dinnertime; family drive through the neighborhoods to see the lights on Christmas Eve. Some rituals we stumbled upon through resourcefulness. It became a tradition for us to go up into the mountains the weekend after Thanksgiving and hunt for a Christmas tree. We trudged through snow often up to our thighs, looking for that perfect tree. Freezing and worn out, we wouldn't stop to eat our meal until the tree was found. One year, we forgot to bring sugar for the hot tea, so Mom had us drop Christmas candy into our cups for sweetener. That became the tradition ever after: grilled hamburgers topped with green chilé and Swiss cheese, and candy-sweetened tea.

Ceremonies. I thought sometimes of the Anasazi people, living in those caves dug into the sides of Bandelier's canyon. I wondered how Anasazi children found their place in family and community. Many times, our family visited those ruins. We climbed the long, frightening tree branch-lashed ladders high into the largest cave: the Ceremonial Cave. Dropping down on another ladder into the dusty kiva, a ceremonial chamber in the floor of the cave, I found myself in darkness. Once I overcame the stench of urine left by desecrators, I imagined the long ago fire that blackened this kiva's walls. I imagined the ceremonies and what they meant to individual Anasazi. *Were they ever insecure about their place in the circle? Did they always relate to the ceremony, or did they sometimes feel out of tune? How did the children find their way in life through the maze of these dwellings in the sky?* I thought of my introversion and realized the parallel: *I'm a cave dweller, too.*

Rituals allowed our family to develop a common consciousness over a certain part of our lives. We were all privy to the expectations and meanings around those particular habits. We all understood the moment. In that shared space, I was able to open up and flow into the family dynamic. Nature often was the outline for such traditions. The camping and hikes we went on stripped us from our usual social context in the community. I found I was less conflicted in those moments, and more able to join the rest of the family in our raw and vulnerable enjoyment of nature. It was a tight, nurturing space out there in the mountains, under the moon in the thin crisp air. The only eyes on us were perched in trees and belonged to winged things. Maybe if nothing more than owls and robins had witnessed my Blackness back in town, I would not have been so conscious of my status in the family.

Dad had his own rituals, brought forth from his childhood. Like Grandpa Potter before him, Dad loved to shout out to us on the 4th of July, as we churned our old-fashioned homemade ice cream maker: "Anyone who doesn't crank, doesn't get any ice cream!"

But it was Mom who presided steadfast over the preservation of our rituals. She made sure that the ways of family that made sense to her continued their course. "We're having a family day!" she demanded, anytime we tried to weasel out of something. It never occurred to me how unsettling this lifestyle must have felt to her, away from her kinship culture in Illinois, as she worked to make her family strong. But she came from nail-tough people. She would not lie down easily.

The piano was one of those ritual places. An upright Baldwin studio piano—made in 1924—my parents bought it for $500 from a professor at the University of New Mexico after returning to Los Alamos permanently. It dominated the living room, and was Mom's spring of joy. The piano bench had a top that lifted, exposing the hollow hold where Mom stuffed stacks of music sheets. "Come sit and play with me," she beckoned to me. I sat close, melting into her body heat. "You press the pedal," she said, or, "You play the right hand, I'll play the left." I didn't know what I was doing, but she did. She was giving me a role, making me a part of her moment. She played, her fingers jumping on the keys like popcorn in the pan. Her voice strong, shaking the large mirror on the piano top. Maybe, in those moments, she was back in choir practice at Woodruff High. Maybe she was just lost in song. But I know one thing: we were playing together, deep in those white and black keys together. Mom knew it, too.

Ease me
I am that place
where river meets the rock
and becomes whitewater
I am that place of
transformation and foam
I need a tide pool
I need a home

THE FATHER TREE

SATURDAY mornings were Dad's show. Waffles with brown sugar syrup, both made from scratch by his hands. He had a joy for cooking his few specialties, and for having the hungry horde of five little ones pounce on the table from their lazy sleep or from cartoon-induced trances. The sound of waffle batter bubbling inside that old-fashioned waffle iron, smelling the mix of syrup reheated in a pan of water on the stove, and frying bacon, the grease popping in its skillet dance. *Yeah, Saturday mornings.*

Dad had the kind of sense of humor that entertained itself, if not necessarily others. He was given to jokes so corny they were painful. *"Who wants a roll?"* he would ask at the dinner table. We children groaned immediately, having heard this one at least 50 times before. Nothing stopped Dad's joke express once started. After the painful pause, someone would finally oblige him. *"I do"* was muttered in defeat. *"Then get on the floor and roll!"* He would roar in his husky voice, followed by his self-satisfied laughter, more groaning by us children, and then on with the meal. It was a family ritual in redundancy, an exercise in excruciation.

Another whopper was the poem he got from his father that he recited like it was the best material on Earth:

"In days of old, when Knights were bold,
Before kerchiefs were invented,
Men blew their nose
In their underclothes
And then rode off, contented."

Some of the jokes he told to company sent us scurrying to avoid suffering our guests' reactions. My mind has protectively cordoned off that section of my brain where memories of his jokes are stored, but I do remember his response to his own whoppers. Soon as that punch line was out of his mouth, the mountain man became little boy made of jelly. Hand to his belly to contain the quake, eyes twinkling, mischievous grin, elfish snickering, whole body rearing back like a champion bull rider, shoulders heaving, full laugh satisfaction.

Dad was a legendary stylist. Sort of. Not once during childhood did I see him wearing anything other than his Red Wings 11-inch pull-on Wellington boots. Similar to what Davey Crockett or Daniel Boone might have worn, the boots were a cross between those worn by cowboys and those worn by construction workers. They were boots I saw few other men wear—just one item in his ensemble of stark individuality.

Dad usually dressed for work in button-up shirts over a white undershirt, with a standard Lab-issue pocket protector filled with pencils and a calculator. He crowned this ensemble with a bolo tie bejeweled by an enormous turquoise stone. Then there were the jeans or corduroy pants that somehow unfailingly succumbed to Potter's Law. Potter's law states that if in the morning you start off with both pant legs either tucked into your calf-high boots or dropped down over the boots, by somewhere around lunchtime, one pant leg will be tucked in and one will be draped over. No mathematical equation or gravitational dynamic could explain it. No one actually saw that mysterious instance of change. One moment, Dad would have it together; the next, his pants were in some sort of randomized entropy. Somewhere far inside the secretive enclaves of the Los

Alamos National Laboratory, there very well may be a postdoctoral physics student who hasn't seen the sun in months, fanatically theorizing and manipulating variables to discover the formula for the ever-evasive Potter's Law.

Truly an original, Dad was a man against the grain. Most people preferred red licorice; he gushed over black licorice. No one I knew could stand anchovies on pizza, so of course Dad thought that was the only way to eat it. Other children coaxed their parents into buying them sports equipment from actual stores. I had the distinction of being the only child I knew whose dad picked up a blowtorch and built him a weight bench, a basketball backboard, and a baseball pitching/hitting net. "Why buy it when you can make it!" he proclaimed.

Whether it was his choice of computer equipment and software or his love for his Land Rovers before they were in vogue, he always treaded a path apart from the norm. Not to mention the two Black children he adopted. It was almost as though he lived his life fanning his nose at the conforming ease of the mainstream, the so-called normal ones. He had a philosophy to support his stance. One passed down from his father. Dad liked to say: "Never try to impress people. Those you want to impress won't be. And, those who are impressed aren't worth the trouble." I realize in retrospect that this philosophy was influential in his perceptions of and responses to the racial spotlight his adopted sons would bear.

Mom spent years pleading with Dad to hire a contractor to dig out the basements Dad was determined to have—first at the apartment, and then later on 47th Street. Never did happen. Dad was going to dig out those basements by hand or hoe, come hell or high water, if it killed him. Greg and I thought we were the ones in danger of being killed. For what seemed like the duration of our youth, we shoveled, picked, mixed cement and sand, transported dirt and cement by the wheel barrels-full, and eventually jack hammered. When the sun was high and hard and we could work shirtless and sweated down in that ecstasy of hard labor's machismo, it was a sweet toil of father and sons bonding.

Dad was built tall and thickly muscled in a lumberjack sort of way, with long curly dark brown hair and blue eyes to rival Paul Newman's. He also had an unruly beard that seemed to have a magnetic pull on the food crumbs that fell from his face while he wolfed down his food. His physical appearance reminded me of Dan Haggerty's title character from the 1977-78 television series, *The Life and Times of Grizzly Adams*. They were both over six feet, burly, soulful-eyed, and the actor Haggerty was even the same age as Dad.

Dad was the kind of father children love. He was not much more than an overgrown child himself:

He was . . .
sneaking Good N' Plenty's
from his shirt pocket, saying
"Put out your hand"
filling my palm with that
white and pink sugar
in the station wagon
on an errand run to town
He was . . .
"Don't tell your mother"
and a grown man's delight in
sharing junk food with his son
He was . . .
Junior Mints before dinner
"Don't tell your mother"
He was . . .
the shared secret of comfort food
like hot fries when we shouldn't
candy bars after a good cry
Oreos before bedtime
warm milk after a nightmare
Dad was there

Just as Mom was music, dance, and rhythm, Dad was not. He was Bee just short of the Bop, Hop without a trace of Hip. Rhythm and he were not acquainted. Music had vacated his bones. Soul was not with him. And yet he was so very soulful. He could be shy and quiet, or when comfortable, forceful with his laughter and storytelling. He also was so passionately deep into the world of physics and science within his larger private galaxy that he could seem to be 'not there' to people engaging with him socially.

If Mom was the howling wind, Dad was the sound of silence. His voice came in thoughtful, efficient bursts that fell between long streams of introspection. When he spoke, his words were well considered and to the point. Laid back was the word with Dad, gentle and patient with us children. He wasn't one to talk too effusively about emotions—his or ours, but he often comforted me in my wounded moments with a vibe of compassion. I didn't feel he was angry at my moods, or that he resented the way I struggled to feel secure with my place in the family and with my race. Dad just tolerated, empathized, and calmed in his own, understated way.

He was a fount of philosophical mottoes and insights, inherited from countless repetitions from his own father. It was the nature of his emotional relationship with the world that his responses to life's flow were thoughtfully packaged philosophy, offered up as explanation, comfort, and resolution. He was the soulful scientist, ambivalent on religion, but squarely positioned within the realm of universal and humanistic laws and tendencies. This was the tree he had fallen from, and in the country way of saying it, he landed right up against the trunk.

At least four of Dad's great grandparents were German immigrants. A great-great grandfather of his, Lorenz Potter, claimed to be of German descent, specifically Pennsylvania Dutch. In the family records, Lorenz Potter appeared out of nowhere at age 21, and was the earliest kin Dad was able to identify with the Potter surname. Dad also identified a German family—descendants of a Potter, Heinrich Oxenbaker (Ochsenbacher in German). Many of them took the name Potter because Heinrich was known as 'Henry the Potter'. Dad was never able to establish a certain connection with this family, but the time and place fit. The rest of my Dad's ancestors were a mix of Irish, Scottish, and English, with some additional German presence.

My great grandpa Potter, James Corbett Potter, was named after the famous fighter who was popular at the time of his birth on February 2, 1893. Great Grandpa, my Dad would tell me later, had an interesting (yet relatively common in my view) perspective on racial difference. From Dad's account, Great Grandpa Potter, a coal miner who had both ears burned off in a mining explosion, "—grew up in poverty, and was often the object of prejudice because he was from a coal mining family. Many farmers didn't want their children to associate with the coal miners' children. He grew from this experience to respect people for what they were as a people." *To a degree*, I thought to myself as I listened.

"He drew a distinction between those Black persons he knew as individuals and Black people as a group," Dad explained. This was a common attitude not only for his generation, but also eventually for my own. My great grandfather saw no contradiction between his attitudes toward Blacks as a group and his feelings for Greg and me. This was a perceptual dichotomy that would prove one of my central sources of wounding.

Throughout my life, I would listen to first White people and later Black people rationalize their prejudices in this way. I grew frustrated with that notion because my own experiences were a daily lesson that it was not possible for a human being to separate feelings and attitudes for a group of people from sentiments for an individual of that group. The former always leaves dust like deadly asbestos in the space where individuals cross paths. With the people in my life, there always remained at least a trace of those racial attitudes in our relationships.

I do not remember my great grandfather well, though if I were forced to describe what sense of energy I received from him, I would say it was room temperature—reasonably warm and friendly, but not obviously embracing or emotionally invested. But then, that was how he had always been on the surface, even while raising his own son. Great Grandpa married Great Grandma when he was 20 and she was 16-year-old Emma Amanda Baldowsky. She was similar in her manner toward Greg and me. She was badly afflicted with arthritis and confined to a wheelchair, which was slightly discomforting to me; but she was warm enough to us that I looked forward to seeing her on our visits.

I felt the same blended affection coming from many of my relatives on both sides—nothing cruel, mean, nor condescending. This was simply the shaded love of people who spent their lives distant from people who looked like me. Children can discern the subtle difference between embrace, ambivalence, tolerance, and disdain. To recognize their presence was my full-time survival consideration.

Incongruent emotion was a great bane to me in most of my relationships. A person caring for me but feeling less than positive about a group of people that I held myself a part of never was good enough for me. My heart was demanding. Unconditional, unstrained acceptance and regard was all that assuaged and reassured my sense of my value. One relative who provided me that was Grandpa Potter.

Harold Potter, Dad's father, was a highly-skilled machinist, of the toolmaker class, for the local industry giant, Caterpillar Tractor Company, popularly known as 'Cat'. He was also a carpenter, block layer, plumber, and electrician who did the repair work around the home himself. Sales were another hand he tried to support the family. At various times he bottled horseradish in the family basement, sold plastic window screens, peddled gas home incinerators, pitched cemetery lots, drove a milk delivery route, and ran a small gas station for about one year. He was a fairly strict disciplinarian who loved to garden, especially tomato plants. He was divorced from my Grandma Marie at age 52 and moved in with his parents, taking care of them in their elder years.

Grandpa Potter was a man clearly swimming upstream in his racial attitudes, especially for his early 20th century era and Midwestern locality. From 1930-34, he attended racially integrated Manual Training High School in Peoria, which was in the south end, an area with a large Black community. As an adult, he was considered a 'Nigger lover' for the human respect he maintained for all others. I have the feeling this was a badge of honor for him—perhaps he spited the mainstream just as much if not more than his eldest son eventually would.

Grandpa Potter often pulled me up onto his lap, where I could feel the love come from him in a middle-aged man's masculine, husky waves. It cascaded down his barrel chest and enveloped me. It was a kind of love I do not recall feeling to such a degree from most other relatives. To my hyper-charged senses, the substance within their hearts was like clouds slow moving over my terrain. I could read those clouds just as easily as the farming ancestors of my Grandpa Danz could distinguish impending rain from coming drought.

Grandpa Potter was an intelligent and introspective person who often concerned himself with the meaning of life. Always pontificating to his children, he often joked, "I missed my calling! I should have been a preacher!"

He was an extremely liberal thinker, always espousing the belief that all people had the same basic desires for a better life for themselves and their children. His value system gave no quarter to class or status. The motto he raised his children under was the same one Dad showered on us: "Whatever you are in life, strive to do your best. If you are a garbage man, try to be the best garbage man there ever was."

Dad believed Grandpa Potter at least partially came by his unconditional, inclusive attitudes as a reaction to his grandmother, a German immigrant with a Polish last name—a woman possibly descended from Jews who was averse to Polish persons. This convolution of heritage, racial respect, and ethnic disdain was a vibrant illustration of the partitioning qualities of the human mind. I was to inherit all those contradictions as spiritual estate from my broader family—a challenge in my making, a blessing in my coming of age.

Grandpa always encouraged me, filling my insecure mind with confidence-building ideas as though he intuited my need. In the greeting cards he sent for my birthdays and Christmas, his messages were inspirational and supportive. His Christmas card to me in my eighth year read:

"I'm so proud to see you growing up to be such a fine boy. I know someday you will be a very important man and will do a lot of good for everybody. Remember, John, that God has a good and special job for you in this world and he knows that you are going to make good and make a lot of people happy.

Love, Grandpa Potter."

Those were deep ideas for an eight-year-old, but they reached me where I hungered. I don't know if he saw something in me, or if he was just giving me what he knew every child needed. It didn't matter. I felt his sincerity, his emotional investment, and rode that wave for all it was worth.

At times, his compassion was a watershed. It swept me into a current where I had no doubts. Once, when I was maybe seven years of age, Grandpa Potter was visiting us in New Mexico. "Johnny, come over here and sit on my lap, and read Grandpa that story you wrote in school," he called to me.

The story I wrote was about a kingdom of black ants that battled against a kingdom of red ants. I climbed up in that grown man's lap and he pulled me close against his generous but firm belly. I smelled his cologne; it was a good scent. His arms were strong in their embrace of me, his love washed over me. I was in a heaven I did not admit externally. I read and he fed . . . fed me his warmth.

As I finished my story, Grandpa smiled down at me. Even at that age I could recognize pride. "Jim!" He called out to my dad, "This boy's going to be a writer!" My self-esteem burst open within me as my inner shore received his high tide of belief in what I could become. *Yeah, I could be a writer. Grandpa thinks so.* In an instant, I bonded further with him, for during those moments in his lap I could *feel him* seeing me.

Seeing me. This was for me invaluable evidence of our connection. Most of all, in that interaction there was love. Grandpa Potter was engaged in loving me in that moment in a way that bypassed my race and swallowed my being, whole and unconditional. Without a direct word about the idea, Grandpa had sealed what was for me a precious deal. I had experienced him regarding me as a part of him. His love had rushed through me like a freight train, but not because he was colorblind. He was very aware of what I was. Grandpa reached through to my essence so cleanly and unencumbered for another reason. His comfort with me was composed of two ingredients. One part was a natural human respect for Blackness in its broader self, even those people extending beyond me, his grandchild. The other part was a lack of fear of that greater Blackness, an absence that extended back into his relation to singular me.

The magical formula that made me feel connected to a person did not have so much to do with whether she or he liked my personality. The solution was much more basic. I was simply looking to sense in others a measure of reflexive comfort with my being. You can't fake discomfort or comfort to a child. I knew my grandfather was comfortable with me through and through. It was not his words or actions; it was not superficial claims of 'transcending' race. Nor was it incomplete, lazy love of the 'me' that excluded my race. It was a vibration, borne in his heart, the heart of a White man, and carrying across the molecules of space to reach me. That night, peace and I were a reunion in my sleep.

Creation claimed Grandpa Potter back in 1984 at age 68. His footprints were filled with compassion. I believe he looks down on me now, smiling and thinking of his own son. *Jim, you did well. You taught your children to love folks wide and well, and for all the haters, to give 'em hell.*

Dad's mother, Grandma Marie, was an extremely bright woman born in a farming settlement called Powder Town in Lee County, seven miles northwest of Keokuk, Iowa. Powder Town was a company town owned by DuPont, which manufactured gunpowder there. Grandma attended a one-room grade school, and later was one of two women in her class who took drafting as a high school senior in 1934. She didn't have much of a social life in high school, living with no transportation in a rural area outside of town. She pursued a traditional woman's career in nursing. She was also an excellent homemaker. She canned vegetables from the garden and sewed, making her own clothes and some of her children's. She was the kind of woman who could reassemble a wind-up alarm clock in an afternoon and handle the house chores in the same breath. At times she sold Avon products and Yardley's plastics. Even when she wasn't working as a nurse, she provided nursing care for her four children. She administered penicillin shots when they were sick, and even gave them polio shots.

Grandma Marie was a registered nurse, trained at Proctor Hospital in Peoria. After the children were all in grade school, she worked as a private duty nurse, caring for clients' family members in their homes or in the hospital. For the last 10 years before she retired, she was a nurse at Hiram Walkers bottling plant in Peoria, in charge of a small staff; and retired at the same time the plant closed. Grandma Marie lived her life clean and tempered and life paid her back. She now is a lively, whip-sharp 85-year-old who recently wrote her own autobiography, a story of life in the U.S. during the early 1900s.

Grandma Marie was always proper in manner and kept a very tidy home. Her electronic organ was one of the few child-enticing pleasures in her house when we visited. I hung out at the organ, fascinated by its range of musical instrumentation, called up at the touch of a key. Grandma wrapped all of us children in her grandmotherly bouquet of affection. I never sensed otherwise from her, and the physical love she draped me in with hugs and kisses was a wonderful signature of arriving at her home. "Come here, sweetie. I'm so happy you're here," she said, her words laced with sugar and tender to the bone. That's all the invitation I needed.

When we were lucky, our cousins Dale and Bert, the children of Dad's sister, Aunt Cheryl, would be over at Grandma Marie's at the same time. That's when Greg and I could let out our energy, though Kristin was usually left behind to negotiate the distance caused by a two-generation span between her and Grandma. "Hey, let's run down to the creek!" Dale would say—music to our ears. Gone in a flash into the wilderness.

What passed between Dale and Bert and Greg and me was an enthusiasm for each other's company that gave me crucial reassurance. They introduced us to their friends with no trace of shame or discomfort, despite their all-White social circle. "These are my cousins, John and Greg from New Mexico," Dale said simply. It was like receiving approval from a big brother, and meant more than he ever knew.

Three years older than me, Dale was a legendary outdoorsman in my eyes, even before he was a man. He seduced trout from ice-cold streams with an ease that left me in awe and envy. On a day in June of '78, in the Rockies, just south of the Colorado border, Dad, Greg, Uncle Jerry, my cousin Kenny, and I were fronting as fishermen. We had seen trout the size of alley cats sitting fat and lazy against the shores of Latir's seven lakes—hadn't caught a one of them. Dale spotted a 17-inch trout in the tide pool of a stream, and set to work fashioning a knife tied to the end of stick. We ate well moments later. In my shy eyes cousin Dale glowed that day.

Bert, a year younger than Dale, was also adopted. He was from Swan River, Manitoba, Canada. Bert, Greg, and I bonded over that shared circumstance, although the heavy cloak of silence kept us from mentioning it to each other even once. But I knew it. And Greg knew it. I think we both enjoyed Bert's special connection with us, affirming as it was. In his presence, we became just a shade slightly closer to normal, even if he was yet another redhead, adorned in freckles like our sister Kristin and later, our youngest siblings, Anna and Rudy. Maybe I should have taken that peculiar redheaded pattern in my life as a message. *All of us stand out in one way or another.*

Whether over at Grandma Marie's or at our cousins' home, the relationship between Dale and Bert and Greg and me was classic boyhood mischief and physicality. Dale and Bert were rough and tumble, young masculinity in high dose. *Them boys were buck strong, Auntie. What'd you feed them?* They loved to bond through wrestling, and they showed their love that way to us, including Kristin. Greg was up for that brand of affection more than I was. I don't know how many things were broken in Aunt Cheryl and Uncle Cliff's home, but our reunions weren't cheap. Their house in Chillicothe was across the street from a cornfield and 11 blocks from the Illinois River. This only excited our adventurous energy. Aunt Cheryl knew what she was doing, letting us run ourselves to exhaustion outside so that we might be at least slightly more controllable indoors.

Dale and Bert had the world's greatest comic book collection. I lost myself in those pages for hours. It was ecstasy. The Incredible Hulk, The Fantastic Four, The X-Men, Thor, Flash, Daredevil . . . I read as long as I was left alone; my imagination voyaging deep into worlds where everyone was a mutant. As I turned pages, I was calmed as if by humming a spiritual. The stories were songs that announced beautiful daydreams into my head; windows through which I escaped to fly away for a while.

Aunt Cheryl was all warmth with a brilliant smile. I had a special affection for her, largely because her affection for Greg and me was so overflowing that it washed away my usual, persistent doubts about the sincerity and depth of my relatives' love. She was one of those aunts so familiar with what drives young boys, being the mother of two and a 'survivor' of two brothers. She intuitively provided experiences when we visited that were memorable treasures. By doing nothing more than indulging our simple desires to play hard, feel good, and eat well, she made herself a strong favorite. Her Sloppy Joe sandwiches made me melt, not only for the taste, but also because it felt so good to eat them knowing the person who cooked them adored me.

"Greggy, are you guys gonna stay the night?" Aunt Cheryl would ask in her sweet tone, making me feel without a doubt that she not only wanted our company, but that it would be special to her. It was only natural to like her back just as fully. The most natural laws of energy rule us, no matter our circumstance: Like begets like. Ambivalence creates ambivalence. No matter how many times we were allowed, we couldn't get permission often enough to stay over at Dale and Bert's. Overnight in that home, goofing around with our cousins, including the babies, Johanna and Heidi, and basking in Aunt Cheryl's warmth, *that* was affirmation.

Two of Dad's younger siblings had followed him out to New Mexico. My Aunt Pamela, Dad's sister, and her family—Uncle Ken, and our younger cousins Brian and Joy, lived in Albuquerque, so we saw them more often than the Illinois relatives. Dad's brother, Uncle Jerry and his family—Aunt Sue and cousins Kenny and Cheri, who were around our age— lived in White Rock, a part of Los Alamos 'off the hill' about 20 minutes away. They were the relatives we spent the most time with, developing time-honored traditions. Like the sibling competition between Dad and Uncle Jerry during Christmas when they tried to stump each other with 'unsolvable' game-puzzle gifts. Aunt Pamela and Uncle Jerry both had Grandpa Potter's soft, compassionate spirit, and it trickled down into their children, our cousins, too. I chose to find refuge in that energy whenever we played together, though I still felt my personality drifted in an orbit different from theirs.

Curiosity trailed along after me, driving me to wonder what my relatives honestly thought about me. According to Dad, my relatives on both sides never so much as asked my parents why they adopted Greg and me. I'm not sure if the absence of such a question was exclusively a positive indication. The subtle vibrations of disconnection and dissonance I often experienced with extended family left me as a young man believing that plenty of waves had crashed within private boundaries. The faint lack of chemistry between us might have been partially rooted in the distinct cultural differences of our Southwestern and Midwestern regional personalities, but not all of it. I cared about things they did not, and vice versa. This could have been dismissed as nothing more than personality differences, but it was happening along a fault line I straddled that was composed of race.

This discordance between my relatives and me was small, but it made its mark. Like a thousand years of raindrops falling one at a time on a rock, it carved me. It would become dull alienation, rather than something drastic. But it was significant enough that I could not surmount it fully and gain a full foothold in the soil of belonging.

I felt that for my family and community, their polite tolerance of the fact that Greg and I were Black was sufficient to deem things well. That was far from good enough for me. The couched thoughts and attitudes and slight behavioral reactions ate at me. Even with those who liked or loved me. The barely rippled air of ambivalence between some of my relatives and me was a tidal wave against my chest. These were good people, and I felt positive about almost all of them. But as would become my theme in childhood, being surrounded by people I liked was frequently a joy diminished by wisps of that one divide between us. The one I was entirely tuned to, searching its frequencies for secrets and safety.

Most of what I received from my relatives was love and acceptance that overrode whatever other attitudes may have existed. I saw that gleam of their desire to embrace me through the haze of old and conditioned emotions and ideas that my Black image activated. That gleam was at once evidence of the distance they perceived between what I was and what they were, and of how much they cared for me. Even the best-intended hearts, filled with love and a motivation to extend that love, can carry forth with contrary streams. I was shown that prejudice is so brazen as to trespass even into the living rooms of loving families.

These weren't the only things I thought about; but friends, sports, and television were often eclipsed by heavier notions. I lived part-time as an old man, pondering the nature of the world. In that persona, I carried anxieties that overburdened my nervous system. In response, I sought peaceful moments and gentle emotions within which I could breathe.

Dad was a calming presence for me. I felt at ease around his easy, deliberate energy. He was an artist working in the medium of physics, so into his work that he was constantly laid out on his stomach on the floor, mind whirring with calculations and conceptions in a distant dimension. His mechanical pencil dropping hints of his voyage onto a green pad of graphing paper. He would stay in that position, working until he passed out into a snoring sleep. When I was small I would curl up next to him, his frame massive and dwarfing me like a mountain range, and there I would fall into my own safe slumber, his scent and weight against me my reassurance.

Dance for us
joke for us
run fast for us
make funny face for us
stick pencils in your 'fro for us
be a 'bro for us
sing for us
scat for us
swing the bat for us
dunk for us
beat that punk for us
grin for us
get drunk on gin for us

just don't remind us
about the back of the bus
be like us
be like us

BUNK BED BROTHERS

"*JOHN*, check out our new room!" my brother Greg shouted with his typical impish glee. He had beaten me up Urban Hill on his bike, and was sprinting out of the brown house to report his find. In December of 1976, when I was in fourth grade, the move our family made four blocks up the hill marked a new season in my life. My identity was to be jumpstarted into an altered consciousness by a series of events. In this new home my demons would begin to strut their plumage and fan their wings. It is when my memories most clearly begin.

The new home was an old government house built in 1952, a simple three-bedroom structure at 7,490 feet above sea level that wore dark-brown shingles for skin. It was situated on a slope steep enough to sled down in the winter. The backyard was set with a stand of tall Ponderosa pine trees that shaded that area, including the house itself. This made our home cooler year-round than it would have been otherwise. In the high altitude, that usually meant a little too cool.

We had one bathroom, usually dominated by the reigning king. Dad could have been reading his entire doctoral dissertation at each sitting, given how long he holed up in there. "Come on, Dad! I gotta go!" was the collective chant of morning and evening ritual. What would eventually be six impatient people pounding on the door was not enough to extricate the immovable object. All bowed down to the Grand Squatter Potter.

The house was a relic. The showerhead was at my chin level by the time I approached my full height. I wondered if people were really so diminutive in '52. The house also had a utility room that our family used for a bedroom. There was also an enclosed back porch addition, and off from that was another small addition—the room Greg and I would share for the remainder of our childhood years.

Our bedroom addition must have been poorly insulated, not to mention the entire outdoor-facing wall being a ceiling-to-floor sliding glass door. The mountain air intruded through the myriad breaches and thin barriers to create a continuously chilled environment. The rest of the house was usually warm during the fall, winter, and the long spring, but as soon as you entered our room, it seemed as though the temperature dropped a good 10 degrees. It was a cold addition to a warm house. *Greg and I . . . cold additions to a warm house.*

Wrapped in blanket layers and shivering in bed, the insecure part of me sometimes wondered whether Mom and Dad realized how cold it was in there. *Why did they stick us in the coldest room in the house?*

A few times Mom remarked, "Ooh . . . it *is* cold in here. Jim, we have to do something about this room." But there was not much they could do besides leave our door open to the warmer, closed-in porch. And then leave the window between Kristin's room and the porch open so the warm air could pass into our room. Dad installed a heat duct extending from the furnace and an external blower, but to no avail. The insulation must have been virtually absent. The wall facing outside was thin paneling and porously fitted glass against the wind. The outside air was too true to its mountain nature. Finally, what remained was piling on the blankets, long underwear, and socks. Still, my insecurity revisited when the temperature dipped outside and in. *Are Greg and I somehow less worthy in Mom and Dad's eyes of being in a room as warm as the rest of the house?*

We shared a bunk bed until I graduated from high school. The rest of the room we filled with a desk or two and posters on the walls, with our clothes stored in the closet space on both sides of the small landing leading into the room. We had our imaginary dividing line, that sacred stripe that children covet as a rare implement of property control. *My side . . . Greg's side. And he better not cross the line with his mess.*

Our toleration for each other in our bedroom was remarkable, particularly given my uncommon need for solitude and space. And because Greg was far from neat while I tended toward the neurotic side of clean and orderly. In all those years in close quarters, Greg and I got into a brotherly tussle just once. Our lack of conflict was generated in part by compassion born of empathy. We were two people on a boat in the middle of the ocean. We weren't going to hardly rock that boat, for fear one of us might fall out, leaving the other all alone.

This was our space. Whatever else was going down in the house, this was the place to which we were either banished or escaped. It was where we plotted our strategies of revenge against a mischievous, tattletale sister. It was where we laughed, and where we tried unsuccessfully to hide our tears from each other in manly, shamed moments of emotional distress.

By the time we moved into that room, Greg and I had already begun to gravitate toward a coltishly clumsy identification with Black people. We created a shrine upon those brown paneled walls with posters that became another degree of security wrapping. Greg put up Walter Payton and Herschel Walker. For me, it was Dr. J and The Iceman, George Gervin—too cool, sitting cross-legged on blocks of crystal-clear frozen water. I adulated to those images almost every moment of sleeping and waking time I spent in our room.

This was a season of burgeoning involvement in sports for both of us, but the posters and magazines we stocked our room with were more than just the usual preadolescent infatuation. This was both sustenance and ammunition for our refuge from the rest of our lives. These were Black faces, like ours, grounding us in a way we yearned for without even full consciousness of the yearning. These were Black faces, reminding us, *We are not alone. There is something worthy out there—something that is a part of us.* These were Black faces apparently not ashamed of their Black faces.

Placing these images around our room was about prideful attitude and our infant expression that *this Blackness means something to me.* The décor was a massage for a part of our psyche that was rarely stroked. Familiarity was not a part of the posters' tonic. Culturally, we were not intimate with the voices, private lives, and thoughts of people like these brown-skinned icons looking down at us. Rather, hanging there large and still, they were like stone lions at the gates of our vulnerability.

As my family and relatives liked to say, I was a serious child. I spent nights staring up from the bottom bunk. Greg snored on peacefully through the night. I looked through the wooden ceiling above me that supported his box springs, peering through that ceiling into a black sky in my mind. There were endless stars. The Earth emerged below me. In that moment, I became aware that I had spirit-walked: I was out in the Universe, at once apart from it all and a part of it all.

In this nightly state, I could see the entirety of the world. I could make out patterns of human interaction, and the way we do the business of life would become clear. Clearest of all was the color of my skin, the tight, knotted curl of my hair, the flair of my nose, and the full swell of my lips. I wanted to tuck them all inside my head in those lucid nights, so that I could emerge more glorious into the morning light. But during those nightly voyages, I knew that I was displaced in this world. In some important way, I was a stray. I so often fell to sleep that way. Sometimes I listened for Greg's breathing, wondering if he was awake, and if so . . . *is he thinking the same things I am?* I was too afraid to ever directly ask him, but I knew he must have been processing something in that stillness of night, after a day of living the same life I was.

Much of my comfort with the night stemmed from the fact that it was my escape. In the daylight I was so different from everyone else. In the night, with the rest of the family asleep, there was only me, so how could I not belong? During those quiet times, I kept myself awake, feeding and thriving off the overflow of thoughts and images stampeding my mind. Everything came to me so clearly in the dark of night that it became my emotional canvass. I splashed all kinds of mess over it, soaking it through with draft after draft of my strivings to pull free from the tormenting emotions of my racial isolation.

But I also hurt most deeply in the night. I bled in the night. It was when I reflected on the moments of the day. What I realized often hurt me to the core—stiletto cuts that usually weren't generated by visible forces or actions that the White people around me might notice. It was a subtle something, insidious, always present—living in people's eyes, in their voices, and most of all in the things they didn't say out loud but betrayed through their spirit's exclamation.

Greg was an outgoing child with a very personable, cheerful disposition. I could never read too easily his deeper emotions and thoughts. I believe he developed early on an extreme talent for masking whatever ailed him emotionally, keeping it locked away in a box he neglected as much as possible. In contrast, I was given to pacing around my box, sitting on top of it, opening it, digging through it, just plain wearing it out.

We were divergent in the way that water and ice are dissimilar: same substance, different state of vibration. But race was our identical composition, just like the hydrogen and oxygen of water and ice. This blend of dissimilarity and common bond created a strange masquerade in our bedroom. I could feel the imperceptible-to-others tremors of Greg's struggle with racial isolation as fluctuations in his vibe, and I knew he could detect mine, but we hardly ever spoke of it. *I feel you, my brother, I'm sorry I can't help you out. I'm feeling it too.*

We portrayed that struggle nonetheless. We signed an unwritten accord of avoidance. But we knew. We could not verbally approach it because it was larger than we were. It was nebulous, vague, shifty, and hard to grasp. Yet, it was a real thing, a force of consequential substance. It filled our chests, drifted toward our tongues and then hung there, just short of being spoken into truth.

I saw my Blackness magnified in Greg. He was much darker than I was and depending upon the moment, my reaction to that difference varied. I either took comfort in the fact that at least there was someone around further from the normative Whiteness than I was, or I siphoned secretly from his darker tone to back my momentary mood of indignation at all things White. Sometimes Greg's darkness made me feel more favored in our White circles. Disturbingly, I was often relieved by that fact. It was a mind warping fueled by my need to fit in and be accepted. *Stop the nightmare.*

We were two young Black boys desperate to feel good about ourselves, like any children. The most important aspect of that feeling good was to be accepted, liked. Given the situation, we were left with no alternative but to greatly value our acceptance by White people. This set off a chain of dynamics that found bitter fruit in a convoluted kind of social intimacy. In that community of Los Alamos, Greg and I, especially as we neared adolescence, came to embody yet another iteration of what I call the 'pet Black' phenomenon.

Just as had our predecessors during the slavery era and beyond, Greg and I found we could gain value with White people through our capacity to entertain and serve as focal points for fascination. We knew we were already valued as people by most of our peers, but we were children, always looking for ways to gain favor with the crowd. We learned to barter our artistry, comedy, and athleticism for positive attention and inclusion in the mix.

Greg found music and dancing could captivate his White friends and peers. He didn't just listen to music. He *got down* to it. That alone elicited impressed reactions. He didn't just dance; he broke off movement something fierce. This was the heyday of breaking, popping, and locking—the capital was on the capacity to gyrate, spin, and contort your body into magical movement. This wasn't sideshow; it was *the* show. Los Alamos was the court, and Greg was King. And he didn't just sing; he rapped, aggressive, raw, and colorful—his words were defensive blows, spirit uprising, and self-description all at once.

Greg saw that comedy was powerful. He became the court jester, shuckin' and jivin' to earn his social paycheck—a slap on the back, some junk food, a meal, a flirtation, or just mention of his name in the buzz of adulation gossip. Los Alamos was neither uneducated nor extreme in its ignorance, but it was a small town with scarce Black people. It was privy to the same dynamics of White response to Black exoticism and expressiveness that have long resided in similar locales.

Greg's naturally comic personality was transformed into something more by his racially isolated circumstance. In our family, we talked lovingly about how "Greg's constantly playing the clown." He reminded us of Richard Pryor, Bill

Cosby, Flip Wilson, and ultimately Eddie Murphy, all of whom he mimicked masterfully. Greg had children and adults busting up as he acted out.

Greg had Flip Wilson's Geraldine character from *The Flip Wilson Show* down pat. He did it up. I wish I had a video of his act, because it was genius. He donned Kristin's mini-skirt and high heels, but he didn't stop there. He applied the make-up, lipstick, and put on the wig. Greg had the hip-swaying, head-bobbing walk down cold. Then he came with the raspy, sassy sister-voice of Geraldine, and it was on. "Heeeyyy!" he screeched out, followed by Geraldine's signature lines: "What you see is what you get!" Or he would tuck his chin, bat his eyes sheepishly and say, "The devil made me do it." My parents fell out laughing. Kristin and I fell out even harder.

The Flip Wilson show was on from 1974 to 1978, which meant that Greg was as young as six years of age when he started doing this impression. Even that young, we identified with the few Black faces that visited our home via an 18-inch 'idiot box,' as Dad liked to call it. I'm sure Greg and I would have connected even more strongly with Flip Wilson's show if we had been aware that Flip himself had been a foster child.

Greg was gifted, but his shtick was also the product of his strong desire to be loved. He had all kinds of friends at his side, an entourage following him home and all over town. His personality was more than magnetic. It was money. Everybody wanted a piece of it. His teachers adored him. Girls drew to him like wet to water. This was going on early in elementary school. He was barely out of kindergarten and holding court.

"Greg's such a people person." You heard that said about him all the time. When he grew into his teens and beyond, he was the lifeguard at the pool all the children loved to play with in the water, or chase around the deck. Everybody in town knew Greg Potter and loved him. A wonderful position to be in—that's how it appeared to anyone without insight into his more telling truth.

Another of Greg's entertainment shows was to pig out on food. The way he did it, with exaggerated movements, snorts, and cartoon-like ballooning of his cheeks, reliably made everyone break out in laughter. Eventually, it stopped being humorous to me, as I watched food become something to him that it should never have been. It wasn't just a stage prop for an entertainer; it was more than that. I knew because the same fears were coursing through me. I knew what desperation looked like.

Greg had another act. He walked around with his shirt off grotesquely sticking out his stomach like he was one of those starving children living in impoverished areas of Africa. We both performed this act, but Greg was far better at it. He pushed his stomach out so far you swore it must have hurt, and that you'd better take cover before he burst. This act was perverse in a way because when we did it, we were like true artists, taking advantage of our inherent racial traits to create an image for our audience. We intuitively knew that sticking our stomachs out would more naturally lead others to associate us with starving African children than if a White child did the same thing.

Black entertainers, athletes, and comics, and starving children in Africa: the images of Black folk that were available to us. We scavenged, reading the National Geographic magazines around the house, or at least looking at the pictures. We shamed to the depictions of nakedness and indigence. And feared the people in our lives saw us in the same way. Other than that, what we had was the television and what it proffered about the nature of our own Blackness.

The 'pet Black' dynamic also hurt my brother's education. Greg had his teachers enchanted by his personality, and his friends loyal as could be. The problem was that Greg, despite being very intelligent, always struggled with his schoolwork. For whatever reason, academic learning did not come easily for him. Where our family and the school system should have made concrete efforts to remedy this, the 'pet Black' misfortune instead crept in like a thief under cover and stole my brother's rightful opportunity to thrive.

I believe that some of his teachers let him slide when he tried to slide, and let him pass through the grades without making sure he was straight with certain skills or comprehension. I don't know whether it was because they had low expectations of him, affectionate sympathy, or did not know how to help him. But I know this: If any of those teachers had been Black they would have been more likely to understand that much of Greg's difficulties were due to insecurities about being Black in an overwhelmingly White atmosphere. His problems didn't originate because of his race, but they were certainly magnified by how his Blackness in that environment affected him.

The two of us started to internalize negative messages about our race at a very early age. Two boys caught in the clinging cloud of the idea that Black folk were not as intelligent as White folk. We both faced the tremulous task of proving to ourselves, never mind to everyone else, that we were just as smart as other children. But we didn't believe it. I spent my first 17 years doubting I had the intellect of my schoolmates. I sensed that they had more of *something* important than I did, and I could tell Greg shared that cursed misperception.

The community's rapture over Greg as an entertaining Black personality unwittingly squandered an opportunity to foster his self-confidence. His academic needs were never identified, much less addressed. People were too driven to make Greg feel good. They could tell he fed off it. Greg was a beautiful person, with a huge heart. He loved people and needed to feel the vital splash of appreciation for his true essence.

Greg's extreme popularity also hampered his academic and personal growth. He was a bright light of a personality. Everyone drew to his luminescence. People didn't often think of his popularity as a negative experience, but in Greg's case, it had plenty of harmful effects. He always found ways to get by when it came to his schoolwork. I've never asked directly, but I picked up on the notion that friends were willing to do just about anything for Greg, including his schoolwork. They just wanted to help him out, or draw his favor. But the less work he did while getting credit for it, the further down the road of 'miseducation' he traveled.

The years went by. Each year, his teachers and classmates assumed Greg's writing, reading, and math skills must have been within the ballpark of where they needed to be, because he was promoted from the previous grade. Or, his teachers knew his skills weren't anywhere near the ballpark, but overlooked it. Somehow, Greg got through to the next level. I feel now that Greg's teachers, friends, and family were all culpable. We all laughed at his act, even I did, a person who engaged in the same act for the same reasons. We all want so sincerely for life to be a happy thing for those we care about that we sometimes fall prey to denial and illusion to create that fairy tale. It was so easy for people in Los Alamos to believe that things were all good and proper for Greg and me. The surface of things looked good. But the most important truths dance undercover, and shy away from surface light.

Greg and I were also successful athletically. Rather, I was successful. Greg was legendary. He was a compact, powerful knot of fast-twitch muscles. He was so quick—even in elementary school—that in flag football he regularly performed one of the most amazing athletic feats I ever saw. He lined up on defense, burst into top speed in an instant at the hike of the ball, reached the quarterback who was 10 feet back in shotgun formation, and stripped him of his flag at the same time the quarterback was receiving the ball.

Greg could burn up a running track, and was so incredibly strong and stocky that he excelled at wrestling and football. We both ran in county track meets all summer long throughout elementary school and into junior high. Our bedroom wall was decorated with the ribbons we won. While Greg's wall was coated in dozens of first-place blue, mine was a little more diversified in its colors. Greg ran fierce. *Brother mine: what pain hides behind the mask betrayed by your eyes? What desperation surges in the piston pumping of your thighs? I see and know. You do not run for ribbons. You run to claim the other two-fifths of your humanness that has been so long denied.*

The athletic success was clearly a part of our 'pet Black' phenomenon. We both showed the skills and talent to deserve our levels of athletic achievement, but that old, familiar sense of serving as entertainment still lingered in the air of our refuge in sports. Greg and I both sensed that the people around us believed in us and were comfortable with us when it came to sports. This was acceptable integration. Being aware of this conditional faith they had in us gave us more faith in ourselves, but only in those contexts.

Athletics was one area of Greg's childhood that he felt he had control over. I could feel him thinking: *This is something I have over other kids, something I can shine in.* And shine he did. He rose inside like a geyser to every cheer at every track meet, wrestling match, and football game. I imagine that Greg's insecurities faded like autumn leaves from undressing trees when he was in his athletic domain. His Blackness probably didn't pain him in those times, he may have even been proud of it. But there were also expectations of us both; because of the success, and jealousy from even our friends.

I tried my hand at the same entertainer game as Greg; he just had greater talent for it. Not to say any of this was required for our acceptance, it simply was a natural outgrowth of underlying attitudes on both sides of the partnership. In Los Alamos, I was embraced by two kinds of love. I was fortunate to be adored by so many people with pure, genuine hearts. But my wider popularity, which could easily have been interpreted as the sign of a racially embracing community, was more complex than that. Slight undertones to a portion of my social acceptance never sat well within my stomach. The popularity was a brand of strangeness in which I was complicit.

During elementary and middle school, I often cloaked my shame about the kinky hair on my head by using it as a centerpiece for making my peers laugh. I don't remember whether I started this particular comedy act, or if somebody else did it to me first. The routine involved putting everything from pencils and pens to paperclips and coins inside my hair. This was hilarious to everyone, seeing pencils spiking my crown, or being able to pull hidden things out of my Afro. They couldn't do the same things with their straight, untangled hair, so I was the entertainment, the source of fascination in an other wise bland school day.

This was not too far removed from the sensation of people watching a freak show at a carnival or circus. There was an innocent, yet disturbing fascination in the eyes of the children around me who witnessed this aberration from what they knew. Even I felt a certain strange and ambivalent enjoyment from it most of the time. *These people are diggin' this!* I kept performing on this same stage in college. I put and let others put a wild array of pencils in my hair, sticking out in every direction, and then skewered pieces of paper onto the pencils. I looked like some kind of whacked-out crack head sporting a junkyard beauty crown.

This was a partially positive experience for me, enjoying the laughter along with my college friends. But later, when I dared look closer at it, a more unsettling feeling came to me. My willingness to behave that way came from understanding that I was different, and that I could do something others couldn't. The non-threatening, simple, and somewhat subservient aspect of what Greg and I were caught up in saddened me. We were contorting ourselves to get by, to get in, and to get over. I wasn't so sure why I was even trying so hard to get into the club.

Our distinctive hair played more than a comic role. We experienced excruciating pain and styling disasters because of the hair care we received, and failed to receive. Mom tried hard to handle it on her own, but she had it rough because she was not at all familiar with our kind of hair or the tools it took to cut it. But we were very isolated up on 'the Hill', almost two hours from a city where we could have found people who could cut or care for our hair.

The words 'tender-headed' had no meaning for Mom when it came to combing our nappy hair. It didn't matter if we were tender-headed or not. By the time that metal, cake-cutter, rake of a comb got through yanking on our Afros, our scalps would be a lot more than just tender. A good deal of yelling, grimacing, and jaw clenching went on—both on our parts and by Mom as she struggled with a mass of tangle she obviously had not been culturally groomed to handle. And that was just the trial of picking out our hair. Then there were the actual haircuts.

I went to school with a shamed sense that all was not right with my hair, although I didn't have much to compare it with. All I knew is that my friends and peers, though their hair was straight, had their styling neat and uniform. The 'holes' in my head, on the other hand, were not few, nor were they subtle. The physical pain we endured to get this uneven cut definitely did not justify itself, especially as we perceived it. *I just know my hair's about to come out of my head*, I thought as Mom pulled with all her strength against it, resorting to every manner of weapon and/or device. She used everything from fine-toothed combs the rest of the family used, to the aforementioned metal cake-cutter rakes that were as menacing in their gleaming, sharp-pointed appearance as they were in their pull.

It got so bad that we both resorted to secretly taking scissors to our own hair, checking things out in the bathroom mirror. That's not an easy task when you have the dexterity of a 10-year-old. My sister Kristin and I—and I'm sure Greg as well—will never forget the time Greg's self-barbering went awry in a big way. He accidentally cut a big divot out of his hair. He must have tried to pick up the piece he had cut out and push it back into his Afro, hoping it would stay in place and nobody would notice. I had done this plenty of times myself. I noticed.

It didn't work for Brother Greg this time around. The family was sitting around the kitchen table eating dinner, when suddenly that chunk of hair fell out from Greg's head and landed on his plate. At first, I thought a tarantula had fallen from the ceiling or something. When we realized what Greg had done, it was on. Greg was embarrassed, so he wasn't saying a thing, except, "Shut up and quit laughing!" The neighbors must have heard the laughter exploding. I was conflicted because it was funny, but I also felt for Greg. I knew that this had to do with much more than physical appearance. It struck at the core of our self-esteem.

The state of our hair lurked as a mini crisis. It was important for me to have a smooth surface to my hair, mainly because I was consciously trying to avoid evoking any Buckwheat stereotypes in the minds of my peers. Greg, once he reached adolescence, put even more attention into getting his hair in proper order than I did. It wasn't just about getting the girls or being The Man, though he did that and was that. We were invested in feeling good about ourselves. For us, the intensity of that need was heightened. We were just about the only ones carrying black cotton on our heads. It took us working overtime to feel good about that.

So, the Mom-as-barber project was a failure. She had given it her best shot, but Greg and I had to give her the gong. The next step was to take us to the local barber. That's the kind of town it was. There was 'the' barber, 'the' movie theatre, 'the' drugstore, and so on. I don't remember whether the barber had clippers. If he did, the problem was that he didn't know how to use them on our hair. His efforts were proud and earnest, but it just wasn't happening for us. Same divots and holes, same rampant loose strands and rebellious clumps, same unruliness.

But my brother and I swallowed what we were fed at that point, having lowered our expectations. Those barbershop cuts were manageable as far as we were concerned.

Greg eventually got hip to another way of doing the hair thing. Around middle school age, he got into the Jheri-Curl flow, but I mostly stuck with the jacked up 'fro of my childhood. It did something to my self-esteem being so foreign to my community that its designated hair-cutting professionals didn't know how to cut my own. Foreign was a firecracker show in my own mind, in my own home. Foreign is as foreign does—I was an alien in my own skin and hair.

Over the years, I heard White people take lightly any complaint Greg or I made about not having anyone around that could 'do' our hair, or give us a haircut; or not having anywhere to buy Black hair care products. They seemed to take for granted the fact that they rarely had to question whether they could get their hair cut halfway adequately. They may have struggled to find someone who would cut their hair exactly like they wanted it, but they didn't have to wonder: *Is there someone in this town or within two hours of here who knows how to cut White people's hair?* And the stores by definition carried White hair care products if they carried hair care products at all.

These same people also appeared oblivious to the fact that my hair needed to be both cut and cared for differently than their own. They so often assumed that every little detail of how they lived was simply the way it works or should work for everyone: *Well, I get my hair cut with scissors, and everybody I know gets their hair cut with scissors. So that must be what it takes to cut that little Black boy's hair.* I didn't have to imagine or guess at those assumptions. I was witness to them over and again when it came to my other personal distinctions. Awareness about some basic Black realities eluded so many people so thoroughly, that in the end, it was Greg and me whose true identity was eluded, with hair as just one symbol of our alien-nation . . .

Do you have to wash it?
nah, it just washes itself
do you have to comb it?
no, I use it for birds to nest
cool, it feels like carpet
wanna see what my fist feels like?
can I touch it?
this is a damn freak show
look, you can stick things in it
I'll tell you where you can stick it
wow, it works like Velcro
my heart breaks for you, Elephant Man
what's that stuff you put in it?
anti-ignorance cream
It's not working.

People took great comfort in my athleticism and any humor that sporadically emitted from my quietness. At the same time, I sensed that some of those people would quickly cease being so comfortable with me if I engaged my intellect and honestly spoke out on what I felt about the world. If I had spoken honestly about race, prejudice, and social inequity in particular, it would have been a whole new scene. I intuited this and almost always acquiesced to what I felt the people around me needed. They needed me to be nice, funny, and to agree with them on their view of the world. I needed to fit in, to not feel that my presence was a threat to those around me.

I had mixed feelings about the times when I served as entertainment for White people, whether the interactions were innocent on the surface or not. I sold out what was in my soul, to make others more comfortable with me. I talked softly on purpose, never realizing the true pitch of my voice until I was well into my twenties. I avoided standing too straight and tall, collapsed my masculinity into folds of timidity to make my male power more palatable. I forced laughter too many times. I acted the 'good boy' so that the stereotypes I knew some of them had of Black people could not be confirmed through me.

Greg took the other route; embodying the popular media's Black personas many were too willing to associate us with. He went hip, hard, and happy. I went bent, burrowed, and benign. We both lost ourselves along the way.

I was Greg's big brother and he looked up to me, though I could not see it from the pit of my low self-esteem. He may have needed me to take the lead on talking about our obvious racial isolation. And maybe I was his role model after all, a negative role model, walking him down the staircase into silence. I can hear his private voice now: *Hey, Bro', how are we going to work this out? Are you feeling as bad as I am? You don't love me any less because I'm darker do you? Do you think we're going to make it out there? Do you think we're going to make it?*

I wasn't there to field his questions. I was not my brother's keeper. I was hiding under a rock, undone. *I was born with a hole in my gut. A hole in the place where I was connected . . .*

My smile was a big part of my identity. My nature was to smile broadly. I felt that kind of passionate joy in life and love for the things that life contained. Mom often complimented me, "John, you have such pretty white teeth." So that was one physical feature I did feel good about. But with each passing year, my smile became more a device of appeasement. Increasingly I smiled as a matter of comforting others, letting them know I was friendly and not to be feared. Like a beauty queen or a celebrity before the greedy glow of camera lights, my smile was often a forced expression I held onto, even in moments or days when smiling was the last thing I felt like doing. The one place I didn't use my smile in this way was in the home. For better or worse, the honest expression of my moods was shared freely with family.

Halloween used to lend me a kind of relief, a pause in the act. I could hide behind the face paint and masks I wore as part of my costume and feel like, for that one night, my Black face was not my dominant feature. I looked forward excitedly to that night, and only now do I realize why. But that one moment was too fleeting. November always came the next morning, and I had to once more put on my smile, the mask I carried the other 364 days of the year.

That was often the nature of mainstream racial acceptance in New Mexico. That particular brand was sometimes spoken, sometimes unspoken. The equation read: Hispanics have to speak English, Indians have to cut their hair and dress *normal*, and African Americans have to dispense with the *African*, and put on a smiling face as an ID card that indicates, "I want to be loved by you."

True to the absurdity of life, my 'pet Blackness' had its advantages. I was so caught up in the blatancy of my Blackness that I didn't realize my popularity until I was looking back on it while I was in college. But the positive attention and good friendships were a blessing, allowing me to slowly construct some good feelings about myself, if not about my race.

At best, I recognized my popularity as a tepid possibility: *Some people seem to like me.* But I was wary of the affection because it appeared to be built upon a vulnerable foundation. I believed that if ever I began to not act like them, and started acting like the distant Black people they seemed to view as alien at best, my popularity would be rescinded in a hurry. It would stagger on spaghetti legs, fall to the canvass, and would never beat the 10-count. I longed for the clean love of early childhood, the kind we had with Tonya and Laura, chasing butterflies and fighting for Grandma Danz's attention.

Greg and I were often complimented. We were seen as 'so cute and adorable' as little diaper vipers, and then 'likeable' as older children, and ultimately 'handsome' and 'athletic' as adolescents. But for some, those affections were somewhat of a facade. The facade revealed itself when the interning college students hit town.

Each summer, the National Laboratory brought in college undergraduate and graduate students from all over the country, and some from other nations, to participate in mentored research experiments with cutting-edge technology and scientists respected globally. The majority of the students who came in were White, but there was also a contingent of Black students, mostly from the historically Black colleges and universities. The number of overall summer students dwarfed the number of Black students, but you wouldn't know it from the way some folks reacted. The 20 to 30 Black students were very noticeable around town, because there were so few Black people there in the first place.

What happened when the Black students came for the summer may not have been perceptible to many people, but it was always obvious to me. The racial tension rose, just faintly. The usual comfortable, friendly light I saw in the eyes of some people during the rest of the year when they looked at me or some other Black person became a look slightly more distant. In the body language and overheard hushed conversations, I saw how a community can become ever so slightly discomforted by the infusion—even though temporary—of just 20 to 30 Black people into its world.

I always knew that part of the reason Greg and I were accepted and tolerated to the degree we were was because we were so rare. We really didn't represent an intrusion into the way of life of people in the community. We were being raised culturally to mirror them. Those who might have had a problem with our race knew they would only see us every so often, and speak to us even less often. People also knew these scattered Black families and children were never going to significantly define the day-to-day culture of the town. *No reason for them to fear or be concerned with us.* But for me as a local, to see how some people in town reacted to just a handful more Black people being around for three months told me a great deal about the most base level of my own place in town.

I realized that many people's discomfort wasn't because of negative racial attitudes; but that it was mostly due to an acute unfamiliarity with Black people. Los Alamos was so homogenous in the physical appearance of its people, in its particular culture and outlook on life, that it scared me. It was so seemingly insulated from the outside world that it existed as a surreal pantomime of that larger reality. Some very warm, genuine people lived there. But its predictability made it feel almost like a movie set.

Even some of the warmest, most kind-hearted people, whom I loved and admired, had a frightening blind spot: the cultural dynamics at the root of most social issues. They lived on that high-altitude plateau, a place almost sterile from outside influences. Each time I returned to that town after high school, I got the sense that time was just passing it by. The country changed, pulsed, and vibrated. But when I came back to Los Alamos there was a kind of stillness to its evolution. It did not seem to have a viable pulse.

There were benefits to such stability—peace; lack of overgrowth; multi-generation familiarity between families within the schools, the churches, and the Lab; relative lack of crime. And the neighborly climate throughout town was always reassuring. But there was another side to this stability. It involved an inbreeding of experiences, perceptions, and stereotypes about what was good and what was 'other' than good. In Los Alamos, people familiar to Los Alamos were good; living styles familiar to Los Alamos were good. But people who brought influences distinctly 'other' than Los Alamos with them from their alternate realities in other communities were likely to be viewed as somehow disruptive of and conflicting with the intimate local rhythm.

It wasn't so much that Los Alamos was uniformly prejudiced racially, just strongly reactive to the unfamiliar. Race, especially the Black race, was likely to bring something with it that was very much foreign. If not through the physical distinctiveness of African facial and hair features, then through ways of walking, talking, dressing, cooking, eating, hobbies and habits, music, ideas, and attitudes. All the textures that give humans flavor.

Because of those things, many of the Black students who came to town during the summer expressed their culture shock. Greg and I usually smiled sympathetically and responded: "Tell us about it."

For most people, my life and Greg's on the surface seemed to be a smooth ride. They saw the things in us that may have been the basis for their own happiness—popularity, athletic success, a loving family, and material stability. They saw these things and assumed we must have been happy. That we should feel lucky to be growing up in such a wonderful town, in such a loving family. They took for granted the thing most lacking but equally important to our true happiness: Seeing our face looking back at us. Most of these people had the comfort of being White in a White community.

My childhood was far from difficult, relative to most lives on this Earth. But the part of it that was a challenge is the very part that few White people ever wished to hear anything about. When they did hear, many took offense, at best—one, because our popularity bred a sour resentment in some, especially from those closest to us, and two, because to implicate my White environment was to implicate those very same people. I knew what the 'true me' had to offer might not be welcome. The resentment I would harbor over this was potent, and left me strayed from my peace.

Full moon preens
to its own beauty
basking on mirror surface
of placid waters

the child I am is envy swollen
I cast a stone and break
that reflection with ripples
silent and hurried
like the desires
wet and unwelcome
that litter my shore

STRAWBERRY BLONDES

IN the beginning, my sister Kristin and I were the sweet simplicity of playmates and companionship. Our desires were basic and fulfilled to overflowing. We had the smother of physical affection from Mom and Dad, a warm home, good food, and plenty of fresh air and green grass to play in. Baths together, splashing each other with squealed delight, story time every night. When I was in my crib, I wanted to be in hers. I once even pulled off acrobatic feats to scale the sides of my crib, somehow reach across space to grasp the top of her crib's railing, and pull myself over and down into her space. She was my steady presence, and life was all fascination and wonder.

When she was a child, Kristin looked like Pippi Longstocking. She even dressed up as Pippi for Halloween one year, her two pigtails suspended on coat hangers sticking straight out from her head like antennae. Her long flowing hair was a vibrant strawberry blonde, though much more strawberry than it was blonde. Her face was a flushing constellation of brown freckles orbiting her blue eyes, straight from Dad. Her skin was milky fair. All by herself she managed to stand out from other children. She and I together made for a real visual spectacle.

I must say lovingly that as a sister Kristin was a champion brat, in the tradition of our cousin Dale. It was likely a family genetic trait. She was constantly up to something to get Greg or me in trouble. "Mom! John sneaked a cookie from the cookie jar!" or, "I'm telling Mom you guys said a bad word!" She was a master tattletale and seemed to take great pleasure in stirring up trouble. Once she and I entered kindergarten, Kristin moved into her own bedroom, next to the room the three of us previously shared. Then it became trench warfare. Greg and I plotted our revenge from the security of our room as we imagined Kristin conniving to develop her next plot from her room.

Kristin was unrelenting in her mischief. Mischief was her love expression in the way men punch each other to display their affection. She came into our room during afternoon naptime and stirred up things. "Come on you guys, let's get up and play." Well, Mom didn't play with naptime. We were supposed to be asleep and quiet in bed until she came to tell us we could get up. So, there we were—three little playmates, violating curfew, unsuspecting of impending doom. Boom! The door flew open. "Who told yous you could get up from your naps!" Mom bellowed. 'Yous' was an artifact of language she carried with her in her migration across the Mississippi.

"They did it!" Kristin claimed, pointing our way, selling us out with such rapid-fire instinct it was a thing of beauty.

"Did not! It was her, Mom, she came into our room!" Greg and I protested in unison. Of course, to the two of us, it seemed as though Mom always believed Kristin. We just knew we were persecution's forever victims in the wake of our sister's wily ways. Whenever Mom did believe Kristin, and Greg and I took the spanking or reprimand, Kristin grinned that devilish expression to indicate: *Got you. Mission accomplished.* I raged at her insolence. The next round of revenge and counter-revenge was underway.

I soon understood that in this world Kristin was one of the 'normal' ones. Beauty was all around me in the bedtime books we read. I saw evidence of my ranking. The story was told in skin and hair. *Kristin, you are Goldilocks, I am the bear. You are the fair lady, I am the opera's phantom, cloaked and masked. You are the damsel in distress; I am Quasimodo, repulsive if not less. I love you so much my dear sister; but you are the beauty, I am the beast.*

As the three of us moved up the social ranks of grade school, we encountered the inevitable neighborhood and schoolyard confrontations, sizing ups, and braggadocio. Kristin loved us deeply and always stood up for us no matter the source of the conflict. Usually it was just a matter of dealing with neighborhood bullies, or another child trying to show off in front of friends. The few instances when racial comments were directed at Greg or me and Kristin was present, she shot to our defense quick as a rabbit. Her love was pure, but her temper was spicy. I just stood back and let her shake the person down. In the moment before she responded, I always wondered whether she would do or say anything. These were my moments of need and hope: *What that person just said hurt, really hurt. What did it mean to Kristin? Does it bother her as much as I need it to bother her?* It always did.

During those times Kristin and I fought, argued, or chased each other in anger, I often nervously expected that she would finally let out what I honestly believed just about every White person in my life felt deep down inside their private, secret space. I feared that in the heat of her emotions she would let slip some kind of racially tinged spite or disdain, and that I would be permanently crushed. I knew I could never recover from that kind of blow. I lived with that fear. One time she did blow and threw a huge metal Tonka truck at my head; but, by the grace of Kristin's heart, my greatest fear was never realized.

I don't know if Kristin ever even used the word *Black* in reference to Greg or me—not that that was entirely a good thing. There would come a day, and times, in which I needed that fact of my being to be spoken to, naturally, by Kristin just like the rest of the family. But in terms of her child's vision of what was real and what mattered, we were her brothers, nothing more and nothing less. I did not find a certainty in that fact until I enjoyed the retrospection of years passed.

Kristin and I went through school in the same grade, though never in the same home classroom. We had maybe one class together, and that was during high school. As elementary school passed into middle and then high school, two streams elevated to run through me when I saw Kristin during the day. We saw each other on the playground during recess or at lunch, and in between classes or after school. It was reassuring to see my sister in that mass of students. Even if just in a passing moment, it soothed my shyness and insecurities to run across someone who had known me almost all my life.

But there was also an element of awkward discomfort, because I knew that the sight of the two of us—fair-skinned redhead and tall, lanky Black boy—was an odd one to many of our peers. I was always conscious of it. I knew encountering Kristin at school was a trigger for others to pause and recognize how I stood out—not only racially, but because I somehow had a White sister.

In my state of poor self-regard, I constantly wavered between brotherly pride and youthful embarrassment over the rare relationship Kristin and I represented in the intense social waters of childhood and adolescence. My heart was confused. I loved Kristin and needed her supportive and loving presence around me out in that community. But that horrible feeling of being in the spotlight, of appearing so brazenly Black and without tether to a larger Black presence, scorched me at a higher intensity when I was paired beside the Whiteness of Kristin. It was a pairing that in my imagination somehow left the Blackness I was ashamed of a more grotesque and salient thing in the eyes around me.

The contrast of my sister beside me became a magnification I did not handle well. Already, by the time the two of us had ascended to the higher status upper playground domineered by the fourth, fifth, and sixth graders, I had developed a conditioned response of aversion to my own sister. I saw her coming from class with her friends and was afraid I was an embarrassment to her. "Hey, there's my brother!" she shouted.

I saw her coming from lunch or from recess and she was the fair-skinned beacon to the world that shone the light of contrast onto my Black figure. *He's not happy to see me*, she thought, deflated.

I saw her coming and she was the truth teller to all the children that not only was I Black, but I wasn't even a regular kind of Black: I had a White sister. I couldn't even manage a second-degree normalcy. *Why doesn't he like me?* She pained.

I saw her coming.

Instead of embracing my sister, I retreated to my safe place inside. I carved paths in the pumice hillside of the playground and raced agate marbles over and again down the slope. Sunlight caught them spinning, swirled with colors, and they were miniature glass galaxies. They were magnificent. They were transportation away.

Our relationship was also being affected by another evolving fact. As Kristin aged, her personality emerged, and showed itself to be increasingly like Mom's. Their voice tones and pitches sounded just about the same. Over the phone, it became difficult to tell them apart. Kristin and Mom's style of interaction with people, their sense of humor, even their colloquialisms took on an almost mirror-image quality. Kristin showed herself to be gifted with arts and crafts like Mom. Her emotional character was clearly fiery and strong, like Mom's.

At the same time, my own personality burgeoned into a more definite tone, and much of that persona was by then sharply duel-natured in its compassion and anger. The compassion was for the way people were hurt in a world that seemed to me insensitive and cruel. Anger was the bristled defense I erected to halt the inward flow of hurt coming from several sources. In addition to my struggles with race and adoptive connection to my family, the muzzling of my personality heavily descended upon me. I was feeling more each year that I could not share myself with Mom; that we were on two completely different pages.

The more Kristin's character resembled Mom's, the less confidence I had that my sister could understand my plight. My drift away from Kristin was one of surrender more than aggression. Betrayal was almost the emotion—a feeling that Kristin, as she socialized into her emerging adult mentality, was beginning to represent and defend the cultural state of mind that had injured me the most. It was a cultural perspective unwilling and unable to peer through the veil of its own reality and see what was going on inside of me. My love for Kristin was quickly deepening in complexity and contradiction. In being so similar to Mom in personality, Kristin was a reminder to me of Mom's inability to see me. Maybe the real root of that irritation was that I perceived Mom's inability as more than inability; I saw it as an *unwillingness* to see me. I resented that. Poor Kristin would bear the brunt.

Although I would not realize it at the time, the popularity I was receiving in great bushels was causing Kristin a throbbing emotional bruise of rejection. "Kristin feels like you treated her poorly because you were popular and she wasn't," Mom shared with me years later. That revelation struck me broadside and left me stunned. My popularity was not something that I could say I enjoyed, because I had mostly not even been aware of it. It was the farthest thing from my mind as I interacted with Kristin at school and home. What she saw as my rejecting her because she wasn't part of the 'right crowd' was a conflict that ran so much deeper.

While Kristin suffered the wound of beholding my popularity from outside its glow, I clung to a solitary and desperate need to feel as though I fit in and was normal. We were both young and insecure. Her torment was popularity; mine was race. For both of us, the emotions were real and had teeth. We grew up never sharing what was in our own bag, never realizing what burdened the other as we trudged forward.

Six billion variations of perspective are what make humankind so volatile. As I shared a family and a life with Kristin, I saw her as enjoying the privilege of a biological connection with Mom and Dad, and later with the youngest children, Anna and Rudy. She had a reflection pond. And her racial harmony with most of our community was a treasure for which I consistently ached.

The whole time, Kristin was seeing a whole different picture. Growing up with two adopted and Black brothers, and as the only girl in that older sibling group, Kristin was feeling like a minority, thrice over. I thought she was on the inside of the circle from which I was excluded: *She's a part of them. I'll never be. When she speaks her sorrows, they all hear her song. They all understand: Mom, Dad, her friends, and teachers—all of these people. She has an audience. They don't know a thing about my song.*

The truth was, Kristin saw herself on the outside of a glass window, looking in: *John and Greg are the special ones. They get all the attention.*

I lived as the freakish alien, wondering what planet I had come from and whether I would ever truly be accepted. To Kristin, I was the star of the show. To her there could be no possible reason for me to be unhappy about anything. I was living the Golden Life. But while Kristin was a minority of one in a peer group of three siblings, I was a minority of two in a family of seven, in a broader family of dozens. I was a token in a community of thousands, an object of scorn for too many in a nation of millions. That weight had my spine bent near to the ground, far too warped to be able to see much of anything clearly, especially something as secondary to me as popularity.

In the ninth grade, Kristin and I played on the same YMCA youth league basketball team. I had decided I wasn't up for playing on the Pueblo Junior High team—too much competitiveness and intensity for me at that time. I was just trying to ball, have some fun. I was also younger than my classmates and still met the age qualification for one last year of youth league play. Kristin wanted to play on the same team and I wanted that, too. I was proud to have her on the same squad—so many of our school experiences had occurred separately, in different classes, with different teachers. In this arena, the basketball court, I was becoming assured and oriented. Here, Kristin's presence did not affect me in the same way it sometimes did on the schoolyard or downtown in public. Here it was just me and my sis' running the court.

She played hard, gave some of our male teammates more than they could handle in practice. We ran the table that season—undefeated. While my friends were playing for the school team, dressed down in their splashy uniforms, Kristin and I were running in white T-shirts with black iron-on lettering and numbers, with whatever shorts we could find. Raggedy and loving it. I was feeling good and free to let my sibling love flow.

Once we reached adolescence, many people who didn't know us assumed we were boyfriend and girlfriend. Telling people that Kristin, with her fair White skin and red hair, was my sister drew predictable responses. This claim was usually met with either laughter, as if I had just told a good joke, or a moment of awkward confusion as the person tried to figure out this picture that wasn't quite right.

When we were even older and out together, I could sense that people who saw us were silently processing their thoughts and emotions about us as an interracial couple. In their presumption, Kristin and I were nothing more than two people caught up in 'jungle fever'. Anytime we traveled outside of Los Alamos, to Albuquerque, Illinois, or elsewhere, and encountered Black people, a predictable dynamic often ensued. First came the quick glance, their peripheral spotting of a Black male walking with a White female. Then came that energy wave of rising indignity, disgust, revolt, anger, and a desire to say something. I could virtually hear their thoughts gritting through their skulls. *You ought to be ashamed of yourself, boy.* Last came the physical look of disgust as the person barely held her tongue, barely concealed his flames. Then the moment would pass, strangers having assumed everything and realizing nothing. I was left yet again to do nothing but swallow my frustrations into a place of latency.

This especially was the case with Black females, who had their own valid reasons for strongly reacting to images like the one Kristin and I represented in our intimate sibling interactions. I understood the origin of the reaction. Years of humiliation and untold layers of betrayal inhabited those emotions. But I was disappointed in those strangers nonetheless. I wished that we African Americans as a people would find the strength to be more dignified and resist the temptation to judge what we saw on the street. I detested seeing people of my own race fall prey to the same kinds of prejudiced assumptions and dehumanizing attitudes that had always plagued us as targets.

I was fortunate to grow up with a sister whose love for me never seemed to waiver, no matter how much ambivalence and aversion I threw her way. Kristin could not have understood all of what I was wrestling with, or how in my mind she had somehow become a part of that opponent. At the time, I didn't understand it myself. All I knew was that the emotions were always there, right beneath the surface of my general happiness. It didn't take much to send those feelings shooting up through my membrane of suppressed angst. I was a garden hose with a kink. The water pressure built up; just waiting for a moment that would release the knot, sending that scalding fester racing through me. Then I would kink back up, pressure building again—a persistent cycle of despair.

My adolescence was preceded by a change in our family. During my first seven years, my mind had been a whir of thoughts, trying to figure out who I was, and what I was a part of or not a part of. Just as I began to orient myself to some sense of my place in a family of five, a new season began. Biology made its reappearance in the form of two new personalities in our home.

By 1974, Dad was close to having endured the challenges of handling graduate school while being a father of three, a husband, a full-time worker, and living many states away from his graduate institution. He finally achieved his doctorate degree in physics in 1975. I vaguely remember the mental, emotional, and financial strain it placed on him and Mom. But the two of them always worked to keep their grown-up stresses away from us children. For the two of them, those seven years must have been a hearty struggle. Money and time had been tight, but now Dad was done with school, and he and Mom were ready to return to one of their earlier objectives: raising a large family.

Mom's body changed over the winter heading into '75. I was fascinated as a seven-year-old, having an up-close view of a woman transforming into a passageway for new life. I was just about head-high to Mom's growing belly and the scene was at turns horrifying and mystifying.

Heaven sent our family one of its angels in the spring. But first, on the night of April 4th and the morning of April 5th, 54 inches of snow were laid down as a blanket of purity. We took this as a gesture of welcome for the little baby soon to come. Everything was buried in white. Cars were invisible beneath the drifts. Kristin, Greg, and I were in a land of wonder. We dug tunnels in the snow and constructed our version of igloos that served as command centers for our snowball wars. Of course, we had to dig foxholes and trenches and stockpile snowballs in the freezer, anticipating a battle that would last into the summer. Before the snow could melt, little baby Anna, truly an angel in spirit, was born on the sixth of May.

Anna was an adorable, cherubic baby, with strong red hair, soulful brown eyes like a forest deer, and her own constellation of freckles, like her older sister. How Mom and Dad, with their dark brown hair, came up with what would eventually be three redheaded babies was always of great intrigue. The genetics of that trick became just one of many family conversations about shared physical traits. My excitement over a new baby sister dominated the moment for me and allowed me to enjoy celebrating her similarities with the rest of the family.

Anna was the most kind-hearted and sweet person I knew. Dad has told me of his great grandmother, Emma Baldowsky, who was a person of lore in her family and community—one of God's chosen people put on Earth to bless others with her compassion. He says that he often sees some of his great grandmother in Anna. As an adolescent, Anna loved to collect angels. In doing so, she was surrounding herself with her peers. She had so much love as a young child that it spilled over into every living thing she encountered. She loved animals and was crushed at the loss of any family pet. I could relate to the strong love that came so forcefully and easily from her. I focused in on that energy, that piece of her that felt like me, and clung to it as a place to embed myself into our family.

Anna and I found our way into a special bonding ritual, helped along by the fact that she was born with a warrior spirit. Her sweet nature also had a competitive fierceness. Just about as soon as she could walk, I strapped the boxing gloves on Anna. I faced her on my knees, and we went at it. She was fearless. I threw shadow punches her way, feinting, and tapping with my gloves. She walked right through my flurries. More often than not, especially as she got bigger, she buried me in an avalanche of punches before I called her off. We actually timed the rounds—three minutes each, with water breaks in between. Out of breath, she kept punching. *I love you, Big Brother.*

Sweating from bobbing, ducking, and throwing, I kept soaking up the moment: *You and me in the same space, Baby Sister, in the same space. This is love.*

She was a champion, hanging in there with her big brother, boxing with me round after round, until we both were exhausted. Anna probably didn't realize that I was bonding with her, but I could see in her eyes and from her enthusiasm that it meant the world to her. Our shared joy of trading punches was an important part of my feeling connected with our family. Mom came in on us sometimes, throwing leather. She just looked at us like we were crazy. But she could feel what was happening. She left us to our madness. To this very day, Anna still beats me down.

In 1978, Rudy became the fifth Potter child, the baby child. We were in the new house on 47th Street by this time, and I was 10 years of age. Rudy came home from the hospital with a squished up nose, Dad's blue eyes, and a beet-red, pudgy face, like the character, Chubby, from *the Little Rascals*. The boy obviously had a rough time squeezing into the world . . . poor Mom. Rudy started out life as one more redhead in the lot, blonder than Kristin and Anna, gradually over the years fading into a true blonde.

Rudy was a huge baby, a one-of-a-kind bundle of energy and intellect. There was absolutely no way to keep that child still. If those days were today, every teacher, relative, or acquaintance would badger Mom: "Put that child on a super-dose of Ritalin and call it a day." But Rudy had at least one parent who could relate to this part of his character, and therefore was able to help Rudy feel normal in that regard.

Dad was always defending Rudy's hyperactivity with the explanation that, "I was just like that as a child." To which Kristin or Mom would respond, "Yeah, and you must have driven your mother crazy." Rudy quickly learned to stand his ground and take on a thick skin. As the youngest child in a family of seven, he was treated unmercifully.

Rudy showed Dad's spirit from day one—quiet, inwardly intense, outwardly laid back, and brilliant. That brilliance had him wrestling himself to get through grade school, because class work was too slow and unchallenging for him. Like Dad, Rudy drifted deep into his own private world of science and ideas. Social graces were not his gift—his talent was reserved for his mind. Dad had persisted in trying to get us older three children interested in science. We ended up in so many science fairs my head was spinning with hypotheses that I could barely remember, much less comprehend. But in the end, none of us held science as a passion.

Dad shared passion and personal makeup with Rudy, and it was good to see how they thrived in each other's presence. It was especially gratifying for me to witness, knowing that neither of them was the kind of person destined to be surrounded by a mainstream of similar personalities. They had each other—their humor, idiosyncrasies, rhythm, and interests—and it seemed to be all they needed.

Mom and Dad may have forged ahead with their master plan for a large family, but by the time Anna arrived, Mom was burnt. She already had three active children running around, each screaming "Mom!" every five minutes, which meant she was being screamed at, on average, about every minute and forty seconds. She had no real extended family support system around her, with her sisters, parents, and other relatives in Illinois. Uncle Jerry and Aunt Sue were handling their own two children, and they were down in White Rock, a good car trip away. Aunt Pam and her family were in Albuquerque, so it was mostly on Mom. Maybe she realized that soon after Anna's delivery, because we three older children were quickly recruited to pitch in and help with this new baby.

'Pitch in', was Mom's vernacular for changing diapers, warming the bottle, bottle feeding, baby food feeding, burping, rocking, dressing, playing, babysitting, reading and singing to, bathing, pushing in the stroller, and cleaning up messes— including spilled food and drinks, spit-up, and other bodily baby expressions. I loved it. Caring for Anna, and later for my brother, Rudy, was an act that was pure and clean. My usual worrying about racial undertones just wasn't there, at least in terms of what these babies were giving me at that time.

Being that intimate with Rudy and Anna from their infancy and into their early childhood was a blessing. Those close interactions allowed me to develop a distinctive connection I did not share with the rest of the family. The love they naturally radiated toward me was something I sorely needed. They just sat there staring at me with total affection and need for the same. *Give me more love, John. That feels good.* I knew that at least during this early season of their lives, these two babies looked upon me as nothing other than a person they needed, loved, and could count on. I was aware that they had been relatively untouched by all those hurtful racial messages the world would inevitably cascade onto them.

But as I stood over them, powdering those little butts, every now and then a fear would flash through my mind: *What racial attitudes might these sweet and pure little souls carry as they grow into bearers of the White standard? Will you still love me the same way?* They would grow up socialized by the same societal biases as any other child, and they would live in a community that would leave them unfamiliar with the human texture of other Black persons. Would they always think of me as they thought of me now? *Love me more, John. Love me more.* The thought of these two beautiful babies catching even one molecule of ambivalent attitude about Black people, and by extension about me, was a fear too hurtful to entertain.

While I worried about how Anna's feelings for me would develop, I remained obedient to the family culture and never brought up my fears to her. As she stretched from toddler to 10 to teens, she never realized our family was different. To Anna, Greg and I were her brothers, just like any other brothers. She grew up with one of her favorite television sitcoms, *Diff'rent Strokes*, giving her the impression that a normal family had two adopted Black children in it. She responded to confused looks from others as they saw our family photos, with a pride born from simplistic loving bliss I only wished I could have enjoyed.

Anna was only 10 when I left for college. I wasn't as in touch with the emergence of her personality as she moved into adolescence. But from all those miles away, in my dorm room, in the most mundane moments of thought, I wondered, and worried. *What kind of racial attitudes is my baby sister soaking up from this society? Is she rearranging her thoughts and feelings for me, even slightly? How is she making sense of what African Americans are; why Black people are portrayed they way we are; and who, then, is her older brother? Is she viewing me as something more, something better than other Black people, because I was raised in her family, in her community?* While she was going about loving and admiring her older brother, her older brother was sifting shades of color through the worrisome blender of emotions and meaning he had constructed long ago.

There had been simpler days. One summer Anna and I walked just about every day from our house down Urban Street's long hill to Urban Park, where we played ball on the outdoor cement court. Along the way to the park, we always stopped at an apricot tree whose branches hung from the backyard of a house over the fence and out over the sidewalk. The days were blue skied and healthy with heat. We paused under that tree; I picked large, ripe apricots and handed two or three to Anna, who was not yet waist-high to me. I loved seeing her smiling face, chipmunk cheeks stuffed with fruit, juice dripping down. Because of the moment, those were the best apricots I've ever had.

At the park, Anna was once more the good sport, with the unyielding enthusiasm to accommodate me. I shot. She rebounded. She grew tired along with me, but she never stopped running after that ball. Never stopped pushing her little body through the heat to please me. I should have known from moments like those that her love for me was pure, but I was distracted by a stronger force. I could have sensed that Anna actually identified more with Greg and me than with the rest of the family, because of her interest in sports and her disinterest in science and technology. But I didn't. Many of the people in my childhood identified greatly with me for various reasons, and I recognized very little of that. My concerns made me more than myopic. I was thoroughly blind.

The fears I had about Anna were replicated in my thoughts about Rudy. He and I were even further separated in our perceptions of the family because of the 10-year age difference. Being the 'baby of the family', the youngest by far of five children, he suffered the classic syndrome of disregard. He had six personalities enforcing their will upon him with a sense of entitlement. Six people bossing, ordering, humoring, and patronizing. In the middle of all that, he was trying to make sense of his place in the mix.

As he would tell me years later, his child's eyes saw this: Two people, the oldest, both with darker hair and slightly darker skin than his. They were called 'Mom' and 'Dad'. There were two girls, one much bigger and one closer to his size. Both had light skin, freckles, and red hair. Then there were two boys, one, tallest of the four, calm and quiet. The other was shorter and more verbal. Both boys had skin that was much darker than his. Their hair was dark like his parents', but curlier. This was his impression of his family. At his age, it was all about sizes, shapes, colors, and personalities. Life had not yet intruded upon him with social complexities.

Over time, these complexities came. In first grade, he was assigned the task of writing a sentence that answered the question, "What color are you?" Rudy wrote, "I am camouflage, so I can hide in the woods." *I feel you, brother.*

Complexity came to Rudy in the form of school counselors asking him how he felt about having two Black brothers. To him, this made as much sense as being asked how he felt about having two sisters who were redheads. Unlike for me, there was nothing in his own appearance or personality that would cause race to be a conscious idea for him. The distinctions he perceived were one dimensional, along the axis of physical difference. By his age, in elementary school, I was already well acquainted with a second axis. I knew different people were valued differently because of how they looked.

This came to me more quickly than it came to Rudy, because my identity was at the center of that valuation. Rudy was following the more gradual path of awareness of most children—that tragic movement from perceiving the world's differences as artistic splendor to experiencing them as symbols heaving with implication. Through that simplistic lens, Rudy saw the world and he saw me. I was his brother, a person to be loved, and a person from whom he hoped to receive love. On my side of the consciousness divide, I prayed that Rudy was seeing things so cleanly. At the same time, I wished he would recognize the racial complexities in a way that would allow him to relate to my state of being.

My path was ambivalent as I moved through the maze that was my family's individual personalities. 'Black sheep' was, for me, an appropriate term in more ways than one. My personality seemed foreign and difficult to interpret for the rest of the family. I often felt as though I needed to translate myself to them. When I did make an effort to express my truer emotions, I often received a brief moment of nothingness, as if they were trying to decipher what I had said. It was as if I was a stranger they had encountered on the road. In many ways, through my habitual reluctance to come outside of my emotional shell, I was that stranger.

So much of what was mine on one side of the abyss and what was theirs on the other side seemed to be writ in separate languages. The disconnection between us when I tried to communicate felt much like the awkward vacuum that looms on a romantic date when nothing seems to click; except in my case, my only choice was to stick with the relationship and endure the absence of synchronicity.

The older I grew, the more conscious I became of the cold realities of how African Americans were regarded by so much of society. The further I drifted into that awareness, the more it seemed I was beginning to reside on a different page—or not even in the same book—from the rest of my family, other than maybe Greg. This race-related schism became something I confused into a writhing inner turmoil. The resulting morass was a hairball in my gut that would take years to cough up.

The many similarities that Kristin, Anna, and Rudy shared with each other and with Mom and Dad were gifts from nature that instilled in them a sense of belonging. I constantly looked to my parents and White siblings for a sign that I existed. I looked for it in their physical appearances, in their personalities, and in the extent to which they appeared to understand me. I needed badly to find something. Finding very little, my identity became 'the outsider'.

Rudy, Anna, and Kristin all had fair skin that burned easily. They might not have exactly appreciated that, but at least they could relate to each other through that similarity. They shared mannerisms and tendencies with one another and with Mom and Dad. Their hair was similar and Mom knew how to care for it. Family conversations noted how each of them had physical traits of relatives: "your father's nose," "her mother's eyes," "his uncle's chin." These elements allowed my brother and sisters to know who they were in relation to other meaningful people in their lives. I looked hard to identify some of those same kinds of connections and came up empty.

I choked on those contradictions. The message I always heard from the world was that blood was thicker than water. *Except for your blood, John. But your blood is of no consequence, because we love you. So don't worry, you're a part of us.*

Jealousy sprang up in me at times. I suspected that my sisters and brother Rudy were not even aware of the ways in which they had been wrapped in a security blanket not of their own making. Things existed in that house, things that were infusing them with cohesion and togetherness. I was a bystander, drifting in circles around the party, kept from joining in by an unseen but very real force field. Maybe at some point I gave up trying as hard as I could have. By the time I was a teenager, I was tired of the effort. I just couldn't latch onto that sense that *I exist in them, in their being.* The broader love we shared was the only glue that kept me together.

My family wouldn't have admitted their enjoyment of similarity, not desiring to make Greg and me feel left out. But the function of similarity was a natural truth—it served a purpose. And the lack of sameness between my family and its two Black children had consequences. My parents had to deal with comments that questioned the connection of their Black children to the family. Questions like, "Is that your child?" or "Where did you get that beautiful baby?" may have seemed innocuous enough, but they were questions I overheard. I took the comments to mean that my being a part of this family was uncertain and unclear to others. To me, what others thought mattered greatly. I was trying to arrange the pieces of my puzzle. Their doubts of my belonging became mine.

Trips to town with Dad or with other family members often involved people looking at us with confusion or discomfort. Going to the hardware store with Dad and having the cashier hear me say "Dad" to the White man next to me produced all kinds of crazy facial expressions. Simple errands and social outings were full of reactions from people that highlighted my adoptive circumstance. It wore on me after about the first few hundred times.

It stung to wait in line with my family and have people not recognize that my brother Greg and I were a part of the family. It made me feel like a little Black castaway, or stowaway. So many times I stood in line behind Mom or Dad as they paid the cashier and then I would start to follow them out. "Can I help you?" the alarmed cashiers would ask, as if they were wondering why I had just stood in line if I wasn't going to buy anything. Or as if they suspected that I had just shoplifted.

Just as reliably, I would go into a store with a sibling or parent, and the employee would come up and ask the other family member first if they needed any help. Then the employee would turn to me and ask, "And can I help you with anything?" *What does it look like, that I was just tailing this White person into the store for some reason, and decided to stop by her side while she talked to you? Do you think I have nothing better to do?*

Misunderstandings like those, even if of innocent intent, were significant to me. The accumulation, day after day, of being on the receiving end of misperceptions and ambivalence grew at least tiresome, even when not hurtful. I was a child, with playful interests. This racial concern wasn't a hobby I chose to pick up. My face was rubbed in it dozens of times for every one time a family member noticed.

My parents and siblings couldn't help taking for granted the physical and cultural similarity they shared within the familial circle. That similarity extended out into their schools, neighborhoods, workplaces, and places of worship. It was part of their social communion, so inherent in the day for them that they rarely thought about it or considered what it would be like to live without it. They had benefited from this since their own childhood. It was a part of their self-esteem, an unconscious natural inheritance, concentric social circles of affirmation.

I had two choices: either believe that my struggle with being distinct was largely of my imagination and overblown, or have faith in what my spirit was telling me. The nudging, usually unspoken tide coming at me externally wished that I chose the former road. My spirit was larger than that. I could not make real emotions turn to vapor, so that I could blow them away and fall in line. I had no choice but to be disturbed by my predicament.

The lack of similarity in appearance and personality between my family and me was not the factor that affected me the most. The lack of active compensation by my family for this circumstance tolled the bell. It was not a natural, common part of the fabric of our family's social life to interact with and seek exposure to African American people or culture. Not only was such interaction difficult given the geographic isolation, but also and more importantly it was not a priority. African American considerations were not an inherent strand in our family life. Of course, this would not have been an issue except that Greg and I *were* an inherent strand in the family life. Our race, rather than being a positive strength to embrace, was something to run from.

On the rare occasions our family engaged socially with African American culture, it felt unnatural, given our normal way of life. It had the feel of a special event involving 'special people', rather than just another family experience. Like the time in high school Mom invited two Black female summer students to our house, with the well-intended motivation of exposing us to some Black people. The two students and Greg and I ended up sitting in the living room staring at each other uncomfortably, not knowing what to say. The four of us shared no real social commonalities. Such efforts would have felt natural only if our family had routinely spent time with other Black people, until my parents and Greg and I grew comfortable and could breathe freely within that space.

I wished I could be free of the nagging, aching emotion crawling around in my chest whispering to me: *I don't belong in this place.* I was not actually wishing I could have been in a Black family. That was a reality I knew so little of that the idea was beyond me. And blessings have their baggage wherever you find yourself in this world. More constant and weighing for me was a desire to not have my skin pretended away, to have my spirit seen, and to have my true and silent voice heard and understood by these people I loved and dearly needed.

Part of what I wished for, though I was unaware of it at the time, was that my parents admit to me what my intuition told me must be true. I knew they had special and unique feelings for each of us children, even if they loved us the same amount. My heart told me that giving birth to Kristin, Anna, and Rudy must have meant something indescribable to Mom. Looking into the faces of their biological children or watching them grow into their personalities must have been an amazing experience for my parents. Admitting this to me would not have made me feel they loved me less. It would have only given me a more honest sense of my family's essence.

Biological children are a reunion for parents with themselves and other relatives. I knew this must have been the case for my parents, but it was as though a secret was being perpetrated to make Greg and me feel wanted. There was discernable pride in Dad's voice when he would try to calm Mom over Rudy's hyper-charged behavior by explaining that, "I was just like that as a child." But just as family conversations sometimes touched upon Kristin, Anna, and Rudy with, "When you were born—," there were never similar references to the adoptive origins of Greg and me. Our arrival was a story wiped from the books. My genesis grew ghostlike inside me, unclean and fungal as it escaped the light of reenactment.

The world was a vast water, overwhelming, and impatient around me. I searched for tangible connections with the one source that could placate my drifting—my family. My tempest stirred, I sought that anchor, floating wildly on sea's belly. But life was stingy with that gift. All that was left on the sand before me were scattered and fragmented shells of what to my family was all the love I needed, but to me was a love incomplete.

We do not honor the One Spirit
of which we are composed
by pretending sameness
but by watering the soil
of our many nations
and feeding that
garden to the
seven
generations
to come

This is love

COLORBLIND

THERE is a belief within Sioux Indian culture about those
who are born with the medicine, or power, of eagles. The belief
is that once such persons live past the age of nine, they will
begin to experience this energy—the ability to fly in spirit
above the world and perceive it with great breadth and
precision. I don't know what that explains about my life. But it
is interesting to me that so much of my formative experience,
so many of the memories I have now, occurred during that
stretch between ages nine and 11. That was when I became
starkly aware of my circumstance. My consciousness shifted
from childlike wonder and overwhelmed absorption to a more
alert and resistant state. In addition to the move to our new
house, things began to happen—strange things.

Maybe the surgery during fifth grade reconnected me to
some greater source. The surgery, to close the umbilical hernia
I had been born with, may have repaired a lifeline of
otherworldly inspiration. Would this affect my ability to form
emotional attachments that I could consistently believe in?
Maybe it had come too late. Was there an expiration date or

statute of limitations on closing spirit ruptures? My newfound state of awareness might also have been instigated by the monstrous needle the doctor slid into the marrow of my spinal cavity that same year, extracting spinal fluid to test me for leukemia. They had found during my hernia surgery that I had an unusually low white blood cell count. *That's me, always in the minority.* Maybe my change was not so romantic a thing. Maybe I just changed. However, it was clearly a new season.

I was 10 years of age and walking under a blue sky through the woods one high summer day. The pine tree canopy framed the bright sky, the overlaid branches playing Twister with each other. The blue beyond the trees looked like Heaven peeking through a green quilt. It was a good day to walk. I came upon a woman sunning herself on a boulder. The boulder was a large basalt formation, a lava ball coughed up from far inside the throat of the Jemez Volcano. This woman was elderly in her face, yet her hands were as smooth as mine. Her hair was wild, thick, and sky bound. It was a tint of silver and white that reflected too much sun into my eyes. As I took in her image, her face seemed to shift shapes. A subtle transformation of bone beneath her skin changed her appearance from American Indian to African and back again. Every 10 seconds or so, this change occurred, leaving me mesmerized.

She must have weighed no more than 100 pounds. Her spine was rounded, but not badly humped. She was cloaked in brown, cotton cloth and a hand-woven serapé, a shawl that was somewhere between clean and soiled and appeared to be half her weight. Her teeth were too white for her age, and the whites of her eyes were moats of faded dandelion yellow encircling milk chocolate irises that held mocha pupils. The skin on her face was a thin, seemingly delicate layer, like century-old parchment, though the life force beneath it was as thick as a newborn's.

I thought she might have been an apparition, but she was sweating. *Apparitions do not sweat.* Her demeanor was far from angelic. Rather, it was somewhat crabby and impatient. She spoke to me in a voice of refined gravel. It was not a soothing sound, yet it was somehow comforting to me. She opened up into words as though we were familiar relatives:

"First of all, you have been disloyal to yourself."

"Excuse me, ma'am?"

"You have allowed your circumstance to rule you. You are what you are, and you must stand for that. Your job is to be the clay, a thing shaped only by the Great Hands, and not to acquiesce to the chipping away of gnats and mosquitoes. Those in your life have dictated your image, and in response, you have denounced your essence."

"Excuse me?"

My understanding of her did not seem to be a concern. She spoke as though her speaking was all that mattered in that moment. "In a world of healthy human relations, we honor a person for who she is, not for what our comfort level leaves us wishing her to be. A tree is a tree. We must place our honor there. A woman is a woman. We must place our honor there. Our presumption of what that person's image should mean or does mean is a spite of Creation. We have no right but to receive what emanates from that person. Honor is a receiving wind, not a dictating wind. Stand up for your wind. Don't let them behold you as something you are not."

With that, she stood up to a height of no more than five feet, picked up a long walking stick that had been lying beside her, turned, and walked away. She had a peculiar way of gliding sideways while her legs strode forward, defying the physical laws that I knew. As she walked, she changed. She became first a diminutive oak, then a sparse shrub, then a butterfly perched on a yucca leaf, and finally, a grain of sand so small the wind caught her and carried her away. It was then that I awoke and realized that I had been dreaming. The old woman was my storyteller, my griot come to open my eyes. She would visit me with bothersome frequency in the moons that passed. In that moment, though, I was left to wonder what the blazes she was talking about.

Either directly or indirectly my parents asked and answered a question that would determine the emotional portrait of my life. *How are we going to deal with Greg and John's Blackness?* They may have asked it to each other, but I am certain they at least asked it as a private thought, and often in moments of concern. Everything about their own upbringing indicated to them that it was most important that they treat all their children the same. What this came to mean over time was tremendous. There would be virtually no mention in the household of our adoptive or racial truth—these aspects were, in effect, erased.

Erasure is an eerie thing. I don't know how many times I heard a White person tell me, "I'm colorblind, I don't see colors." The older I grew, the more aggravated I became hearing that claim. People stated it so proudly, as if they had just crowned themselves with the title 'The Most Virtuously Unprejudiced in the Land'. But there was a vital flaw in that convoluted attempt to simultaneously embrace me and seek moral absolution. Being 'blind to color', or treating me the same as anyone else, had very little to do with how racially unprejudiced the people were. And though I was highly averse to people fixating on my color, the last thing I wanted them to do was ignore the obvious fact of my race. It was a difficult distinction for my family to make as they strained to understand my needs. Even in the midst of self-rejection, I burned with a need that others embrace that very part of me that I shunned.

Just about every single White person around me—my family, friends, and community—had grown up White in a country in which White people were the social norm. They had been raised and socialized around mostly White persons, having inescapably developed a personal culture of dealing with people as if those people were White. It was therefore impossible for them to act 'colorblind' toward me. I understood the term was meant to equate color with race—

meaning that, "I don't have a problem with your race. I basically ignore it."

Mom and Dad had developed ways of relating to people almost entirely based on their cultural styles and values. They couldn't see it that way. To them it was just 'normal' attitudes and behavior. But I was Black from the beginning. This was not only a fact of biology. And I was so in spite of the lack of a Black cultural presence in the early years. I was Black because I shared with most African Americans a common cultural ground resulting from society's reaction to our physical Blackness. I was no different than White children in that I derived my sense of belonging largely from how others who looked like me—in my case through scenes brought to me in books, television, and movies—were accepted or rejected. I lived in a Black outpost, but in dealing with the phenomenon that was my race, I was just as Black as any Black child. Maybe more so, because of the constant reminders.

One of the most difficult things for me to later communicate to my family and others was that everything about the way they thought, assumed, and acted had a cultural influence. I attempted with exasperation to explain that much of this world did not wish to be treated as though they lived by the same cultural styles and values as the White norm that defined 'colorblindness'; that relating to people through colorblindness could be disrespectful of and demeaning to their beliefs, values, and lifestyles. There are folds and flaws in the blankets of every cultural ideal. 'Blindness' is a term that implies you do not see something that is there to be seen.

My essence was manifest in the way I saw the world 'seeing' me and those who looked like me. My family chose, for the most part, to be largely blind to that essence in the hope that a contrived sense of sameness would help me feel at home. I may have been in the same home, but I was not entirely at home.

The Fourth of July did not mean the same thing to me, once I learned of our nation's racial legacy, as it did to my family. For me, July 4th, 1776, represented more than a moment of liberation for a nation. It marked also the beginning of a freedom to continue conducting the tragedy of slavery on an entire people. That the Fourth of July meant something different to me than to my family was not the problem. The problem was that I sensed my attitude would not be respected or tolerated by teachers, family, or friends, much less collectively addressed. So, I rarely gave it breath. I was expected to "Join in the celebration," "Don't take things so seriously," "Let it go, move on to the present." I had attitudes and convictions about endless other racially related social issues like this, but kept them muffled.

Reciting the Pledge of Allegiance, with its ". . . and liberty and justice for all," or singing ". . . land of the pilgrim's pride, land where my fathers died," meant something entirely different to me even as a schoolboy. While other children focused on the harmony of the singing, sometimes I found myself working out the off-key contradictions of the lyrics. My patriotism was no less. But I saw more folds in the blanket. And I was a dreamer. I expected the ideal to be real.

I took great issue with my country's racial past and present. I burned up inside when I saw negative portrayals of African Americans and other ethnic groups on television. The 'cowboys and Indians' shows tore me up—I fully related to the American Indians and their plight in the face of arrogant and superior-minded White 'pioneers', 'frontiersmen', and other 'heroes'. Heroes who stole their land, spited them as savages, and killed them as though their lives were worth less than cattle. I was offended daily by infractions against the human spirit that I witnessed in the community, through the media, and in my textbooks.

I am sure I wasn't the only child feeling this way, but I bore a special sense of connection to the 'others' who were outside of this White standard. I related to the American Indians and the Hispanic Americans in the New Mexico area, and in a similar way to women in general—as they all struggled, in real life or in fiction, with the absence of respect on their behalf. Not far from 47th Street, there is a landmark peak in Los Alamos, called L.A. Mountain. So many days I wanted to climb that peak and scream out, "This is not the way you treat a human being! Can't you all see this?"

I never felt comfortable saying anything. A few times, I might have weakly mentioned my disdain for social injustice. Receiving nothing in response other than muted sanctioning, I quickly dropped the idea. I could tell when people were reluctant to go down a conversational road. Their lips shot out euphemisms, their tongues retreated like turtle heads back into the shell-protected comfort spot near the back of their throat. Their tone and composure were much like 'upstanding people', quick-handing change to a beggar: "Here, take this and go." They said things like "People can be so hurtful," handing the phrase out as quick charity: *Take this and go.*

'Colorblind' people related to Greg and me through a denial of our essence. They sincerely believed they were treating us with high morality, but as they ignored something so central to our identity, so critical to our place in the world, and such a salient aspect of our connection with our heritage, they somehow diminished us, in their minds and in ours. The enduring invisibility plunged my esteem into negativity and eroded what confidence I could muster.

So much of what was happening was motivated by people's desire to make us feel accepted, loved, embraced. Family, friends, and teachers—they all must have intuited on some level that we may have been experiencing a kind of isolation. But they tried too hard. They ignored our race so vigorously that they succeeded only in making it a grand spectacle and a poorly attended reality.

I worked ceaselessly to figure out these strange contradictions, but my young mind was limited. It seemed as though the message from my parents was that the way I looked physically shouldn't matter to me, because it didn't matter to them. But it was my season of life to tune in to things the 'big people' had tuned out. I noticed things about physical similarity that didn't agree with this vague message about my race that I was hearing. My thoughts grew increasingly confused: *It seems as though to everyone else, these physical features they share in common give them some comfort. But my family is telling me not to care about the fact that my physical features are different. I don't understand. Is it like when we see a person in a wheelchair at the mall, and Mom says not to stare? Like we're just supposed to ignore it? And if that's the way it is, then is there something wrong with me looking different? Am I handicapped, too? And why, when Rudy was born, was everyone talking about whose eyes his looked like, whose face his looked like, whose personality he had? Why do the grown-ups all seem to care so much about things being the same, when they are always telling me not to worry that I'm different?*

The madness was cascading. I became a crack in my own spirit's sky:

Who am I?
crying
Who am I?
lying
Who am I?
dying

One of my most embarrassing, self-conscious days at school came during the fifth or sixth grade. The teacher laid out a large map on the floor in the center of the classroom. The map was of the entire world, showing all the continents and oceans. All the students became excited as they learned what they were supposed to do. That is, all of the students except me. Our assignment was to crowd around the map, and one at a time point out to the class where on the map our ancestors originally came from. We had to mark the country in some way, so that it stood out as a bright and shining reminder. This activity required us to have an understanding of our ethnicity, to be able to identify our nation of family origin.

I was horrified. When I realized what we would be doing, a wave of panicked heat rose in my chest. I became nauseous as the children began marking their family origins. As I had anticipated, the map began to fill up with markers clustered around England, Germany, France, Scandinavia, Austria . . . Here I was, in my mind, successfully downplaying my difference from my friends and peers through my behavior and speech. Now all of a sudden, in plain and close-up view of everyone, I was going to be asked to, in essence, stand before them and acknowledge my shame, like I was in an Alcoholics Anonymous meeting: "My name is John Scott Potter, and I am an . . . African American." How could the teacher do this to me? How could fate be so evil? In a moment, I was going to be pulled out of the shadows and placed squarely in the spotlight I so desperately wanted to avoid.

Before it came my turn to point out my ancestors on the map, another crisis reared itself within me. I was suddenly and completely confused. Who were my ancestors? Were they the predecessors of my parents? This would mean that they came from somewhere over in Europe. Where exactly in Europe, I wasn't so sure, but then many of the other children knew nothing more specific than that their own family came from somewhere in Europe also. Or were my ancestors the people who came before me in blood? The lack of clarity spawned a new hurt inside of me, as I realized I was some type of mutant—an offspring lost somewhere between worlds.

If I placed my origin as being in Africa, I would be the only one marked in that area of the world, or anywhere near that area of the world. Standing out like that is a child's worst nightmare. To add to this crisis, I was ashamed just at the thought of my people coming from *Africa*. Africa was the jungle, dark and uncivilized. This is what we were taught. And we were also taught, not so much through things said or read, but through things unsaid and unread, and through neglect, that Africa did not matter much in the scheme of worldly things. All the literature we read through those elementary years was about English culture and flowed from English pens. Or it concerned White America, White pioneers, colonists, and frontier heroes. But Africa? Africa was the edge of the Earth, and if the Earth were flat, I was sure at the time that few of my classmates or my teachers would be upset if Africa fell off that shelf into the unknown abyss.

All of these thoughts and feelings surged through me as my classmates took their turns proudly pointing out where their ancestors came from. All of their colored, round-headed pins were now clearly grouped together within Europe on the map, with a lesser amount scattered in Mexico. I imagined their thoughts turning to me: *Where is he going to put his pin? Wow, hey, his people come from the jungle.*

From the jungle. I was tempted to place my pin in Europe somewhere, just dump it off with the rest of the crowd, because at least that way I wouldn't have to stick out so loudly. But I knew if I did that the whole class would immediately be hip to that blatant lie. There would be no hiding on this one.

I knew I might have a 'Europe exemption' or an honorary White status for this game because I could claim my parents as my lineage because of adoption. But I wasn't sure. Was adoption allowed as a substitute for blood in this game? I was suddenly faced straight up with questions that I had to resolve: *Where do I come from? Which group am I more a part of: my adoptive family's ancestors or my Black ancestors? Who in the heck am I?* The questions battered the core of me. Circumstance had made yet another intrusion into my self-security, my peace had gotten itself up and on down the road. The crossroads of the moment were glass shards beneath my youthful feet. I walked forward from that crossroads, trailing red footprints in my wake.

I finally motioned to the teacher. I was ashamed, confused, embarrassed, and wanted some kind of escape from this mini-torture. I asked my teacher, "What do I do?"

She responded, "What do you mean?" She had no idea what I was talking about. I think she was proud of herself for thinking up this activity. In most ways, she should have been.

This was an activity that could put children more in touch with their past, and help them to better understand the nature of their parents, grandparents, and family culture. Only in this case, she hadn't reckoned on the fly in the milk.

Had I been better prepared for this, maybe through a conversation with my parents the evening before or through a conversation with the teacher, it might not have been such a horrible experience for me. But my parents didn't know we would be doing this class activity and the teacher hadn't thought of my complication. The moment was vicious in its suddenness, and demanded of me an immediate judgment of myself on issues I wasn't prepared to face.

In response to my teacher's puzzled response, I said to her, "I don't know where to put my pin. I . . . I'm adopted." I whispered the last part of that statement in a soft, quiet voice with my eyes downcast in shame. I couldn't bring myself to actually use the words 'Black' or 'Africa', so I hoped that she would understand my dilemma. In part, I think she did. Recognition dawned in her eyes and she whispered back to me something like, "This activity is about your family. The Potters are your family, right?"

"Yes." I said.

"Okay then, go ahead and put your marker down on where you think they come from." She was empathetic, and she thought she had settled my trouble, but she didn't come close to calming the demon I was wrestling. She may have understood my unspoken reluctance to put my marker down on Africa, because as a teacher I'm sure she knew that kind of social isolation was the equivalent of the end of the world for a child. I think I even saw a glimmer of shame in her eyes as she realized the position she had put me in. But she didn't know a pivotal struggle ensued within. I was battling for an adult's understanding of race, family, and ancestry, but I was battling as a child.

I ended up heeding my teacher's advice because after all, she was the teacher. I put my pin down in Europe. But nothing about that move felt right to me. I felt at once like an imposter and a betrayer, and I sensed my classmates' own confusion and judgment about my placement. This was an innocent activity, a well-intended one. But true diversity ruins the colorblind game.

Storyteller's whisper in my night: *Son, you're like a baobab tree. Your roots appear to be stuck up in the air. They got no soil to feed on. You can live long that way, but the question is, what will be the quality of your living? Yessir, you can sure 'nuff live long, but your roots will be up in the air all the while. That ain't no way to fly a kite. You so lack peace right now that if you were to go and stand still out in the woods, the forest would feel assaulted from the vibration of your agitation.*

Maybe my stage fright in the face of life as a whole was borne in part from humiliations I suffered on actual stages. In maybe the fifth grade, my class put on a theatre play for the school community, including parents. We entitled our play, 'Tall Tom Jefferson'. It was to be a wonderful celebration of one of *our* national heroes, the third President of the United States, *and another redhead.* My classmates quickly leapt into frantic excitement, unleashing their brimming energy into a structured activity of casting, costume and scene design, rehearsal, and finally, the performance. I am sure that the teacher and my classmates' parents hardly questioned that this would be a great experience for the children. We would have the chance to learn more about a role model of *ours*, a great man, someone *we* could look up to.

First, there was casting to deal with. It was at this point that a sizable lump formed in my chest and the familiar dread and self-disdain reappeared. My classmates clamored to be chosen for various roles, with the role of Tall Tom of course the most sought after. Our teacher and my classmates approached casting with the intent to be as accurate as we could in matching children with the physical traits of the key roles in the play. A tall child with auburn colored hair was chosen to be our 'Tall Tom'. But what was going to be done with me? We had studied President Jefferson in class, and we all, including the teacher, understood the uncomfortable truth of the historical reality of the times we were preparing to portray. Given that colonial era context, the only accurate role I could have played would have been that of a slave.

Neither the teacher nor our history books had betrayed the more precise truth that my most accurate portrayal would be to play a slave of Tom Jefferson in particular. But it was enough just to know that during that era, and in that setting, the only Black people on the scene were slaves. The quandary I had realized immediately was only a percolating awareness for our teacher, and probably many of the students. As my teacher looked at me, I could almost see her thought spelled out on her face: *Oh, dear, what are we going to do with John?*

I was horrified. I had no idea how this was going to play out. Fear draped itself over me as I imagined I might actually be asked to play a slave or that at least the sticky situation of my race would be discussed—with me in private by the teacher or out loud in class. I lacked the perspective then to realize that those frightening possibilities never were likely to occur. True to the tendency of most every adult around me, my race would never be so brazenly considered, much less highlighted by casting me as a slave.

The resolution, quick and disregarding, was to cast me as just another colonist, white wig and all. I was relieved to once more escape the possibility of calling attention to my race. That relief was soon wiped away and replaced by a dreadful embarrassment. I was certain I was going to look like a fool up there in front of the whole community, donning a white wig and high stockings. I wasn't too familiar with the social undertones of actors appearing in black face, but I knew enough to know that White folks jumping around on a stage with their faces painted black looked ridiculous. I knew I had a good chance of looking at least as ridiculous. Everyone would know I was a hoax, a fraud . . . a misfit. What could possibly bring more attention to my Black skin than playing a White colonial 'gentleman'?

I looked for the nearest rock to crawl under, but in the mountain desert all you are likely to find under a rock are scorpions, ready to sting. I tried everything I could do to get out of the play, except tell my parents why I was so reluctant. That was something I did not feel, based upon other instances, they would respond to with empathy or parental pardon. I told Mom I wasn't feeling good—the eternal child's ploy. That was a no go. I begged the teacher to let me out. I even admitted my dilemma to her: "There weren't any Black people like Thomas Jefferson, Benjamin Franklin, and all of them. I don't feel good about doing this."

She seemed slightly empathetic and guilty. "John, you'll do fine. It's just a play. Make believe. You're smart and people like your smile. Just be yourself, you'll do well."

The night of the performance, I was in a panic that had no voice. I was getting used to enduring those moments in silence. My classmates were buzzing around me, primping and posing in their costumes. This was make-believe to them. It was also a celebration of a moment in time. I identified myself enough with being a U.S. American that I also saw the play as representing a proud moment. But I was conflicted. There was an aspect of this that felt wrong. My knowledge of the slave presence in this same story left me ambivalent. And it flamed in me a spark of indignation.

Showtime. There we stood on the stage of the auditorium, virtually my whole world seated in rows that seemed to never end—facing us. Curtains were parted, parents began their applause of support they are genetically encoded to exhibit, and then we were on display. It did not matter to me then whether the audience was choosing to ignore my blatant miscasting. I knew I was a farce. I forced my few lines out through gritted teeth and waited for the slow motion moment to end. Not all of me left the stage that evening. Some amount of self-respect, a portion of my sense of belonging, stayed behind. I skulked home with a new layer of humiliation. I knew I would be taking it straight to my room, past my parents and siblings, to marinate in that well-worn mute pose.

I wasn't old enough at first to understand that I was beginning to feel resentment, but by my high school years the words were beginning to emerge to outline my thoughts. *How can you ignore my Blackness? How can you treat all your children, both White and Black, the same if when the Black children go out the door and into the world, that world treats us differently?* My anger was growing.

I believe those in my life thought it was in my best interest to rarely ever be identified in terms of my race, or to have that brought up. But, though many of my fears had to do with standing out, I later realized that as a child I never wanted my Blackness to become nullified, denied, or erased. Often I did wish for a temporary escape from the oppressive bonds that my skin color brought. But more than that, I just wanted it to be placed in its proper context within the set of characteristics that made up who I was.

I wanted my skin color, physical features, and cultural heritage to be appreciated and valued. I needed people to not pretend they didn't notice my Blackness when they interacted with me. It was obvious to me what they were doing. I felt like what an obese person must feel like—aware that others notice the obesity but refuse to acknowledge the truth of it in any way. Unlike obesity, my being Black wasn't inherently a sign of poor health, though my experience with race sure led to its special brand of illness.

This ignoring my race made me feel as though my Blackness was a dirty family secret; something that wasn't supposed to be talked about because "we are all really the same on the inside." That towering, trite lie glared too brightly for me not to see it daily. My Blackness *was* dirty. Something I might one day be told, in a crushing moment of honesty, to go and wash off. Erosion was working hard against me.

Mom and Dad inherently were engaged in cultural parenting. They were constantly attending to their White children's ethnicity simply by relating to them through the White cultural styles that had shaped them. In the way they went about living, they modeled for all of us children how we were supposed to talk, walk, dress, eat, cook, clean, think, dream, and relate to the world. By osmosis, social learning, or whatever term it may be called, they were immersing us in the waters of their essence.

The growth of any positive identity in me was not inherently present just by being loved. I longed to be basted in affirmation. I needed my family to be the first and last bastion for my racial validation. I needed them to actively plant the seed in me that this racial part of my person was a good thing. Silence and inaction, unspoken thoughts, and uneasy avoidance of racial issues my mind and heart were tethered to—these were a message in and of themselves. And the message hurt.

Mom and Dad often spoke of their desire to have each of us become who we were meant to be and find our own way in life, with their undying support. But I also have to believe that their hope—conscious and unconscious—likely was that their children would emerge from that water in adulthood with the wetness of Mom and Dad's essence still coating their skin. They were, in a very human way, hoping that their children would take on their same 'color' in the world—color in this instance meaning their particular cultural personality. It must have been hard for them to resist that impulse to want to see me grow into their image, when it came to my race.

My parents meant well and were motivated only by a desire for our well-being, but in order to treat their children all the same it was necessary to, at least partially, avoid focusing on their children's individual needs. It must have taken a significant effort on their part to avoid thinking about and addressing something so radiantly obvious as the Blackness of two of their children in a family, town, and nation dominated by Whiteness. Some kind of emotional strain must have existed, though they never acknowledged it.

Race, like disability or giftedness, was a character distinction that demanded some kind of honest address. But, my race was so discomforting an issue that my parents did not confront it head on or consistently. They almost never talked about Greg and me being Black. Rarely even alluded to it. The words 'Black' and 'African American' must have seemed like sand particles grating their tongues.

Being Black was about much more than color to me, even in the earliest years. My race was culture and culture was my 'everything.' My culture was my essence, the substance I was born with. It was my personality, my beliefs, my experiences in life, and how I chose to react to them. Culture was my rhythm, and my rhythm rarely seemed to match the larger one in our household. Culture was how I valued my devotion to the principle of loving and respecting the full spirit within each human, including her or his race.

Culture was my seething and wounded indignation from the injustice splashed over so many brown-skinned people all over the world, without, it seemed to me, hardly a whimper of condemnation. Culture was my disappointment and rage when newspapers reported the loss of thousands of dark-skinned lives in a mudslide or hurricane as brief text presented with the priority of a weather report, while single White lives lost were upheld as the rightful tragedies they were. This was my culture, my race . . . my color. The last thing I needed to hear from my loved ones was that to them, color didn't matter.

Storyteller comforted me with a soliloquy:

"Culture is as small and precise as the way we kiss a lover's neck or whether we feel it normal to kiss that neck at all. And culture is as grandiose as the faith that dictates which God we pray to. Culture is that impulse in the shortest moment of them all before we feel what we feel about a thing. That flash of light in our mind before stimulus beckons thought. That premature morning glory blossom before sunrise reveals the reason for the petals to open. It is our rationale for why the cardinal is red, the bluebird is blue, and why the color black seems to make some folk fall back. Culture is how we make sense of life itself. I should hope to never live in a world that has transcended culture."

I said Amen.

Growing up in the image of my parents meant, in many ways, becoming less like most other Black people. I was over my head with that challenge. I came to know several Black adults later in life who had grown up in circumstances similar to mine. Their adult personalities portrayed for me a wide range of management styles for that peculiar tension between resembling family and identifying with Black culture. Some had become heavily oriented into African culture; others swept into the cover of White culture and dared not step out from under that tarp. Those who had struck a balance had not done so easily or without stumbling.

During a visit to Los Alamos after I had moved away, a long-time friend and I fell into a discussion about how it was for me growing up in my family and in Los Alamos. After my friend had listened to me for awhile, he responded. As with many other White people I knew, there was almost resentment in his voice in reaction to challenges I described. "You were so popular in Los Alamos. You were successful in sports, you were on all those dance courts like homecoming, and everybody loved you. I don't see what was so hard." To him, apparently, those were the prerequisites for happiness.

I realized he felt that way because as a White person who grew up in his biological, White family, surrounded by a White neighborhood and town in a White-dominated country, he had taken certain things for granted. Issues of connection to his parents and family never haunted his thoughts because it was a glaring given; he was born to them. He never had to deal with the fact that everyone around him in his own house, much less the town, had different-colored skin, different hair, different facial features. On a larger scale, he never questioned his place in our society, because all of the important faces in his schoolbooks and on his television had been White. He never had to question whether his Whiteness was something that belonged.

His question to me essentially was "What right do you have to have felt emotional pain growing up? You had a good, loving family, material comfort, and you succeeded in everything. People would kill to be you."

Family members and other White people implied to me the same thing, over and again: "You've had so much, what do you mean it was painful for you?" My silent answer: *Social and athletic success is worth very little when you feel like an ugly, trespassing freak of nature with nappy, Buckwheat-wild hair, a nose like an ape, lips twice that size, and the intelligence of something less than human.*

It didn't feel so wonderful to be popular, when that loving embrace was coming from people, many of whom had negative or lukewarm attitudes about Black people in general. Too many of those persons who had love for me were victims of the split heart of prejudice. I could sense their broader racial attitudes. My mind and heart could not reconcile these two truths. I was not able to see myself apart from people I shared the Earth with, especially other Black people. I could not feel at peace with that contorted popularity, even as I ate it up as one of my few affirming meals.

Most people never saw what I saw lurking behind so many eyes in the community. They never played the inescapable role of the adopted Black freak ("Do Black people go bald? Do Black people get sunburn? Do you have to wash your hair?") who tries daily to monitor his every action and word so as to make the White people around him—who he knows often feel threatened by him—more comfortable. It was difficult for those close to me in my early life to understand why love and popularity weren't enough. Their difficulty had little to do with prejudice, but much to do with a lack of awareness.

I knew no other parents more steady and true with their love. Mom and Dad hurt when I hurt, and they were there with kisses and hugs when they believed I most needed them. Mom sacrificed all her youthful energy and nerves to raise five children without the benefit of supportive relatives living even within the same state. She endured the subtle and sometimes not so subtle isolation from the prejudgment by others in the community because she had Black children. People didn't quite know what to make of this woman who, capable of giving birth, had *chosen* to adopt two Black boys in the late sixties. *What was she all about?* Mom stood up to that—all those strange looks and muted whispers, and was there for us unwaveringly.

My parents also provided for us beyond their means. Despite what might be assumed of the income of a physicist, our family never did seem to have much free money floating around. We were a family with five children, and three of us were on the scene before my dad even finished graduate school, so we weren't exactly rolling in cash when he started his full-time livelihood. I heard, "We can't afford that," coming from my parents so often, I swore somebody must have been siphoning off our bank account. And Mom thought she was slick, adding powdered milk to the whole milk container to make it last longer for her high consumption brood. We all knew it, and knew why she had to do it.

A big night out for us was going to McDonald's, and frequently we could not afford even that. But Dad worked day and night to pay our bills, feed our growing bodies, and provide us with material comfort beyond what we needed. He worked late into the night at home, after having worked all day long at the office.

Mom and Dad put us first as a rule. I don't recall ever worrying about where the next meal would come from. They wore out a succession of station wagons driving us to and from school, boy and girl scouts, and sports. I often sensed that other children were decked out in clothes and shoes a little more expensive than what we had and their school supplies seemed slightly more extravagant. But perceptions are relative, and Mom's utilitarian thrift had much to do with our lifestyle. This was Los Alamos after all. Our provisions were bountiful compared to many children nationwide.

We were spoiled with a diet of love, support, opportunities, and education. But love is more complex than the concept we dress it up as. My parents' only source of security in their decision to adopt us was that they would simply love and treat the Black children just like their own biological children. They had to believe that this loving environment would be all that we would need, because it was all they could conceive of offering us.

This is where my whole family, including me, was mistaken. I was not my sister Kristin. Greg and I were not the children my parents were when they were children. Our circumstance was unprecedented for them. The bonding I developed with the family, and my achievement of positive self-worth and esteem, were dependent in part upon things my parents provided excessively: compassion, empathy, humility, and honesty. But even those qualities were lacking in the context of my issues with race.

Mom and Dad's love did not assure them the capacity to acknowledge and work through any latent prejudices or racial unease, or a willingness to learn and grow along with me through challenging cultural and racial implications my life brought up. Their love did not allow them to serve as or bring into my life Black role models, actual or fictional. Their love did not lead them to provide a sincere family audience for my expressions of race-related pain, joy, doubts, concerns, or ideas. As with all loving hearts, theirs only took them so far.

My sense of safety was contingent on my ability to express my true personality in the presence of my family and be understood and embraced for that. But too much of my person was entangled, for better or worse, in my race. And my race was not a thing my family's love enabled them to accommodate. Mom was a two-river woman walking through her love for me. She was the heart of inherent love and affection, and the adult consequence of a little girl socialized to harbor a less than positive regard for Blackness. She fought a tug of war with these two forces in raising Greg and me. And in the hypersensitive dance of human relations, a *less than positive regard* can be all it takes to do the damage.

Hate-spewing banshees and race destruction soldiers rarely were the problem for me. I could have handled all that if only the 'good people' had been more able or willing to relate to me fully. But that 'good-hearted' majority harbored my truest enemy, the polluted energy of unclean love. They had settled somewhere safe but untested, in between the extremes of honoring the full human spirit and prejudicial spirit itself.

I swallowed those subtleties. My relationships with other humans were not built upon broad gestures and claims. They grew from flash auditions contained within the space of milliseconds. They sprouted from minute waves of emotion that barely rippled the air between us. Those modest ripples bred quickly into tsunamis with the fertility of time. That's how I drowned. Love's multiple personalities created a cacophony of jazz and jambalaya from the first moments in my tender life. A nightmare chased me as I contemplated whether my frightened running would ever stop:

This child never breast-fed. He's never going to bond properly with anyone, ever. He's hopeless.

Dear God . . .

Who is my love?
who is my enemy?
can I love my enemy?
should I enemy my love?

you gave me love in white skin
now bring me to the killing field
to watch white skin
murder black skin

am I supposed to know
skin from sin?
good grin from bad grin?

can I love my enemy?
should I enemy my love?

dear God

ALEX HALEY'S *ROOTS*

IN 1977, when I was almost 10 years of age, I heard these words from a father to a mother on a television screen: "We still have one son." I was branded forever after. The miniseries, *Roots*, Alex Haley's impassioned and fictionalized tale of the history he uncovered of his ancestors, drove through American hearts. The novel, *Roots*, had been published in 1976, and this subsequent television drama reached all the way back to the days when the Kinte family lived by the side of the Kamby Bolongo (The Gambia River) in the village of Juffure, The Gambia, West Africa. At the time I was in the sixth grade, and increasingly conscious of my racial difference in the midst of my social world. My 'hood' was a White one, and my classmates, teachers, principals, and people in charge were the same.

Before I witnessed *Roots*, I was already caught in a downdraft of racial self-aversion. In my perceptual state of mind, my skin and lips and nose and hair were all giant glowing flare lights to me that emanated in the darkness to illuminate the fact to everybody that I was Black. Steadily my self-esteem crept downward. It was the frontier days of my sexuality and social self-concept, and I was already on the edge.

Nightly I watched the scenes of incredible horror unfolding on the screen before me. I absorbed those whippings, lynchings, and the separation of families, as though they were happening to me. The capturing of Kunta Kinte on that beach, his cornering by evil-eyed White men with ropes and nets and knives resembled too closely the capturing of a wild animal. I felt raped, like I had just been snared in the same cruel trap. I felt the screams of millions from four centuries back surging through my chest.

My eyes grew huge as I took myself into Kunta's heart where he fought, strained, and was desperately frightened of his impending capture. I could feel his breath on me, and smell his panicked sweat as it rolled down his skin and fell to the hot ocean-side sand. I was dying inside as I knew he was about to be taken forever, and then I died again as his father later came back from the search party holding only Kunta's necklace. The look in the father's eyes as he had to face his wife and let her know they *still had one son*. The soul-shattering in the mother's eyes as she heard words she could not believe had been spoken, her unearthly wail and sinking to the ground. I was broken-hearted.

The following nights of the movie were a mixture of evil, pain, sorrow, separation, hope and crushed hopes, and searing human tribulation that cut through the core of me. That's when I believe I first understood what it meant to be free. I was watching a tale of reality in which White people were viciously treating Black people as animals. I was in a melodrama classroom, learning what resides in the hearts of too many—a tragic surrender to inhumanity.

Heart bruises emerged as I realized that the White people in this movie represented attitudes and intents of many White people with whom I now shared the Earth. The most painful cut of all was that my own family—most importantly, my parents—were White. I could not accommodate both truths— the White-faced evil on the screen and the White family around me. I was more than torn. I was terrified. In a panic, I kept repeating to myself words that would become a mantra/prayer/plea thereafter: *But this, . . . this horror is not my family. My family loves me.*

Because I had already developed a sense that the Black part of me was nearly forbidden territory for my family to approach, I had nowhere to turn and put the mountainous anger, rage, and hurt that *Roots* was unleashing. Of course I buried inside my shell.

I was watching images of Whites in hoods and robes, riding cowardly, terrorizing souls in the night. Little White girls with a sickening air of superiority in their interactions with little Black girls and Black folk in general. Daughters sold away from ruined mothers; Black males treated with the pathetic fear that still pervaded the climate of my times—fear of their physical strength, fear of imagined retribution. Retribution that the White perpetrators knew they themselves would take if roles were reversed. Lynching, whippings, and the rapes—*But this is not my family. My family loves me.* The electrons and photons jumping off the television screen landed on my skin and must have mixed with my melanin, because a chemical reaction took place whose byproduct was righteous anger.

My faith in the truth of these television images was unshakable because I had already sensed the remnants of such attitudes and potential behavior in the White society I knew. My wound widened and deepened.

My spirit walked and became Kunta. The absolute rage and humiliation that his burning eyes told as they looked up at the overseer became my eyes. As Kunta, on his knees, tied to a post received the whip, my spine contorted to the lash's sting. Scarlet sorrow opened up on *my* back and shoulders, branching out in fluid lines that swept south and met at that location on my back directly behind my heart. There, those lines became a delta. And there I drowned. Dad became the slave master, and Mom the slave master's wife. Greg was my Fiddler. Our bedroom was the slave quarters where wounds were licked and secrets told. I saw Kristin in Missy Anne, the girlhood playmate of Kizzy, who grew older and betrayed Kizzy (me) as she fled across the racial divide. That acute pain in Kizzy's face as she could do nothing but stand and receive Missy Anne spitting her racial condescension at her was a pain that haunted me. I would come to half expect it around every corner I turned.

I didn't want these thoughts; but as I watched the Haley's drama unfold, they just kept coming. *This evil is not my family*. My fears were a current that swept me downstream into that horrible imagination. It would take years to convince myself that both the idea and the possibility were but phantoms come to taunt me.

Given the acutely sensitive child I was, it was only natural that I quickly fell into a sullen, angry mood and behavior as I watched this real-life drama play itself out on the television. I hurt for what once was, for what I knew still to be, and for what, somewhere inside, I sensed would come to be. I was wounded because I had seen a magnificent, shaved-headed, muscular, proud man who was Kunta's friend slain by White evilness on a slave ship. I felt his death in me. I lay on my bottom bunk at night, imagining Greg and myself in the hold of a slave ship, stacked tight on saltwater-soaked planks.

The wooden bottom of Greg's bunk above me was the foundation for another row of slaves. I imagined the shackles on my wrists, ankles, and neck; the surging sea; the uprising of my stomach; the darkness and interminable days. This was no macabre emotional dive. It was not even a negative experience for me. I was spirit walking—stepping into the truth of people I felt myself a part of. It was empowering, grounding, motivating.

The saga continued. I was traumatized because I knew Kunta's mother, Binta, died a spiritual death in that moment of realization that her son had been taken from her forever. I broke apart at the image of Kunta's father, Omoro, shamefully returning to his wife, having failed to bring home her son. I was stung repeatedly, with each of the wounds dealt to the soulful humans portrayed. I had endless reasons to funk, and did I ever. My visage was a sign post reading: *This way to fury.*

I had no one else but family to direct my rage toward, but I needed to or it would have torn me apart. I targeted my family not only because they were White. It was also because of the particular types of racial discomfort or at least avoidance I had long sensed residing within them.

Mom was watching the same story as I was. She must have wondered all along how I was reacting, what I would do with my thoughts and emotions. *His heart is so tender, should he be watching this?* Human nature dictated that she in some way associate herself with the White people acting out their tragedy on the screen. Any association, any identification, must have ignited at least a wisp of guilt within her. Guilt brings defense.

"You've been acting weird. I'm not gonna let you watch that show anymore if you don't straighten up," she warned. I would not forget those words. They carried so much meaning to me then, and even more to me now. Mom had never asked me if anything was bothering me, what was bothering me, much less what I thought of *Roots* as it was broadcast over several days. It was clear to both of us why I was acting 'weird'. I knew she sensed that part of the energy I was emitting was an accusation of complicity aimed at her.

Her words contributed to my growing distance from my family. In one of my most obvious moments of need for consolation, communication, understanding, and evidence that

I was loved, I found no trace of such feelings in my parents' hearts for my Black self. Instead, I was scolded for feeling the pain that consumed me.

Another layer of difference had just been applied like thick paint between my family and me. I understood the message loud and clear: *Don't you be blaming us for any of what went on in that movie. And further, whatever you are feeling from watching that movie is an overreaction.* The questions my parents had later in my life about why I wouldn't ever share myself with them, let them in on what was inside of me, had their answers square in the lap of instances just like this one. I knew that the things I felt about slavery and the treatment of Black people were not the things my parents felt. They may have experienced a related pain and outrage, but not nearly approaching the intensity and inner destructiveness of mine. Even so, *Roots* was a missed opportunity for sharing and bonding.

Mom had full-bodied emotions. When she became angered by any one of the endless frustrations that five children can easily elicit, her words, tone, and volume penetrated me and lingered. Because she came from a thick-skinned family background, she could not easily relate to my hypersensitive soul. The frustration in her brought on by my sulking, withdrawals, and moods displayed itself in the form of an angry tone, with cutting words as the blade. This only served to broaden the distance between us. I confused how Mom's personality affected me with my own insecurities about race and adoption. All of that hurt collapsed itself into a ball that took years for me to untangle.

In times of perceived family betrayal such as during the *Roots* broadcast, I retreated to my bedroom. Back there in my solitude I faced the pain—jagged, ripping daggers that knifed through my chest. I felt actual physical damage taking hold in my heart. This scene played out over and again: me being hurt by someone or something as near to me as a conversation in the family kitchen, as intermediate as the grocery store downtown, or as distant as the nightly news. Then I would retreat to my room for the solitary battle within.

The emotions of those moments were frightening in their sharpness. What strength carried me through wasn't mine at all, but came from something great and beyond my smallness. I balled up, fetal, clutching my stomach or clawing at my chest, the tears drowning out my vision, every smell and sound enhanced. My head exploded into migraines and blood red ribbons invaded the black behind my eyelids.

Something very central to my personality occurred each time I weathered that storm of pain alone in my vacuum. I was developing an unhealthy independence in dealing with my emotions. I was dealing with the pain on my own, and surviving. Every repetition of this distorted success was making me more closed off to the world, more dependent on myself to handle the storm. An island continued its evolution. My thoughts heaped upon themselves until I was buried beneath their weight. *They don't understand my pain. They can't see what I'm going through living in this place, in this town, this house. Every time I am upset she responds in exactly the same way. Every time I am hurt, she responds by hurting me more with her cruel, cold words. I don't need them to handle my pain; it's up to me, because they will never understand.* I longed not so much for a Black family in those moments, as for people around me who would react with the same emotions to the horror I witnessed in *Roots*.

You're acting weird. The words made me feel as if I was the discontent field slave planning an uprising against the big house, and she was the Master's wife, discovering the treachery of Nat Turner in my eyes. Perhaps even Dad's lack of words during that two-week stretch of time contributed to my sense of alienation. Regardless of my parents' best intents, I felt so utterly betrayed.

If Mom had pulled back the membrane that was my anger, she would have found fear. Greg and I gained a slavery consciousness from that point on that oriented us in a new way within our social relationships. This was when our sarcastic "slavery is over" comments began slipping from our lips. My presence in the family would come to remind me just a little too much of the ownership relationship between White slaveholders and kidnapped Africans. That left a layer of irritation somewhere within the other layers of my emotions that pertained to family. Whether a product of my 10-year-old's imagination or intuitiveness, that thin band of discordant truth colored the panorama I was deducing of the world.

It was not until I read a magazine article in my mid-20s that I discovered I wasn't the only one for whom *Roots* had elicited such feelings. According to the article, Black children all over the country had reacted with emotional disturbance and physical conflict to the pure, undeniable wave of testimony that *Roots* unleashed on the nation. The movie took all U.S. Americans to task for the reality of our past, a past not separate from our present, but imbedded deeply within it.

The resentment I had to work through later had to do with realizing that I was made to feel wrong for responding the way I had as a child. Adding to my anger was the jealous discovery that other Black children were able to at least turn to their own parents and family for some type of emotional shelter as they were struck by the unrelenting blows of *Roots*. These other children were at least able to turn a teary eye toward Moms or Pops and see a glint of understanding in these grown folks' eyes. And if these other children were inclined, they at least could feel safe to ask questions about why these terrible things happened.

But even through the experience of watching *Roots,* I was able to derive some pride, convoluted as it was. For a while following the broadcast I acted out scenes in which I pretended I was Kunta Kinte. During recess, my classmates and I chased each other around the playground, alternately designating someone to be the one chased by the mob. And since I was the only Black child, when it came time for me to be chased, I became impassioned with images of Kunta Kinte escaping momentarily off of the trading block, and through quickness, balance, and reflexes, eluding the crowd of White men trying to recapture him. On the playground, being chased by a crowd of White children, it was easy to imagine myself as Kunta. I took pride in being able to run, cut, fake, dive-roll, and scamper my pursuers into exhaustion.

I don't know whether the other children understood the tragic and convoluted fantasy I was playing out, but for me it was something real. I was the African, running for my precious freedom, and my classmates were the White slave owners and overseers trying to steal my liberty. By the time recess ended I walked back into the classroom with a mess of grass in my Afro from tumbling around on the ground. I've never been more proud of a messed-up hairdo, but the scenario didn't make me feel any closer to my peers.

Responding to my very specific emotional pain was a formidable challenge for my parents. I do not know how thoroughly they worked through those painful issues of our shared racial legacy. But I needed them to have done just that. I didn't need them to utter magic healing words each time I was stung. But my heart did require a certain depth and insight from them. Unfortunately, the horrors and indignities of slavery and racial domination may have been too much for them to have fully reckoned with in spirit, at least before I ever came along and provided the reason.

Conversations we might have had regarding race may have led to outbursts, misunderstandings, and conflict. But over time the balance, I believe, would have tilted in favor of the benefits of our communication, rather than the alienation that emerged from avoiding those issues. I also may well have chosen on my own to avoid thoughts of race during various seasons of my growth. My parents could not have predicted when I needed such subjects to be left alone, and when I needed them to be addressed. And I did not need them to dictate to me how much my focus should have been on my race, ethnicity, culture, or on race relations as a whole. But what I yearned for then was a simple emotion. I desired to feel welcome to bring race to our tongues if my heart needed it.

I had lesser emotional experiences with other portrayals of Africans and African Americans throughout those years, and they all left behind a kind of residue that coated my strained identity. I think the whole family paid particular attention to one of Anna's favorite shows, the situation comedy, *Diff'rent Strokes*. The show was about a rich White family that adopted two Black boys. Gary Coleman's character delivered the tag line we all repeated: "Watchu talkin' bout?" The parallels with our own family drew us in to the weekly story line, especially since the *Diff'rent Strokes* family included a White daughter who was born to the father.

Greg, Kristin, and I tuned out the real world and were held in the trance of our mirror image—two Black brothers and a White sister. Seeing a version of you represented on television can have a powerful and strangely validating effect. Still, I was uncomfortable watching that show. It first came on in November of 1978, and by that time, I was rejecting my circumstance. The show tapped that troubled inner spot, and recalled the alien orbit in which I was caught.

Other television shows left their mark within me. *Sounder* broke my heart, at age five, when it was aired in 1972. The powerlessness of the Louisiana sharecropper Morgan family to live freely was not something I could witness and then let go by the next morning at the breakfast table. *The Life and Times of Miss Jane Pittman* left me enraged and seething. I was only six years of age. I was triumphant when she spit in Master Bryant's cup of water. And in the last scene of the movie, when, as a centenarian she defiantly drank from a segregated drinking fountain for the first time, the expression on her face spoke familiar emotions. Emotions a six-year-old should be virgin to.

Then there were those *National Geographic* specials, displaying naked-breasted African women that shamed me. These women and men were being portrayed as uncivilized or, at least, less civilized than we in our 'greatly advanced' nation. I feared that my family and people in Los Alamos might be witnessing these images of African people and transposing a subtle and demeaning disgust on to me. I rarely walked around the house without a shirt.

The distance that unraveled itself between my family and me like an invisible carpet was stealthy and stubborn. It crept forward even through the midst of the warmth, consistency, and reliability that held our family close. It wrapped itself around my heart like a constrictor snake despite all the many joys and magical moments I shared with my brothers, sisters, and parents. Before I realized it, the free-loving closeness of my first years was something else.

I slowly but effectively built up a formidable shell around my emotions, like creating a sandcastle on the beach, and dug a wide, deep trench around it so that the ocean's liquid paws could not invade. I was truly becoming an island inside, and this was a dysfunctional fact that I would carry with me into adulthood, to be faced and eradicated on that future battleground.

Hidden pain must be one of the signature aspects of childhood. The more I felt incapable of articulating myself, and the more unsafe I felt doing so, the thicker became the cocoon I wrapped around myself as I licked my wounds in private. I was a Black child in a White family, cast in the role of learning how not to upset my family or community by being too direct or too frequent in expressing that it was precisely their Whiteness and their related attitudes that were at the root of my pain. And so, I took my pain indoors into my deeper places. It festered there as my habit grew roots—my personal tradition of allowing comfort to others by suppressing my discomfort, entrenching itself by the day.

As with most people, the emotional pain of my childhood shaped me at least as much as the joy of it. My pain forged inside of me a fierce disdain for prejudice, racial prejudice most of all. My childhood was ground zero between Black and White. I reaped the whirlwind of that bitter blight, the poison we stew in the cauldron of our hearts, and then inseminate our loved ones with so steadily. I learned the pattern at an exceedingly young age. People hurt each other and scorn each other due to differences they can detect. Human beings broke my heart as they went about being human.

Every day I stepped out the doors of our family home, and every single day, that outside world noticed my race, and treated me accordingly. That daily ritual transformed me. Feeding this metamorphosis was a powerful inner current. Sometimes a surge through my chest caused me to ball up. It felt as though all the pain in the world was passing through my body. I could feel the shrieks of lives shattered on the other side of the world, and back in time. I often found solace in the pine tree forests surrounding our neighborhood. Those woods served as my private castle. I was protected by the tall, strong trees, and bedded my fears down upon the pine needle mattresses I swept and kicked into piles—not aware of the insecurity I was banishing.

My life's purpose was born in this way. The nights I spent scraping my nails in despair on the underside of my brother's bunk accumulated in me through the years, as did my conviction to grow into an adult who would change the way we treat each other on this planet.

Adoption and race demons made my solitude and alienation explode like a piñata within me. What fell out to clutter up my inner peace wasn't anything sweet. The nation's racial illness was a movie reel flickering steady in my mind.

Everything these images brought to my shores was tainted with a salty residue of reality gone askew. I knew there was a flaw in these patriotic ideals that drifted up to me through endless tides. I knew there was another truth. *There is no way I belong to all of this.* I was an abandoned island, adrift from a larger body. I asked repeatedly: *Why me? Why am I here?* The rest of the house slept, Greg snored above me, but I could not fade into unconsciousness with the tide so loud, crashing with unwanted salvage from the salty sea around me. Worst of all, I had no name for what was tearing me apart.

I grew familiar with the tracks my tears would take down my face, over the expanse of my high cheekbones, down off my face and into my pillow, or onto my sheets. I came to know what path the tears would take depending on how I positioned my head. I was intimate with the warmth of those tears. At least I was releasing my river.

"Quit moping." "Quit hanging your lip."—Mom's expressed frustration with my sulking presence. I translated the meaning of those words into the language my insecurity had developed: *Crybaby. You're just an oversensitive crybaby.* I felt that she was right, that my emotions were unjustified, which only made me feel worse about myself.

I stole away to do my hurting, because in the household that I knew, we were not supposed to mope or hang our lips or be thin-skinned. And when the world outside beat me down in any way, that way had better be a way that Mom could relate to. Otherwise, my emotional reaction might leave her confounded and frustrated. I was a ball of confusion and turmoil, a ball that couldn't explain himself to her. Mom was frustrated. Dad was stumped, but he allowed me to go with my flow. When I was alone and awake with my thoughts as the family slept, I made one promise, over and again. I promised myself that I would do whatever I could when I grew up to make sure no other child danced so regularly, so passionately, with whatever this tormenting thing was that encumbered me.

There was a time, up until I was about 10 years of age, when I enjoyed an open and unbound ability to love Mom with nothing held back. Mom and I had a routine we shared in the evening that is bittersweet in my memory. When the sun slid down into its bed, and the moon came calling, we would sit together in the living room to watch the sitcoms. I sat on the edge of the couch, and she sat on the floor in between my legs, with her back resting against the couch. I brushed her beautiful, long black hair with my most tender strokes, and it meant the world to me to give her that deserved break from the day's work and tensions. I think that she regularly asked me to do this for her because my personality was patient and enduring—I sat there with her for hours without falling into a child's restlessness.

The blue glow from the television screen engulfed us, as twilight became full night. Then I would massage her scalp for what seemed like forever, with fingers made strong and conditioned from hours at the piano. I massaged her shoulders and neck, wishing nothing more than to make my mother feel good. I could feel the tension drain from her. She was happy. My simple knowledge of that filled the cavern in my chest with the sweetest contentment. I wish I could have loved Mom so freely and openly for the rest of my days to come. But circumstance conspired against us both.

I was Black in the midst of Whiteness
but yet I was the brightness

I wanted to retreat into the shadows
of bittersweet night,
but fate bid so that even dark shelter
would bathe me in light

lilliputian only in esteem,
freak of circus
gilded with gleam of Negro grin,
my entry way / permission slip
apology note / deferential plea

wide Negro grin
those were the conditions

That was me

TOKEN IN THE SPOTLIGHT

MY racial isolation was much more than a numbers game. Its potency was rooted in the psychology of expectation. Expectations others held of me to behave, think, and feel as they did. Determinations I held to do what it took to fit in and be loved. Expectations burned the air next to my skin, and gave me an aural glow. Yellow. The book of human isolation has many chapters, and I have to believe that a Black child standing in the racial spotlight wrote several of them.

My family relied heavily upon stock responses to the struggle I expressed over being racially distinct. The message usually had to do with the idea that, "You can't worry about what other people think of you." Or, "People can be ignorant, you just have to ignore it." Or, "All people are the same, color doesn't mean anything." But to me, color meant just about everything. It was the bold paint splashed over my skin like a bull's eye target. My parents' messages, intended to reassure, did as much damage as good, because they placed between us a contradiction of values.

I was dealing with a host of race-related issues, and my parents' simplistic messages didn't cut it. I was contending with my own subtle, insidious twin contradictions of social isolation and strangely tinged popularity. I was also constantly processing all the messages from media, school curricula, and my community that on the underside told me a very disturbing tale about the nature and worth of Black Africans in the States. Race would not leave me. Perhaps I would not leave it. It was in my footsteps and my breath. It was background whisper to my conversations and back lighting to my social interactions. I went to sleep with it and woke to its undulating choke around my neck. We were bound and dysfunctional, but faithful, Race and I. My parents wished, for my own peace and theirs, that I could ignore the attention directed my way, and that I would find strength to rise above the ignorance I tasted. My spirit was not so strong in that early season.

My personal culture of pensive and reflective searching required a more substantive address by others. I needed honest and textured conversation about these issues. I wanted racial prejudice to be directly spoken to, for it to be worked out verbally and sincerely. Not just with my parents, but with my friends as well. My spirit would not have been settled unless those conversations went all the way to the point of specifically accounting for the roots and history of White American attitudes toward Black people. My peers and I were too young to articulate these things with precision and polish, and my parents were unprepared to do so. But it was what my restlessness demanded. Instead, I grew onward toward the anger of my young adulthood.

Evasive responses often accompanied my claims of racially motivated attention directed my way. I received rationalizing comments that veered from the truth like a jackrabbit from a coyote: "But how do you know why they were looking at you, or that they were looking at you at all? It could have been your size, or your smile because it's so attractive, or your shirt that they liked, or your shoes, or the tree behind you, or your imagination." God forbid it might actually have been my Black skin, hair, or features. I understood their reasons for trying to explain away racial attention, but was far from appeased.

I was quickly fine-tuned by my daily experiences to the point of keenly being able to discern racial attention from other kinds of attention. I knew the scent and vibe of racially charged discomfort, fear, and aversion as well as I knew anger, sadness, and attraction. And it was not paranoia, imagination, or fixation. No more than a woman might be fixated on navigating herself through very real social streams of male bias. She is simply responding to what is there. I might have been crying wolf, but my wolves were real.

Dad often sought to comfort me by saying, "People stare at me all the time because of my beard." I ached with indignation at this. It was a cold slap having racial reactions to me equated to the reactions to Dad's beard or clothing. The inhuman attitudes that spawned and maintained slavery were never as benign as fashion opinions. And Black skin never slid so easily through society as a hairstyle out of vogue.

I seemed to be stuck in a glass bottle alone with this experience. My voice was muted to those outside the bottle. Those many nights I cried in that bunk bed I shared with Greg, I was embarrassed that he could hear me. *I'm supposed to be strong for him. Some kind of big brother I am.* I believed I was in the clutches of a cruel fate. *Why was I placed here? Why do I have to be a freak? Why does it hurt so much in my chest to be me?*

Not once, though, did I ever ask, *Why couldn't I have been White?* It might have been easy to mistake my outward behavior and attitudes as indicative of a desire to be White. But much of my behavior and expressed attitudes had more to do with a desperate need to fit in and to be accepted, or to just not stand out, than with an actual desire to biologically change races. I wanted the benefits that the straight hair, the lighter skin tone, and the more narrow facial features brought to those who hold the magic traits of social standard. I wanted their apparent ease and self-security. I wanted normalcy and to receive the societal confirmation of my goodness and worth that was allotted to everyone around me. I was greedy for the membership card.

I was truly ill from people doing the double take and focusing on me. As I became older, I didn't want the employees' eyes to follow me around the store, while those same eyes didn't follow my friends or other youth. Or for children, as they passed me in the stores or at the park, to pull on their parent's hand and point back at me, whispering things I could only partly make out. Things that usually included the words 'Black' or 'skin' or 'hair'. I was emotionally spent from witnessing the uncomfortable reactions and stumbling words of their parents in response.

I didn't want people to describe me as the *Black kid* or the *Black one* over there. I didn't wish for the whole classroom's eyes on me whenever we covered slavery or the Civil Rights Movement in our lesson. Or to have entire families staring at my White family with two Black children because we looked like something to them that they didn't understand or approve. I didn't want to be the subject of the tiresome game: *One of these things doesn't belong. One of these things is not like the other.* I hated that after-school TV show tune. I repulsed seeing the glances and stares from people at the movie theatre, at the swimming pool, everywhere, when Dad and Mom introduced me as their son. And finally, once I left Los Alamos, I was just tired and didn't want to be around any more White people who were rarely around Blacks. I didn't want their curiosity, their fascination, their attraction, their ignorance, their stereotypes, their prejudice, or their attention.

No, it's not that I wanted to be White. I just desperately did not want to be Black in a White world . . .

I am that troubling thing
threatening to expose the ugliness
we all bring
I am that fawning, servile thing
I'll bow if you just
fit me with your approval ring
I am that stuttered over thing
that B-B-Black
ad-d-dopted being
I am that taciturn thing
turned inward
steady cannibalizing
sorry can't sing
I'm too busy eating

My childhood could be described as having been a smooth and
easy ride, other than for the race thing that hovered, a fog just
about at chest level, penetrating my heart with its dampness. I
could have ducked beneath the fog, but then I would have
been ducking. Shrinking myself. I could have risen above that
haze, but I didn't have the jumping legs. I was still the wobbly
colt. What was the verdict? Shrink myself. I did. And what was
the sentence for my crime? Walk as two beings, cleaved down
the middle of my make-up, conspired to silence, passivity,
acquiescence, and the noxious grip of my self-imposed
suffocation.

Throughout my elementary and middle school years, and
into high school, I was extremely quiet and shy, virtually mute.
I was afraid of my own shadow, not to mention the shadows
of others. My elementary school teachers frequently became
frustrated with my intense quiet. They weren't able to get more
than a word or two out of me most of the time. My parents
received more than one call at home from these teachers,
wondering what to do with me. I withdrew so far because the
spotlight singed me that much. So few Black people were

present that I was certain I was an alien. I was actually startled any time I saw a single other African American face.

The racial spotlight was real. Children read another person's vibe as easily as they can read a pop-up book. The vibe I read was no harder to detect than if I had been standing in a room full of mourners. The spotlight had nothing to do with the valence of the attention. Whether it was negative or positive was a secondary consideration. What affected me was to know that in their scanning of the human landscape, people's eyes got caught up on my visage. I was the stimulus for their double take. I caused pause. Because of this, I hated showing my skin.

This was a problem because our family spent almost every day during the summers at East Park Pool. Kristin, Greg, and I started swimming lessons at pre-school age, and the pool became our backyard from that point forward. The paradise of sunshine and water was embellished by our consumption of a sickening amount of junk food from the concession stand whenever we could coax it out of Mom, or sneak it without her permission. We were young and funky. Our bare bellies dripped with the melted sugar of Fanta Orange Soda, Cherry and Grape Taffy, Pop Rocks, Bottle Caps, Lemon Drops, Lemon Heads, Atomic Fireballs, Red Hots . . . I'm not sure how we still have teeth.

The sweetness had a flip side. The swimming pool highlighted my Blackness. My skin, ashy from the chlorine, was more exposed. I had nothing more than bathing trunks to conceal it. I wrapped a towel around my waist, just to cover my legs. I was self-conscious with that much of my skin showing. At least at home or school only my head and hands and arms showed. Donning a bathing suit was like turning on a red flashing light. *Attention all shoppers! We currently have a special running on ashy Black boys. Aisle five, down by the deep end of the pool. Pick you up some lotion on the way, 'cause that poor child is gonna need it.* My skin was the substance that set me apart. My skin was the thing . . . *the thing.* By age 12, I was well aware that only 15 years before, much of the country practiced pool segregation. It wasn't the most pleasant knowledge to carry around with me as I dove and splashed around in the water. Sometimes the sun and water left me dozing on the plastic poolside reclining chairs. And when I slept, my . . .

Nightmare went like this

got up, wiped the sleep from my eyes
pulled on my jeans, threw on a shirt
went down to the pool
day was hot, skin was fryin'
thought I'd take me a dip
got poolside heard the word
that sent my heart to spin
everybody out! Black boy's getting in!

Not only was I isolated racially, but also mine was the particular race most physically divergent from White racial characteristics. My race was also the race most historically at potent odds with White America and I knew it. My peers, even in elementary school, knew it. I carried that awareness as a key part of my token status. I knew that I invoked feelings and thoughts that many people had invested much energy in suppressing. They usually were free to live their lives in that state of denial, because they rarely ever encountered the subjects of that denial. I was that reminder. I could see the recognition alight in their eyes, and their muscles clench taut.

By explaining away why people were staring at me, my loved ones were trying earnestly to protect me, but they were also protecting their own self-esteem. To acknowledge the flawed nature of a people you identify with is to have to contend with a threat to your self-image. So, they tried to minimize and rationalize.

I imagined myself to be just like the animals at the zoo. People coming by, "oohing" and "aahing," and making comments about my hair or something they thought was interesting. And like zoo animals whose keepers take pride in how well the creatures are being fed, cared for, and loved, I was not thriving. I was detached from my element. So I retreated. I wanted out of the spotlight and into the shadows, so I did as little as possible to draw attention to myself. I spoke softly, rarely, and unassertively. I tried to be a 'good little boy', and not act too wild. I tried to play by the rules. Anything to get people to just not pay attention to me.

I am trudging through another insomniac night. *Tick of the clock.* *Trying to sleep before sunrise.* I hear Storyteller's serapé flapping. She doesn't wait for my dreams this time, slinks in on the crest of my delirium and yaps like a mosquito in my ear. "You can't divide what is indivisible. Y'all keep trying, and all you get is dying. You can't take a flower from its root. You can't take the black from soot. You can do that, but then you got to ask yourself, 'am I prepared for the consequences?'"

"Raise a child . . ." she begins to opine. "Raise: to make rise. A thing don't rise by virtue of what you put into it so much as by what is already in it, that you let out. You don't get to choose the formula that makes a thing rise. All you get to do is bring the sun, then get out the way and let it rise. It will seek the sun, along its own course, at its own pace, through its own form."

I hear her and grow drowsy on purpose to flee her voice. As I fade off, I wonder: *What in the world is she telling* me *this for?*

The most important thing in my whole world was to feel like I belonged: belonged in my family, as a part of the group I hung with in my neighborhood, and at my school. Emotionally, I was skating on ice in July, awaiting the melt's crack when I would be treated, even if ever so subtly, as though I was in some way different.

My family and friends seem to have perceived me in much the same way people look at a beautiful woman. People see the attention bestowed upon the beautiful woman—her 'popularity'—and they assume that she must be perfectly content. After all, what more could she ask for? Further, they assume she knows she is beautiful, and perhaps they even experience some jealousy and resentment. What they don't realize is that this beautiful woman very likely is dealing with her own personal wounds, whatever they may be. They don't realize that the attention she receives does not make her feel good, but in fact contributes to her self-consciousness. They don't realize she wrestles with low esteem and feels anything but popular. And when she does dare to express how her life feels to her, she receives scorn and flippancy from others who believe she has no reason to complain. She bears her 'beauty', all the while feeling as ugly as she can.

Bubbles burst. I will never forget the day one of my closest friends tore a trench through my heart after a high school basketball practice. I was a junior at the time, and all the players were at the drinking fountain in the lobby of the gymnasium. It was early in the season, soon after the squads had just been chosen—the 'C' team, junior varsity, and varsity. My friend, a junior like me, was on the junior varsity team. At that time, I didn't realize that any of the players had ill feelings about me being on varsity. I assumed that at least my friends would be happy for me.

But my close friend said something in that moment at the water fountain that told me a handful of truths about the racial realities of my life. He said, *"They only put you on the varsity because you're Black."* I didn't know what was behind his words. But it hurt sharply because I knew that I deserved to make that team, and I more than held my own that season. It stung mostly because this was my friend, and he was revealing a resentment he carried for me. How many other resentful hearts was my radar failing to detect?

You only made the varsity because you're Black. I was shocked to realize that apparently many people, including my closest friends, spent my childhood years looking at my Blackness as some kind of advantage for me. I would again hear that hidden attitude escape periodically on the breath of sarcastic, humor-veiled remarks. My race was my most foreboding curse and yet people thought it was my great fortune. *These people, including my family, have shown me that they can't relate to my reality. I'm gonna stop trying to relate it.*

Basketball . . . walking onto the Griffith Gymnasium court on a Friday night for pre-game warm-ups, a chill passes through my being. Here we are dressed in shorts and jerseys, baring our bodies to a cavernous crowd piled high on bleachers ascending toward the farthest reaches of the gym. The cheers overwhelm us as our community urges forth a fighting spirit. The bouncing of balls echoes in slow motion reverberation—a sound studio in use. Lay-up drills form. Bodies move with practiced grace toward a rim that defines our objective. This is a boisterous pit of adulation, screaming fans, band blaring with air-rippling drumbeats, and young women in skirts and smiles flipping and flying through the air. This is high school ball and it is madness. *I am shrinking.*

I am a Christian in the Coliseum and all around me are Romans, not roaring for my demise but for my victory. *And I am shrinking.* Too much of my brown skin is showing. The whole town is watching and here I am—all naked brown limbs in motion. My greatest fear is transpiring on a wooden court. This is the pinnacle of being at the center of attention. The spotlight is heated to infinity. Most of my teammates are eating up the attention, soaking up the splendor of flexing athletic wares before transfixed eyes. *Too many eyes.* My nightmarish imagination hears subtle murmurs of thought through the bleachers: *Look at that Black kid running around out there.*

The game starts. The referee throws up the ball; it teases as it rises, like a balloon with just enough helium to defeat gravity. Up, up it goes. My body, coiled, now springs, and I am catching air, racing another body to a ball hanging suspended in the sky. We are chasing a comet. The gymnasium crowd is a mass of agitation I cannot hear. It is my body against another body, willing to tear muscle fibers to stretch and claim this ball and . . . this game is on.

I post up on the low block, my back finding familiar resistance in the defender behind me. My strength tests his, my left hand outstretched, a target for a pass. Now the ball is mine. I spin on my pivot foot, swing the ball around and back to my right hip, out of reach from his digging and swiping. Two hands holding the prize. "We are . . . L.A.!" The crowd's chant is rising. I am seeing everything now. My heart is pounding and old fears are flooding my insides as early game sweat floods my outer surface. Mortensen on the far wing, Lujan at the top of the key, Williams, Newsom shifting hips and shoulders like bullfighters, throwing defenders off balance, cutting to open space. They are the shooters. I am the 'banger', blocks and boards are my delicacy. *I should pass the ball.*

"We are . . . L.A.!" The crowd is deafening. My man is slow moving laterally. I ball fake right, throw the ball down to my left, dip my right shoulder into a wet jersey that backs off oh so easy. The path to the rim is mine. One power dribble is all it takes. I gather and release in an instant, with full clearance for take off. I achieve air space capped by a hoop at altitude 10 feet. My right hand, holding official Spalding leather, moves up through atmospheres passing by like rungs on a ladder—first the bottom of the net, then its middle, then to the higher rungs where the netting is less tightly webbed. Ball, palm, and fingers pass by that 120th inch and keep going. This dunk is mine. But I am shrinking again. I should not jump this high *don't stand out*, I should not shoot *don't speak*, I most definitely should not dunk *don't shine too bright*. Too much spotlight. Too much glare. My biceps contract at the very moment they should release. My fingers part gently, too gently. They are flower petals and not the angry vice grips necessary for the dunk. The ball whimpers out of my grasp, a lay up when I could have been king.

Basketball was my savior. It was the swelter pit of crowd attention in which I broiled, but it was my savior. I started playing relatively late, around the fifth grade. My friends, Kent and Dean Mortensen, pulled me into it. Until that point, I spent much of my time chillin' in the back yard with my GI Joes with the Kung Fu grip. Slowly and imperceptibly, basketball changed my life. Chiefly, I benefited from the confidence basketball instilled in me. I was a late bloomer physically, lanky and deliberate in my athletic motion, and I didn't fill out until college. But from one year to the next, I developed skills. More importantly, I developed relationships with teammates that gave me emotional ground to stand on.

Until high school, I was used to playing basketball almost exclusively with and against White or Hispanic players. But now it was high school and games against teams from around the state. The opposing teams had more African American players. When we met on the court, I saw them peering in my eyes for that look of connection. They didn't find it there. They were so unfamiliar, so notably different in the way they played the game, that I was intimidated. I was ashamed to share the court with them, because I was playing on White teams against them. I felt like Benedict Arnold and Uncle Tom rolled into one pitiful power forward.

I spent much of my time wondering what these other Black players thought about me, rather than paying attention to the actual game. I was silent, never daring to talk smack. I was afraid if they heard me speak, sounding as White as could be, that they would fall out in laughter. "You're soft," one of those players said to me once as we shouldered each other for position during a free throw. I knew what he meant. He meant, *what the heck are you doing playing with these people?* He only called me soft once. My rage found *his* soft spot, right on his jaw line. I was intimidated by life, but not harmless.

The crowning achievement of my senior season came when I played in the North-South State All-Star game. Standing at center court during the pre-game ceremony, I awaited my turn to have my parents introduced to the crowd of thousands and be led out to stand beside me. Mom, as always, was radiant with pride, Dad, awkward in the public spotlight. I hated myself in that moment. What felt like the entire state of New Mexico, an arena of White faces, was witnessing the secret I bore: besides not being White, I was not even a normal Black person. My parents were White.

At times during elementary school, having my parents show up at school to pick me up comforted me. It showed other White children that I was semi-White by virtue of adoption, and therefore worthy of their sanction. But on this night, at center court, I could not even fully enjoy the pride Mom and Dad were taking in being honored alongside their son. I kissed Mom and hugged Dad, full of love and gratitude for their constant presence. But I was all guilt. This night, this game, this honor, and this award plaque—were things I did not deserve. My blood cells grew sickle in shame.

When I was in the ninth grade and still in middle school, I sat one night in the top bleachers of Griffith gymnasium and watched a huge, Black, muscular man-child in goggles dominate the high school varsity action in a way that made me sick with unfamiliar pride and awe. His name was Carlos. Carlos was only a sophomore but he was bigger, faster, stronger, and leapt higher than everyone. I did not know him, had never seen him before. But my eyes never left him that night, not even when he was on the bench.

Carlos was the image I wished for myself. Who knows what insecurities he himself was battling as a Black giant in that town? All I knew was that to me, he seemed indestructible, powerful, and sure of himself. Two years later I played with him on the varsity team. I spent the season with my chest fluttering as chests do when you live out a dream of playing ball with your hero.

My senior year, Carlos' cousin, Nate moved to Los Alamos from Indiana. Nate was a different kind of experience for me. I knew that to the folks in Los Alamos, Nate represented many of the stereotypes they held for African Americans. Nate had the Jheri Curl going on. He was big, handsome, and wore a mustache, which added to his threatening Black presence in the midst of all of us baby-faced adolescents. Nate drove a fast car, wore stylish clothes Los Alamos had never seen, and walked with rhythm and swagger too full of soul for this straight-laced place. He also talked like a city brother, and had that confident and defiant attitude that was so easy for folks to call arrogant.

I paid close attention to the little things about Nate— seeking to gain information about how I was supposed to carry myself. I studied how he cared for his hair, dressed, ate, and spoke. I was an eager student. But in the end, I fell prey once more to the combating tidal waves within me. I had great affinity for Nate yet suffered discomfort with him, for he represented the stereotype through which I so feared I would be judged: *that kind of Black person.* . . .

Nate was experiencing extreme culture shock in Los Alamos. Other than his cousin, Carlos, he found no peers he could relate to in any way. At least in me, he had my race, so he latched on, a life buoy in deserted waters. One day he told me, "You and I are going to have to hang tight this year. We're the only ones." Conflict splashed around in my stomach. His offering of friendship boosted my esteem. I wished to reciprocate unabashedly, needing to have that connection with him. But I was more powerfully pulled by a need to not be ostracized by the people who had been my friends and point of orientation all the years before. I feared they might abandon me or at least diminish their friendliness toward me if they saw me growing close with a 'different' kind of Black person.

Retrospect showed me that Nate and I were dissimilar personalities, but I had affection for him that had to do with sharing our racial reality. That bond alone was meaningful, but not powerful enough to drive me. Though we did become friends and knowing him took me farther down my own road of growth, I regret that I held back from my relationship with him out of my habitual need to defer to the comfort of my White social circle. Nate, Carlos, Greg—we faced the same peculiar challenges under the veil of our supposed successes. *Los Alamos is a great place to live*, persisted as the sound of society in my head. I concurred: *So was the plantation back in the day, if you weren't a slave.* My issue wasn't with Los Alamos as a place. It was with the power of subjectivity to determine what 'great' is.

I was fortunate to have in my life, especially during adolescence, a family who over the years was like a second family to me. Through my friendships with Kent and Dean Mortensen that started in kindergarten, I steadily became a part of the Mortensen family fabric. Kent and Dean's older brothers, Larry and Russ, and their father, Gene, coached Greg and me in baseball, football, and basketball. The mother, Gail, and the sisters, Tammy and Debbie, had such tender, sensitive hearts they must have detected my insecurities. I basked in their warmth and hospitality. By middle school, I slept over at their house as many times as Mom allowed. Dean was my classmate and the most gifted comic, along with Greg, I have known to this day. Like Greg, the young ladies loved him. Because of Dean's overwhelming cool and popularity, he was a singular source of my basking pride. I stayed close by his side.

By high school Kent and I were each other's shadow. Kent was the most considerate, sensitive soul I knew. This made him a safe place for me to land. I put roots into him because he seemed to value me all the way to the core of my spirit. He seemed to somehow need me. This was new and empowering. I felt my inner pot holes pave over as our friendship grew. His love for music by Black artists was no small invitation for my bonding with him. I wasn't just cool with him because I was a different kind of Black person. I was cool with him because he was cool with Black, period. His place in my life was an esteem-building machine. Ultimately our friendship would stand as a redwood among the forest of my life's relationships—always there, deeply rooted, an extra umbrella of protection above the canopy.

The Mortensens were partly of Norwegian descent, and always joked about their outrageous character as typifying the 'History of White People in America'. They were a sports-loving family like none I've seen. They went whole hog when they became fans of a team. Every member in the family was a fan of the Packers and the Celtics—their homes plastered with team paraphernalia. Perhaps mimicking that team mentality, they had an intense loyalty to one another.

The Mortensens always seemed to be celebrating their own culture, even if they would not have defined it that way. I appreciated this aspect of their family. They found the simplest ways to celebrate their values. The Mortensen stew, the family rituals, like being as late as possible for every moment of the day, these things made their culture. The substance that came to them via the vessel of generations shaped how they interpreted life and people. I saw that inheritance as being shaped very much by their ethnicity. They probably saw it as being normal. Either way, what was bound up in their Whiteness, they honored without shame. This *being-ness* without apology reminded me of what I was missing. I yearned to celebrate and share my African heritage with family and friends in a way that wasn't questioned, ridiculed, or resented.

It was difficult for me to hear the social message that race didn't matter while a counter truth played out around me. People's affinity for their race and heritage was evident everywhere. The proof was in the homogeneity of the community. These people didn't just happen to live here. This community wasn't an accident. It was a consequence. Choices had been made. People were comfortable with the particular residents with whom they shared this high mountain space. At least some amount of that comfort was a matter of race.

The affinity people had for living among other White people wasn't what bothered me. To me, that was a natural inclination. I understood it and wanted it for myself. I was conflicted by the lack of honesty about that affinity. The Mortensens, in some strange way, exhibited that honesty for me. Not by denouncing other people, but by not pretending their comfort with their own racial and ethnic atmosphere didn't exist.

In that way, the Mortensens were a refuge. If I had to hear another person tell me that she or he didn't care if a person was black, white, yellow, or purple, I would have turned purple myself and left my nausea all over their clothing. 'Color' was never the real problem. The culture—the lifestyle and values— that those colors represented was what threatened so many, and left me doing a sickened jig through life. I was fatigued from hosting people's testimony that color mattered nothing to them. I knew that was only true assuming the palette of crayon-colored humans they imagined before them was, at heart, a parade of White people dressed up like the rainbow.

Because I was so dissimilar in personality from my own family, I began to spend more and more time in the Mortensen household when I was in middle school. They had interests and habits similar to mine: sports, sleeping in late, staying up late, eating fast food—this was heaven to an adolescent. They also had a sense of humor I could relate to. Most importantly, I felt penetrating affection and love coming from them that I did not feel from most others in the community outside of my family.

The Mortensens loved me as a son and a brother. They fed me, comforted me, laughed with me, shared loss with me, and fiercely defended me. Between Mom, Dad, and the rest of my family, and the Mortensens, I received a double dip of family protection that compensated for much of what I lacked otherwise. But I also never fully revealed myself to them, out of a withering fear that their possible racial attitudes and my racial truth would ultimately conflict so badly that I would become the 'bad Black person' in their eyes. It would have crushed me to discover, so I smothered any inkling of opinions or attitudes that might have caused them to categorize me with other Black people. For 17 years, I connected to people through that sad dysfunction.

The years gave me counter-evidence to my fears about the Mortensens. I experienced them sharing a consistent compassion and incredible hospitality with people of all ethnic backgrounds. But as long as I lived in Los Alamos, and for a long time after, I smothered so much of my being to curry their love. I feared certain fine particles of bias or prejudice might drift, latent, in the bottom-current of their spirits. I clung desperately to the affectionate substance of their hearts that rose up like wisps of heaven scent and enveloped me.

The Mortensens existed at the core of a priceless social circle in my life. Along with Kent and Dean, I became friends with Mike Hannaford, whose family was also from Illinois, and Dan Guevara. Mike and I spent hours playing in the woods, both of us more comfortable with the cover of nature than with the mercurial streams of human interaction. Dan and I were the two persons in the inseparable friendship circle who were not White. He and I talked about this, years later. We realized that we both had long struggled with the contradictions of love and racial bias found in the friendships with which we had been blessed.

Our friendship circle would endure, become potent in its tenure. The relationships would surpass 30 years, keeping me anchored, even as I voyaged deeper into my African American self. I do not know how successful I would have been at resisting my own pull toward racial prejudice if not for my family and these long-time, faithful friends. It took bleeding, crying, and loving together to make my fight for a clean heart worth enough to work for.

In Santa Fe, New Mexico, every fall there is a festival of celebration unlike any other I have encountered in the United States. La Fiesta, the oldest civic celebration in the nation, is passion unleashed. Since 1712, the people of the area have gone plum crazy in the streets every fall during the weekend following Labor Day. Mariachi musicians hold the stage, Navajo fry bread scent makes anyone with a pulse famished. The streets are filled like Mardi Gras; Latino fervor floods the avenues; and, for a day, White people become the ethnic minority, in cultural power if not in numbers.

In the evening, as dusk becomes heavy, mysticism sets in and a giant takes the stage. A 50-foot, white paper monster, with huge black eyes and enormous red lips stands facing the boisterous crowd of thousands, many laid out on blankets with coolers of food and drink keeping them well satiated. The monster is a caricature of a bully. Huge, glowering eyes are plates that roll in their socket. He wears formal dress for this occasion—a black cummerbund and bow-tie. His long arms hang down to where you would imagine his knees are beneath his white floor-length apparel. The left hand is bunched up in a fist, with the thumb extended like a hitchhiker—he surely would rather be anywhere else but here. The giant's name is Zozobra, the High Priest of Gloom. His name means *worry* in Spanish and he is an effigy extraordinaire.

Then the southwestern sky goes from powder blue, to purple blue, losing its daytime enthusiasm. As darkness comes, fire dancers costumed in red begin to gyrate around the monster. Soon Zozobra agitates to their nuisance. He does not understand why this attention must always be upon him. The fire dancers light torches and threaten with their flames. He feels their fascination and ambivalence as fire hovering too close for comfort. Finally, they lick at the parched paper that is

Zozobra's clothing. His clothing cannot make him one of them. He is too much the giant.

He feels like wailing. He erupts in flames—his wails come, a deep moan that fills the sky. Fireworks explode from inside his head, shooting out his eyes and mouth in great yellow sparks. The crowd explodes in pleasure: "Viva La Fiesta!"

The fire dancers are different from the monster, and with that difference, they have scorched him. His arms flap in torture, his mouth falls open in agony. *Why am I on a stage and surrounded? Why am I burning?* As Zozobra, the great monster, is vanquished on black embers floating toward the clouds, thousands of people, the normal ones in relation to this beast, explode in a victorious roar. The great monster is Black and the crowd's embrace is suspect. He (*I*) wishes to find the clouds. The normal ones cheer at him (*me*). His (*my*) ears take in only rejection. All the gloom and poor fortune of the year are now gone away until 12 moons have passed again. His (*my*) own gloom has crested and he (*I*) cannot imagine passing another dozen months again this way.

Looked for you under the bed
in the closet / down the hall
at the kitchen table
in the shopping mall

looked for you on the street
in the church / at the ball

couldn't find you playin' cards
slappin' bones / playin' saxophones

couldn't find you anywhere
but on the t.v. / dancing as Ali
cutting up as Flip / doing Geraldine
but only on the screen

I mean
what do I gotta do
scream?

ME & MUHAMMAD ALI

STORYTELLER whispers in her intellectual voice:

"A White child born into a White family in a White dominated
society requires a million instances of reassurances over 18 years and
beyond to feel secure in his belonging. This, despite all the
consistencies of biology, personality, and physical appearance he
enjoys to bolster his sense of belonging. Given this, how many such
reassurances should a Black child adopted into a White family be
expected to need? At what point should the child be judged as mal-
adjusted, oversensitive, needy, ungrateful, antagonistic, or troubled?
Within what boundary should the behavior and emotions that led to
such labels simply be viewed as nothing more than healthy indicators
of an increased need for reassurance, given the context of the child's

life? Who is dysfunctional here? The child with his reactions, or the people who squirm at those reactions? We all need to be stroked endlessly. We all need heroes, not that we may love them, but that we may imagine them loving us as perfect in their eyes."

One of my few sources of racial pride growing up was the storybook I had, *John Henry*—the folk tale of a strong Black baby who, legend had it, was born with a hammer in his hand. In the story, John Henry grew to be big and proud, and went off to become a steel-driving man for the railroads. I gazed in wonder at John Henry's Black image, feeling an admiration and intimacy. John Henry was my man.

I didn't realize what *John Henry* had done for me then until later after college when I saw the book in a bookstore and immediately broke into a grin. *John Henry, my man!* My memories flooded back, and I wondered what had ever become of my original book. Of course, I bought the copy I was looking at on the spot and promised myself to keep the book around for any children I might have. It was then that I began to fully realize the value of such *little things*.

I read comic books almost fanatically, soaking up the dialogue and colorful images. I bought them new and used, and spent many nights when I was supposed to be asleep under the covers in our bunk bed, reading to the weak glow of a flashlight, ever-vigilant of parental footsteps coming toward the room. The comic book hero that brought rare pride to my chest was *the Black Panther*. This cat was bad: swinging above ground in the jungle or cruising through the hood. Sleek in his blue-black, skin-tight uniform, a mask covering his face. The alter ego of the Black Panther was T'Challa, royal prince of the fictional African nation, Wakanda. He was just a bad cat. Never mind that his creators, in conceiving of him, associated the Black alter ego with the panther, a creature they themselves described in the comic book as a savage beast. I took my heroes where I could find them.

My only problem back then was that it was always hard to find copies of the *Black Panther* comic book. Somehow, I don't think *the Black Panther* inspired the same kind of emotions in the other children (or adults) around Los Alamos. That superhero wasn't too high on their totem pole of self-image. I ended up wearing out the few issues of *the Black Panther* I did have. I still have one issue to this day: Issue number 9, Marvel Comics Group, 1978. Price: 35 cents.

John Henry and *the Black Panther*—those were among the few scraps of racial pride that I managed to gather to me as I grew. The entrance into my life of sources of racial pride was rare and inconsistent. I found them where I could, and when I did, I held on for dear life. One of those sources was Muhammad Ali. If only I had known then what I would learn later about the connection between my biological family and my love for Muhammad Ali. Life is an incredible circle. It's just that our vision is usually too limited to notice the arc.

Dad and I shared a magical night back in September of 1978, when I was not yet 11 years old. Dad took me in his Land Rover up into the mountains on a cold night to attend a Ham Radio convention. I had no real interest in the convention, that lifestyle was over my head. I just wanted to go and spend time with my dad. But I was also torn because Muhammad Ali would be fighting Leon Spinks that same night in an attempt to regain his heavyweight title for an unprecedented third time. I was dying to watch that fight on television, but Dad wanted me to go with him and I wanted to go as well. Dad promised me I could listen to the fight on the radio. That was good enough for me.

Dark had come by the time we got there. The mountains grow cold quickly when the crickets start to sing their night serenade. I bundled up in the Land Rover and made Dad find the radio station before he joined his Ham comrades over at their gathering. The fight started, and my body temperature rose in anticipation. I was decimated when Ali had lost the title to Spinks in their first bout. I couldn't believe Ali had been licked by a man with only seven professional fights under his belt. But now Spinks held *the* belt. An aging Ali would have to dig deep into his reserves to reclaim it. Nerves flipped under my skin, my heart got jazzy. The rounds wore onward. Conversation and radio chatter buzzed only lightly in the background. My whole being was tuned to the voice of the radio announcer. Ali was moving and jabbing, keeping Spinks at bay, summoning old energy.

With each round my hopes rose. I forgot the cold. Ali was doing it. Jab, jab . . . bull rush by Spinks; Ali holds; back on his toes, moving, jab . . . straight right, fighting in backward motion like only Ali could. Spinks coming forward but thwarted by skill and a champion's will. My head bobbed to the scene I imagined. Dad came back now and then to check on me, and on the fight. Ali was in control. He just needed to hang on. I needed this. I prayed the whole way through. *Please, God, let him do this.* Ali did this. The 15 rounds they fought in those days were suddenly over . . . endless pause for the decision. And then the voice: "And the new!—" All the rest was lost in an 11-year-old boy's triumphant roar.

That night, over 60,000 people packed the Superdome in New Orleans, witnessing history at sea level. But 1,000 miles away, and 8,000 feet farther into the sky, in a forest clearing filled with radio static competing with crickets, a boy jerked and twitched to every blow like he was ringside and sprayed in sweat. What a night that was. A man and a boy—the man doing what he loved, sharing that passion with other men whose passion was the same; the boy, warmed by sharing a night with a father he loved, ecstatic that his hero had come through again. A father and a son, doing what they loved, doing it together. That was one of those sweet moments when I felt connected to Dad in a way that goes beyond love and enters the realm of spiritual communion.

Muhammad Ali represented my unknown biological father to me when I was young. I don't think I realized that then, even if the fantasy danced in my head a few times. I loved Dad, and admired him like most boys do, so my conscious thoughts of fatherhood were nearly always about him. Still, I knew that I loved Muhammad Ali, this beautiful, Black, proud man. And I yearned to see him float across the television screen.

My parents, Mom in particular, may have been slightly threatened at times by Greg's and my occasional tendency to identify with other African Americans who drifted, even if superficially, through our life. Often we imitated the cool and colorful street mannerisms of some hip character we had seen on television: J.J. from *Good Times*, Rerun from *What's Happening*, or some supporting character from the *Jeffersons*. At times, the object of identification was a person or character of less than exemplary nature, which explained some of Mom's defensiveness. But it was this very act of reaching out, imitating, relating, comparing, connecting, that was our instinctive grasp for completeness.

"Stop that!" Mom would say, responding to our imitations. "Do you want people to think you're a hooligan?" *Hooligan.* My impressions of Black characters had activated old images in her. Mom knew exactly how some White folk thought of Black people. She didn't want those thoughts associated with her children if she could prevent it. *Stop being Black* was the message that screamed, loud and clear in my ear.

Heroes, idols, and images that may have seemed unimportant or even threatening or negative to my parents were just the social nutrition that I required. In my case, my identity was born of my imperfect management of three constant tensions: 1) fitting in with my White world, 2) needing to feel a part of my adoptive family, and, 3) needing to feel good about my Blackness. The third tension most often conflicted with the first two. My wounds accumulated in the crevasse left from that conflict.

I needed, with a vicious hunger, to reach out to whatever Black substance I could find. At that time, Black people were a foreign species to me, but they were *my* foreign species. I was given periodic reprieve from my identity dance. And, in one case, I found an encouraging Black man between the treble cleft and the bass cleft.

Mom's iron cast discipline grabbed us by the collar and took us into the world of music at the age of four. Kristin, Greg, and I took piano lessons, whether we wished to or not. What ensued were years of repetition, focus, concentration, failure, and achievement—experiences that bolstered our character. Our piano teacher was Ms. Sydoriak. Her personality was what you would expect of a piano teacher—demure only outside of the world of her piano. She was patient, prodding, challenging, and encouraging, a steady after-school presence in a dimly lit home—a place where I learned to glow a little.

I thrived. Musically, yes, but much more in the way I regarded myself. My long fingers negotiated the keys and scales more easily than other children's might have. And my personality lent itself toward the extended periods of tedium, concentration, and delayed gratification that practice demanded. I learned of a thing called rhythm, as the large buckeyes from the trees in her yard dropped to the ground, thudding like the harbinger of a great hailstorm.

I grew from scales to songs, from being terrified of performing in front of her, to being petrified of playing at recitals in Fuller Lodge. I cannot recall whether playing Scott Joplin's ragtime music was my choice or Ms. Sydoriak's. But I played it. The up-tempo, color-rama of the *Maple Leaf Rag*, *Peach Time Rag*, and my favorite, *The Entertainer*, flowed out of my fingers, an inspired stream. My skills took off. I played like it had resided dormant in my bones, waiting to splash onto the piano keys and become a ghost's holler about having once been *a serious toe-tapper, dapper and all*. Was this choice of music Ms. Sydoriak's awareness of my need for a harmony of culture? Or was her encouragement of my ragtime love affair only a recognition of my musical inclination? Joplin's music massaged me on the crossroad of my soul and circumstance. And it never escaped me that I was playing a Black man's music. I played like it was a protest.

There was a place, called *the Cave of the Winds,* not half an hour's walk into the woods from our house. The cave was a large hollow on a rocky hillside overlooking canyons thick with pines. The wind howled over the mouth of the cave, making the place seem like a gathering place for spirits. This ground was a sanctuary, though few dared the darkness of the cave itself. I went to that spot sometimes to perch myself on one of the hillside boulders and listen to the wind's chorus. One day, I sat downwind from a man approaching me from the rear. I smelled the bacon scent from his clothes in the hearty breeze.

"Caballero, qué paso?" he asked. He was in his fifties, maybe, with a twinkle in his eyes. Skinny as a laundry pole.

"Nada, amigo. Nada." I responded.

He sat down on the boulder beside me. We stared out over the canyon in silence. After a moment, he spoke again. "Mira, Hermano. Eres negro de negro. Me comprendes?"

"No. Qué estas diciendo?" I answered, unclear on his meaning.

"Todo qué digo es qué . . . All I'm saying is that you are black of black. You can't let your Blackness consume you. You got to use what you are to consume the black. Wherever you go, make sure to bring the light with you."

I was not ready for his words. I was more than a little taken aback by his directness and what might possibly be clairvoyance. I wondered what it was he was seeing in me.

"I see a Black man who eats tortillas," he chimed in, disturbingly on beat with my thoughts. "I am a child of old México who can't do without his grits. Go figure. Sometimes, such is such."

His manner was soft, easy, but penetrating. He pulled me into whatever flow he was orchestrating. "I feel so at peace out here," I said. "Why can't I get in rhythm around people?" I asked, now assuming he would have an answer.

"Mira, Hermano. Let me ask you this: Would a world of blind people even know that they could not see?"

"I don't know what you mean."

"I'm talking about the grand illusion of *sameness*, mi'jo. When everyone in one place sees the world the same way, they become convinced that they are seeing the world the right way and the only way. They figure, 'everyone else backs up my point of view. I must be seeing things right.' In fact, all that is true is that they all share the same blindness."

I was half past lost at this point, but I was curious. He continued, "Don't fret so hard that they don't see you. Remind yourself that you are real. You got to do that sometimes around blind folk. Or else, you'll begin to think you yourself are only a product of your imagination."

We sat through some more moments of silence. I sifted through his words for meaning, but the wind's howl made more sense. Eventually, he got up, wiped the dust off the jeans covering his nonexistent backside, and announced, "Time to get some grits and take me a nap. You tired me out."

He paused about 20 yards away, turned back to me and said, "Caballero. You don't have to ride alone. One day, you will find a flowering señorita, and in your garden, she will become a señora. I'd bet on my wife's cooking, which ain't saying much, but it's all I got to offer—I'd bet on my wife's cooking that this señorita, she will see you. You won't even have to translate for her. Now, that there's a hero."

He turned away again, calling out, "Take care around these spirits, they won't let you sleep. Vaya con Dios, Caballero. Vaya con Dios." He walked away, his gait deliberate, banging his head at one point on a branch that overhung the path. He cursed tarnation, stirring up dust devils that nipped at his heels. Only then did I realize I had been sitting with a man who was clinically blind. And that it was my Storyteller.

I am sitting on a hard wooden pew in the Immaculate Heart of Mary Parish, the Catholic church that we attend. I am small and this large room is packed with people. They are larger than I am and they seem to know something I do not about what to do in this place—how to be and act; how to breathe, stand, sit, pray, sing, and all the other things they do. *Is there a secret they are not sharing? How long have they been privy to this state of being?*

Voices vibrate in this acoustic theatre of God. The ceiling pillars themselves seem holy as if doves will emerge to perch upon them at any moment. And there at the front of the worship hall, up high on the wall, larger than us all is the image of Jesus, near naked on the cross. I too am naked, for this intimidating mass of people huddled around me, dwarfing me, and this great Jesus on the wall are both in the image I suppose must be that passport to the great secret they all share. I am naked of that image. It is not my image. I am not clothed of skin like that. No matter how hard I try, and I do try hard, I cannot be as holy as they are, as He is. I have my Sunday best on. Still I feel indecent. Mom stands beside me, singing so beautifully and unafraid. I do not dare.

The congregation is praying aloud now. It is the prayer they always pray, every Sunday—a prayer I have heard so often, in this space, with these people, with that Jesus on the wall. I have heard this prayer so often that its words are a mantra hard to resist as truth. Their voices rumble amazingly deep for a room that is half female. The chesty vibration is rising and filling the air, all the way up to the distant rafters. They are that image that I am not. *I am naked, where are my clothes?* Their voices are in prayer . . . "—on Earth as it is in Heaven . . ."

And I wonder: *Is this how it is in Heaven?*

Check this out:

porch monkey
jungle bunny
spear chucker
watermelon lips
tar baby
buckwheat
flashlight
chicken eatin'
ball playin'
go back to Africa
sambo
stupid negro
toby wanna be

and they think I got messed with
'cause of my size 16 feet

sticks and stones may break
your bones
but your words
they sure did hurt me

HATRED'S WAKE

THERE are things in the dark. Things with long, saber-toothed grins that tear at the flesh of my young heart. Black silhouettes in the indigo where I drift, lurking, waiting to pounce. Things with blood in their eyes, stench on their breath. They stalk me, because I am a child and small. Intimidate me because they can. Most of all, these things are invisible to everyone but me, because everyone else is looking elsewhere. Anywhere other than toward the place where those stalking things leap at me, taking a piece of me away. I am alone with them, the terrible things. They will not stay under the bed, or in the closet, and they do not come out only at night. They are too hungry to wait, too bold to hide, too emblazoned with righteous arrogance and justification.

Those things are the shadows of clerks and security guards and store managers, following me as though they were my shadow. But I know my own shadow does not lurk and creep and smell like vituperative suspicion. I know my shadow does not have eyes that burn through me with judgment and expectation. Expectation that I will not be able to resist my genetic temptation to commit a crime in the playground of these shadows. No, these shadows are not my own. So, I try my best to act normal as I am being judged. But it takes legions of my ancestors to keep me from raging against those dark shadows—to keep me from committing a murder of wishes; or a slaying of dragons with white scales who do not wish my presence in their lair. Liars. When they say, "Can I help you?" It is not a question. The sound of it—*can I help you*—is the sound of gnashing teeth. They are consuming me, because they will do even that if that is what it takes to make me vanish.

Storyteller is growing bigger. She's a good 5'9" now. This rendezvous is in the canyon where I have built so many forts of widow maker pine branches, with eaves of needles and leaves. This canyon is host to my hideaways, but she has found me. "Go on over there and smell that pine tree."

"Smell the pine tree?" I can't imagine what she's up to this time.

"This isn't a spelling bee," she barks, "Stop repeating after me. Go on over and smell that one there."

I do. Taking a deep draw with my face close to the thick, hard bark, I am filled with a rich, sweet smell.

"What's that pine tree smell like?" she asks.

"Smells like maple syrup."

"A pine tree that smells like maple. What's that tell you?" she pokes, looking for the light to dawn in me.

"I don't know. That pine trees smell good?"

"Boy, I'm not so sure 'bout your intelligence. The point is that the substance of things isn't always faithful to presumption. Life is designed to contradict folks' tendency to draw thick lines around everything and call it a done deal. We freeze frame what is fluid. Life thaws that illusion and makes it motion. Lines become smoke and puddles and can't nary a one of them hold its form."

"Are you trying to tell me something?" It's too early in the day for her abstractions.

"Only that you can let them draw a line around you and call it a day. You can do that and suffer the storm. Or, you can go on ahead and find your peace and your definition in that there sky above your head."

"The sky has no definition," I reply.

"Exactly," she huffs. With that, she places the Indian paintbrush stalk she's been chewing in the side of her mouth like a farmer would a piece of straw. She stands, sprouts transparent wings and flies away, a dragonfly, leaving me wondering about the strangeness of her mind.

Even the hyper-educated, socially aware community of Los Alamos was speckled with acerbic acid spilled from hatred's cup. Even in the parade of smiles and friendly hellos, there crouched pockets of clawed disdain. Every so often, some of that touched me. 'Every so often' was all it took to amplify the way I shook. Mothers, wholesome, 'all-American' mothers, pulling their children slightly away from me as they passed me on the street and in the stores. I always wondered what 'all-American' really meant. I knew it didn't look like me, and it didn't love like me. If these mothers were all-American, then my impulsive love for them was bushels of wheat left as an offering unrequited on a field grown rotten and bare.

For every 50 instances of sincere embrace and affection, there was one spoiled moment that largely eclipsed the loving I had received. There are moments like this: I am old enough and grown large enough to scare those who would be frightened of a shy, brown adolescent frightened to death himself. Two elderly White women are sitting on a bench outside. They are the kind of women so many assume as adorable, harmless, and golden-hearted with grandmotherly love and affection for family and strangers alike. I walk by them, trying to catch their attention with a smile. In my wake, I hear the whisper: "How'd you like to come across that in the parking lot in the middle of the night?" The voice is thin, laced with disdain and chills my every living cell. "I was at a party one night with my husband and one of them put his hand on my shoulder. My skin crawled."

The other voice whispers, shamed and awkward in response. "Well . . . I just don't think that way about that."

By the time I pass out of earshot, I am swollen with rage, hurt, and shock. I am floating on that morass and can't get my feet to find the ground. I want to run back, shout, and scream. I want to list my qualifications, accomplishments, and validations for being human. *How can you call me a monster? You don't even know me. Lady, you are the monster, the absolute never-ending nightmare of my life.*

There were times when I could not contain my storm, my latent but very serious temper, connected by a hose to that chamber holding all the racial slings and arrows. One fuse in particular was certain to trigger my eruption. Beneath the surface of my daily interactions with other children, there was the current of an unspoken but undeniable truth: I was Black and they were, mostly, White. Every now and then, this truth broke through the calm surface in the form of racial references, and when it did, I blew. Two thousand bees buzzed the space inside my skull where only an instant before my brain had been. In those moments of absolute rage, I was a spit of resolve away from hurting someone badly.

Being called 'Nigger' takes on a particular sting when you are the only one within earshot to whom the label might apply. There were just a few times on the schoolyard at Mountain Elementary where the usual name-calling spilled over into racial territory directed at me. When that happened, the bees sent me screaming and sprinting toward the offender, hell-bent and set to kill. The result usually was that the other child and I would be sent to the principal's office.

Sitting there before the principal's desk, facing our final judgment, the whole world rained down on me. The principal would say something like "We don't allow name-calling or violence here." That was the sum of his judgment. Then the two of us would be made to sit on the ominous Think Bench. *Equal punishment. Equal punishment for two children: the other child for calling me 'Nigger' and me for having the audacity to be upset.*

I could not see how the two acts merited the same discipline. As I saw it, the other child had just sunk to the lowest, most evil level of living by what he called me. All I had done was to try and run him down so I could make him see the error of his ways, and the ultimate consequence was that I was judged as being just as wrong as he was. My alienation grew like wildfire. In those moments, I learned something about how many people weigh the White perpetrator and the Black reactor on the scales of justice. *That, Mommy, was what I learned in school today.*

Mom did fly into indignant anger the one time she found out about one of those incidents, and stormed to the school, berating the principal for responding so casually to the incident. That meant a lot to me, but it wasn't enough. Safety was an idea that for others may have meant protection from physical violence and abuse, and the presence of a big home, solid money. My safety was bound up in protection from spiritual abuse come to me on the lash tip of denial, rejection, and devaluation.

Something in that principal's eyes when he spoke his judgment revealed an ocean of truth about how this nation, and many of the White people surrounding me, chose to deal with Black humanity. *I am not truly a part of this place, I cannot be.*

I carried a thin ground layer of fear, however rational or irrational, that at any time old hatred would boil over and the 'civilized' demeanor of Los Alamos would transform into a lynch mob come for me. I knew that hatred. I had studied it like my own face. For that reason, even in this generally tolerant and placid town, the back of my mind was a place where the possibility of my violent end settled in, waiting.

My nerves were seared by my unrequited need for those who raised a racial hand against me to receive their reckoning. Not finding sufficient enough punishment for the transgressors' actions in the light of a Los Alamos day, I retreated underground and retaliated internally. My dad had helped me to hang a red EVERLAST heavy punching bag in the basement, to indulge my passion for the sweet science of boxing. There was nothing sweet about the way I vented my rage on that bag.

Shirtless and gloved in worn, brown leather, backed by the radio on high volume, I destroyed all my demons for hours on end. Hook, hook, uppercut . . . *Nigger* . . . triple jab to the face, overhand right . . . *Black bastard* . . . hook, hook, uppercut, straight right . . . I was relentless. I cried as I punched, sweat and tears flew in a 10-foot radius. I was trying to cave in the Jemez mountains around me. Grunting, gritting, groaning, I kept on and kept on . . . digging at my pain, clawing to get out of the coffin of alienation smothering my soul. When I finally ceased, my knuckles were bereft of all skin, raw and bleeding. Chest heaving, eyes burning, I turned out the light, went back up into the house, and showered off my salty catharsis.

I assumed then that Greg's experiences with racial hostility were less numerous than mine because of his outgoing, charming personality. I know now that his exposure may have been more acute and frequent. Maybe it was because of his darker skin, or because of that very same outgoing personality. Maybe it was even because he touched an old and sensitive social nerve with his popularity with girls, most of whom were White. But somehow, my wounds imagined his wounds, and in that way became deeper. Greg was so warm and loving that it hurt me to know that every once in a while someone was throwing a poison dart his way. His skin was not as tough as it may have seemed. Sensing his wounds festering beneath his skilled disguise left me crying for him some nights.

The malefic wind didn't have to blow directly Greg's way for him to receive the stench. His dance was a teeter-totter tune, much like mine. He loved people who loved him but rankled at his race. The contradiction crept from its costume and bared its teeth at Greg, a cruel backstabber. When Greg's good friend, Harl'o, an African American from South Carolina, moved to town when Greg was a sophomore, Contradiction roared. Harl'o came up to Greg one day and asked, "Are those friends of yours?" pointing at a group of Greg's best friends.

"Yeah," Greg answered, nervous with an intuition of what was coming.

"They called me Nigger." That's all Harl'o said. That's all he had to say. Between two Black youth, the message was clear: *Those people you call your friends have a hatred for the Black in you just as surely as they do for the Black in me. What are you going to do about that?*

Greg didn't want to believe they had uttered that word to Harl'o, but he knew better. Harl'o was 'that kind' of Black. The kind that riles 'those kinds' of White people. The White people whose fears breed internal hate. Soon after, Greg overheard those friends in the locker room speaking the same hate. The confirmation stretched him thin as a silk strand. Only he was not nearly so strong. Pieces broke off from his wholeness and slid into the sea of his despair. *Who am I? Who are these people I call my friends? Everything around me is spinning now and a lie. Who do I tell? Not Mom or Dad, I don't know how. Not even John, I am too ashamed.* Yes, there are tricksters in the desert, and love can be a grand illusion. My brother's life changed forever then. And though I wasn't aware of the incident as a concrete thing, I felt its pulse. My passionate disgust for prejudice marinated in my brother's tears.

Greg and I were destined to be viewed, at least somewhat, as 'the boys who cried wolf'. No one would ever know how often or in what way we were being scalded. Yet, several times I was told how happy I should be to have grown up in such a wonderful, tolerant place. I don't know how many times I heard that I never had to deal with many, if any, racial incidents. Apparently the people who made these comments didn't take the time to realize that they weren't by my side most of the time things happened. Their view of what I did and did not experience was based on an incomplete reel of my life's film, a skewed and self-serving perception. It frustrated the peace out of me to have my interpretation of my life questioned consistently.

People are quite effective at not seeing what they aren't looking for. Those persons who cared for me were pained to consider that I might be exposed to any kind of racial animosity. I saw them literally wish it away from their minds' possibility. I saw the pain most vibrantly in Dad's soulful, almost teary eyes—the absolute desire to have his son free from that kind of rejection. His recognition of my emotions seemed almost to be a flashback for him, to his own brand of childhood alienation.

My loved ones and peers also weren't tuned into the presence of racial prejudice around me because of a very simple and forceful aspect of human nature—self interest. They weren't the subjects of the aversion that darted in and out of my social interactions. This allowed them to move other concerns to the top of the ladder of their priorities: popularity, intimate relationships, academic performance, politics, . . . the rest of life. My days were spent brushing by a totem pole of priority and preoccupation, decorated richly, but crowned at the top by my race and everything it yielded. That totem pole was everywhere I was—in my bedroom, in the front yard when

I left the house, at school when I arrived in the morning, in every store, restaurant, and public space I visited.

Most often my parents' capacity for dealing with racial wounds left them only one way to comfort me. They dressed down the offending action and my resulting wound as being less than what I perceived them to be. It was similar to when they attempted to soothe my banged up knee after a bicycle accident by tenderly telling me, "You'll be all right. It's not that bad."
It is that bad.
Sometimes, it was helpful for me to hear alternative ways of interpreting an experience. Being a child, I am sure that I often failed to see the whole picture. But the minimizing and rationalizing became too consistent a pattern of response. While my parents were trying to diminish my hurt by making things seem less ominous, I was receiving another message. Their responses began to suggest to me that they felt I was seeing things that weren't there; and that I was making a whole enchilada out of what was simply a tortilla, so to speak.

Maybe what I really wanted, in those moments when I returned home from the day's blue skies and rain, was to have honest and explicit conversation with my parents—where I could ask questions and they could explain humanity, as they understood it. Conversation about why people are prejudiced; why so many White people have the kinds of feelings and ideas about Black people that they do; why Black people are not what those prejudices claim; what was it about being Black that I should be feeling good about. I wanted us to walk verbally through that unfortunate valley, together, turning over the rocks that revealed ugliness, kicking clutter from my path.

I didn't realize that they might not have been able to have that conversation with me, because they might not have ever had it with themselves. What in their lifetime would have forced them to face that ugliness until it hurt? Would I have consumed myself in Black legacy if I had not been kin child to its swallow sea?

My parents weren't constructed for such conversations. Mom wasn't given to long talks about things outside her immediate priorities. She could talk to you for days about raising children, but broad philosophical discourse was for the deep thinkers and intellectuals. She came from farmer and railroader stock. She matured in the gloaming of girlhood's surrender to grownup practicalities. Things like, "just get by," and "toughen up," and *Handle this crisis right here before me, right now*. Perhaps I was no different. For me, my crisis was often race, and it was before me, right here, right now.

Dad was expressive when inspired, but otherwise his voice, as if to balance Mom's, was a minimal, truncated offering. Then his energy would shift and, in spirit, he just wasn't there any longer. You could feel him out there, perhaps drifting back to his own boyhood moments or into that boundless acreage where isotopes and ionic particles roamed free like stallions, the stars in his subatomic dreams.

My shell grew thicker. I developed a strong habit of not telling my parents about racial incidents. I didn't want to upset them, or be told again just to ignore it. I sought to avoid Mom's silent anger: *Damn them for hurting my baby.* And her anguished frustration turned toward me: *John, why do you have to be so sensitive?*

I didn't wish to again have a hell moment in my life's scrapbook be diminished with a quick philosophical statement from Dad—"Some people are ignorant. You just have to ignore them." I didn't want to call attention to the life experiences of mine that were unique from the rest of the family. I wanted to belong.

But I did wish. I wished that just one of those times, my parents' response would be something that filled me up, satisfied the ache. I had no idea what those words would have been, not then. But now I know them, and they roll like this:

"You know, it must be a painful thing for you to look different than everyone around you, and to have those people with tainted hearts look at you through prejudiced eyes. It must be difficult having no one in your life who can relate to what it's like for you being Black in this White family; this White town; this White society. It must be hard to feel badly about what you know has happened to other Black people in this country, and not have people around with whom you feel comfortable sharing those feelings.

"We can relate to how it feels to stick out, but we can't assume what it must be like to be surrounded by the very group of people that has done Black people the most harm. We respect that it is hurting you deeply, even if we don't fully understand the pain itself. There is nothing wrong with the fact that these things are hurting you. We will always grant you the right to struggle through this. This is the way we can be here for you, and we will."

Even outside of my family, I rarely spoke of racial incidents. I had learned that the common responses would be disbelief, patronization, and irritation that I had brought up the issue of race. If anything, I minimized and largely swept under my emotional carpet much of what happened to me. I could not afford to dwell on those incidents—they were too many. Like so many millions before me, though I did not know it, I carried the weight and went on.

With each passing year, I became aware of an apparent contradiction between Mom and Dad's backgrounds, personalities, and lifestyles, and the fact that they had adopted Greg and me. I began to wonder: *What is really in Mom and Dad's hearts? They don't seem connected at all to this aspect of me.* I developed a need to understand what they felt about Black people generally, and in that way become secure in how they felt about me in particular.

My curiosity about Mom and Dad's racial attitudes began almost as soon as I developed an understanding that there were many people out there in the world who didn't like Black people. At that point, I became a stealth shadow to my parents' conversations. I paid close attention to the tone and substance of rare comments my parents made about the few Black persons in town. I hovered right up over words as they came out of their mouths when they spoke about Black actors, entertainers, athletes, and leaders. It meant the world to me when Dad spoke affectionately of Muhammad Ali. When Mom expressed an enjoyment for Nat King Cole, Diana Ross, or some other Black vocalist, warmth became an internal blanket that covered me through the night.

I didn't notice them ever speaking with any depth to each other about their opinion of Black leaders. I was looking for more than appreciation of entertainers. Connections between my parents and I were too few for my peace of mind, so I searched with the seriousness of a boy consumed with his place in the world. I had received a broad message from my parents about how all people should be treated the same, but this told me little about how my parents felt specifically about Black people. How did they explain, for their own concern, Black poverty that spanned generations? I gained no clear answers.

There weren't many Black folk for my parents to socialize with in town, so I couldn't very well judge their inclination in this regard. But those rare times we came across other Black persons, I was watching Mom and Dad. I tuned in to tone of voice, eye contact, facial expressions, body language, energy— everything. Usually, there was not much to pick up beyond a general acknowledgment of the other person's presence, a friendly hello, or a quick and shy smile. I was gathering priceless insight. It was my opportunity to peer into that secret place in my family's collective heart and understand something more about my place in their lives. This was all scarce fluid I was seeking and siphoning to feel good about myself. I was a maddened child social scientist, tuning out the world as I sought data for my hypotheses, light to illuminate my theories:

Knee high then waist high
I watch you absorb you
crane to catch sight of you being me
being me happy as good things happen

to brown faces on the screen
being me sad as same souls surrender
being me talking about caring about
wondering about planets that churn up
my personal gravity calling me carving me
chest high I sigh softly silently wanting so
badly to see you
seeing me

As I grew older, I developed an awareness of subtle racial attitudes that my parents harbored, especially Mom. My parents were no different than so many other White families, including families who had adopted Black children. They had grown up White in American society. No such person fully escapes the ideas and emotions of the U.S.'s prejudice toward African Americans, not without first experiencing some kind of transformational, painful reckoning. I did not believe that my parents had ever been forced into that reckoning.

It was not that I felt my parents hated or disliked African Americans. They were openhearted to everyone they came across. They taught that lesson as a matter of priority to their children. But accumulated moments led me to sense in them a distinct yet slight discomfort with the *idea* of African Americans. It was a hard-to-grasp but tangible combination of barely perceptible discomfort with spending time in Black environments, and interacting with Black persons. More importantly it had to do with what was not said.

It felt to me that they had a verbal and energy block when it came to discussing, in a natural way, anything having to do with Black Americans as a group. It just didn't feel natural to me. The energy seemed like that energy you get from someone you try to engage in a conversation about something that makes them uncomfortable.

That kind of discomfort is truly prejudicial, because it emerges from a categorical prejudgment of people, even if the prejudgment is not overtly negative. You cannot have discomfort for a group of people unless you have in some way prejudged that individuals of that group share characteristics that discomfort you. Though seemingly benign, I knew this to be the core of prejudice—seeing individuals as a homogenous group. Prejudice was a projection of sameness that blotted out divine uniqueness. The extreme, hate-laced attitudes I witnessed in the world were another story. My more immediate concern was with this silent, covert attitude in my family.

I developed this sense that for my parents, Black people were these 'other' people, somehow separate from people in their lives. My deductions led me to a contradiction that halted my attachment to the family. *If Black people are something separate to my parents, how can I, a Black person, be a part of my parents?*

I began to see that prejudice was not an evil within evil people, but that it was a human flaw within most all people. This was what living in this world did. It made pure hearts fecal hosts. I saw that good people can be prejudiced, and that certainly White families who adopt can also be prejudiced regarding the race their adoptive children represent. Adopting us had never been sufficient evidence for me that my parents had positive, easy regard for African Americans in general.

As I moved into my adolescent years, and I studied the nature of my relationships with friends and others in Los Alamos, I learned well the nature of prejudice. There were those people whose wells were tainted. On the cold, hard floor in the basement of their souls, two energies lay side by side. The one, a festering racial negativity, unleashed the fumes of decay as a bath onto the other, the inherent tendency toward love. The contamination did its damage until it was hard to tell the two energies apart. In fact, they rose as one convolution into the main chamber of the soul. There, that tainted love expressed itself outwardly in human relationships as a grievously contradicted personality.

I saw how the minds of people who cared for me had a powerfully effective way of fragmenting the world to allow existing prejudices to breathe. I saw how Black babies were decidedly less threatening than Black teenagers or adults. Their race could be excused into a corner of the mind. Their physical features were experienced as exotic, unique, and cute. Their heritage and the meaning of their future social personality went easily without ponder. Strong and enduring negative racial attitudes could remain dormant and somewhat undisturbed while families went about adopting and loving children of that very category of people.

White people I grew up with told me numerous times how they liked me because I was 'different' than other Black people. The message couldn't have been clearer if they had splashed it on my face as paint. I had heard their general conversations, and their negative and presumptuous attitudes toward African Americans and other ethnic groups were obvious. When they told me I was exempt from their prejudice, it only injected me with more dissonance and conflict. I wondered whether those I grew up with, including my family, were less comfortable with me as I grew into being more like 'other' Black people.

No one ever did me a favor by liking me as an exception to his or her rule about Black people. I felt that if a person had a problem with African Americans, she or he had a problem with me. More divine words exist for the things my spirit demanded: *In as much as ye have done it unto the least of these my brethren, ye have done it unto Me (Matthew 25:40)*. I feared that whatever it was Mom truly felt about Black people, however mild, would reach out of her chest one day, spiting me down. I feared I was forever within one violation of the 'Act White' code of being banished.

I had an extra sense that picked up the slightest tremor of racial aversion, or even racial 'otherness'—the spiritual state of my disconnection from others. My sensitivity for picking up this vibration was jacked up past maximum. It helped me survive. I could feel that peculiar energy in Mom as she related to me. Her skin perspired it. Her words betrayed it. I knew it. The friction within me was rubbing me raw.

When a child's human relations are not what he needs them to be, sometimes he is lost to that human world. But sometimes he is fortunate to be carried by impulse to seek out that Greater Spirit and the Mother Earth that is Its flesh. I grew close early on with the natural world as a place next to which I could breathe and be naked in my personality. As young as the age of three, I spent extended time with ants, butterflies, ladybugs, caterpillars, and every other insect I could find.

Mom allowed me to begin my own garden in the back yard, next to hers. It was meditation for me to prepare that rich dark earth, to plant the seeds, water the sprouts, and watch the sunlight beckon the emerging green life like a snake charmer in the sky above. I grew morning glories, daisies, sunflowers, radishes, tomatoes, carrots, corn, squash, and a few other plants. This was Mom's culture. It was what she had watched her father do when she was a little girl, and now it was a pleasure I shared with her. It was Dad's culture also, for his mother and father had coaxed life from the Earth when he was young. But more than that, this garden—that soil—was silent, giving, and received me without ambivalence. I did not fear rejection from it. Not with the way it clung beneath my nails and filled my lungs with its fertile bouquet. Not with the way it needed me.

The world of people was unpredictable and cloaked in a way that forbade me from knowing precisely how I was being regarded. Here, in nature, the reception was faithful. The canyons around our home were blankets I pulled around me as I walked deep into them—into their forested domain. In the shade of pines, cedars, willows, and cottonwoods, I studied entire ecosystems of insects living in the water of streams, wondering how they regarded one another. Scorpions, rattlesnakes, centipedes, tarantulas, and black widows with red hourglasses on their bellies competed for the title of most menacing. I found salamanders beneath logs, tadpoles in evaporating ponds, and snakes, horned toads, and lizards scampering at my feet. Rather than being afraid, I was comforted. With them I felt normal, just another variety of life in their world. They didn't doubt my humanness.

There was a reservoir of water in a canyon, a few canyons over from our house—not far, if you are a child eager to explore the wilderness. Miles become the candy treat of your travels. I spent hours there next to that reservoir, gazing out at the smooth reflecting surface, skipping stones and watching the ripples they caused move toward shore, then bounce back and become a reunion with the others. *Predictability: water returning to itself.* I picked raspberries, strawberries, and blackberries from their thorny perch surrounding the shore. I caught crawdads from the water with plastic cups, buckets, and small aquarium fishnets. I fished for the trout lurking beneath the muddied currents—more entranced and awed by their mysterious nature than interested in capturing a meal. Deer were everywhere. I knew black bears, mountain lions, and elk were tucked away in the woods, not too far out of sight. I was not a Nigger in this place. I was not even 'there', in myself. My spirit had traveled out into the water, bathing in total surrender.

Then there was the Jemez. Our town was set in the breast of that great mountain range. Rising above the community, the Jemez was a defining backdrop of life for the area. The mountains were much like a wise, enduring father figure, sitting still and giant, enticing me to come and sit in his lap. On the road driving up into the Jemez, I looked out at the scenery blurring by. My eyes caught red swatches of Indian paintbrush flowers dotting the ground beneath white-barked aspen trees that shed themselves in sheets of paper, revealing black undercoats. That mountain road was swallowed in aspens, cedars, small-sized gambrel and pin oaks, maples, elms, and a tossed timber salad of pines: juniper, piñon, ponderosa, blue spruce, Douglas fir, and others. In the fall, an arboreal display was unleashed with all the flash and grandeur of fireworks on Independence Day. Oranges swirled; Reds shook their hips.

The Yellows tap-danced on the Greens. When great trees blush, what can a small child do but imagine Wonderland?

At a high plateau in that wonderland, the mountain suddenly opened up into a gaping sea of grass. The Valle Grande (the Great or Big View) was the caldera or crater mouth of the largest extinct volcano in the continental United States. The caldera was 14 miles across—the largest in the Western Hemisphere. It had reached its maximum height 1,000,000 years before, and then blew, releasing a discharge of a force 100 times greater than the eruption of Mt. Saint Helens. It now stretched outward as a giant sea—bare of trees and carpeted in a low-lying grass grazed upon by thousands of cattle. The grass was a green blanket of waves undulating to the seductress mountain wind. It was a dominating, almost unreal vision, especially for a child. Trying to escape to an alternate reality, I imagined I had traveled to an unknown and unpopulated planet.

My senses constantly sought some beyond place, even the rich coffee scent of piñon nuts roasting took me backward to the days when the ancient ones, the Anasazi, lived in that high desert land. I favored the cacti among all plants, because they were such an alien presence in the fauna panorama—bizarrely shaped, coated in thorny armor, and able to withstand intense drought. I identified with that character, and brought many species home to care for through the years. My only voice was the vibration of my being, and the harmony struck with this nature was all the communication needed.

It is a cold, rainy day and I am 15 years old when I discover the name for the kind of monster I am: Gila Monster. I am reading through stacks of magazines and books at the public library downtown and begin a slow descent into a fascination with the words I am reading about this peculiar reptile. It was a creature I had seen a few times in the wild myself. . . .

Gila Monster (definition):

The Gila Monster is one of only two venomous lizards, whose territory is the Southwest desert. It is a shy creature, among the surviving members of an ancient beaded lizard family. Spending most of its time underground, the Gila Monster is seldom seen. It is a living fossil, honored by primitive man, and if not carefully guarded, doomed by civilized man. It is a large lizard; its skin covered in colorful beads, with a big head, big feet, and varies in body color from black to coral pink. Young Gila Monsters can consume more than 50% of their body weight in a single feeding.

Gila Monsters do not have control over their venom. It is always injected instantaneously when they bite. Their bite is defensive and does not deliver enough venom to be lethal, however it does cause excruciating pain. Gila Monsters are hard to fool when in familiar ground. Their primary enemies are humans. *Couldn't have said it better myself.*

age 9 months
What an adorable little baby
age 3 years
that's a cute child
age 5
my, isn't he handsome
age 7
look how he's growing
age 9
isn't he a little old to be trick-or-treating?
age 11
I wish he would smile more
age 15
Honey, just what kind of relationship
does he have with our daughter?

THE LAST HALLOWEEN

IT was the season of the color change when the end of my childhood came. I was 10. That fateful Halloween evening I was revved up for another round of trick-or-treating. My sweet tooth was serious, and this night was its euphoria. When the aspen leaves started showing off their chameleon color change and the temperature dipped, that's when I fantasized about a pillowcase bulging with candy.

This particular Halloween started out like all the others: walking the neighborhood, hitting any lit porch that seemed halfway welcoming. I came to a house, one I would deliver newspapers to in years to come. I stood, alone, on the porch, a greedy grin plastered on my face as this neighbor's door swung open. In the next few seconds that grin and the remnants of my innocence vanished.

"Trick-or-treat!" I held out my bag.

An older woman, white-haired and blue-eyed, clenched the partly open door. Her eyes froze me. They were eyes of fear. She hung back, partially obscured behind her door. Then her voice dressed her facial expression with disdain. "Aren't you a little old to be trick-or-treating?" she said. She didn't so much as say these words as push them out and against me, as a whip to chase me off her property.

Shock hit first, then hurt. I didn't know what to say. My face went slack; my body slumped. My chest throbbed as though she had punched me with all her weight. I descended from her porch having said nothing. *All alone in this.* I said nothing to my parents. I dropped hot scalding rejection into my pillowcase and went straight home. It was then that I knew playtime was over. The teddy bear had become a grizzly bear.

At that time, I was about average in height for my age and still slender, so I knew my size could not have intimidated that woman. What I saw in her eyes when she opened the door was a look I had seen before. It was unmistakable aversion. It was the things under my bed; the saber-toothed things that chased me through the indigo haze. I can't recall what costume I wore that night, but the costume did not matter to that woman, my neighbor. What mattered to her was the permanent mask I had coating my face. I was discovering—as I did that evening—that my mask could act at times as nature's most powerful repellent. I was also learning that the adult Black male had long been America's truest bogeyman.

Becoming a grizzly bear is an amazing transformation. The change unleashed in others their truer emotions and strains of racial regard. What before might have been ground water, moving privately through water tables of their hearts, now was at times sent violently up and outward in geyser plumes of revelation. My changing adolescent persona and physical size elicited in others a more honest release. Parents of some female friends looked at me differently now, surely in part because their daughters and I had both reached that age that causes parents insightful panic. But in a few cases I saw another, more disturbing element in the way they held me—one that was familiar and haunting. Merchants in stores and adults around town seemed to look on me with a more polarized split: the usual affection, or distanced ambivalence, if not discomfort.

Racial prejudices that had been latent when I was younger were now emerging around me, as I began to more closely resemble that figure of so much scorn: the adult Black male. I learned up close and personal, in Los Alamos and elsewhere, that people truly feared Black males in a way they did not fear Black females. We lived in a microcosm of the larger White society, which provided me a constant laboratory in which to digest these human relations.

My maleness was evoking too much of something. Too many Black men had portrayed too much violence and transgression on too many television and movie screens. Something was *too much*. Maybe it was the combination of my size and people's fear of the imminent possibility of my sexual intrusion across racial lines. The pendulum was swinging in my social world quickly away from that primal inclination to react with easy adoration to my previously small and vulnerable toddler and child image. I was reminded of Kunta. The psychic scars on my back raised up like cackles. I was on alert, aware that I was being seen, if only by a few, as a sexual being, a powerful being, dangerous and unpredictable. I unknowingly absorbed those expectations, and took on their image.

To my family, I would become in a solemn, troubled way, that dangerous, unpredictable creature I was expected to be. The more I turned inward, gliding on my adolescent inertia toward independence, the more I agitated against my family as the scapegoat for the racial negativity I received outside the walls of our home. When Mom snapped at me in frustration over my typical juvenile sloth, self-centeredness, laziness, sarcasm, or angst, I transformed her energies into a racial stab even before the wave reached me. I snapped back. Sometimes my response was more than anything a cry, a wish to be taken into her arms and comforted, like when I was small and milk-starved. Sometimes my snapping back was over blood spilt away from home by a hurtful interaction that day, or from a month before, or from all the years before.

By the end of my 15th trip around the sun, I was crusted with a protective wall and harbored a fatal imbroglio in my unseen places. The face I showed at school had a smile on it; the moods I exhibited at home were unpredictable and perilous. Privately, I often wished I could die. I was not suicidal. More than anything, I desperately needed a way to escape that emotional storm battering my heart. I wanted it to end. I was a water balloon stuck on the faucet too long, at the verge of swelling to explosion.

For a decade and a half, I had kept just about every drop of this particular anguish contained. I had no faith whatsoever that my family or anyone else wished to or was capable of finding compassion for my experience. I clawed at my chest and prayed nightly to a God I did not yet understand for my deliverance. My prayers were mournful. *God, why have you placed me here? Why did you make me a freak like this, ugly like this? Please, take this pain out of my chest. Bring me back to where I belong.* I became fixated upon this God presence as a possibility for the end of my suffering. I came to know this Divinity in desperation. The relationship was strong yet misguided. God was everywhere, an intense hum filling my ears. I opened up and received all that I could of this . . . River. It flooded me. I swam not with it but against it. I was lost.

Hot tears, long nights, and my adolescent hormones ratcheted my emotional pain up to the maximum I could tolerate at that time. The pain bore a hole through the place where my stability should have been. It led me into perilous places, desperate to have someone pay attention and see me for the deeply insecure and frightened sinkhole I was. *Little Johnny so loved and popular. He has it all. Everybody loves him; they love him at home, at school, on the basketball court, on the prom court. Everywhere he goes, he is loved, loved, loved.* I hated, hated, and hated myself. That self-rejection, along with my need to escape from my own skin, took me too far into the indigo.

I needed to scream but felt stifled beyond reason. So I grew more self-destructive—knotted into an emotional cactus whose quills drew blood from my family. Why does the drowning man flail in the water? Is it to keep from going down? Maybe he flails because the drowning has unleashed his strongest instinct—the instinct to make someone, anyone, notice that he is about to die.

In the daylight, I walked the schoolyard with a wide smile, my natural love for people taking over the abyss. No one could have known the terrible theatre of my mind. In the Los Alamos summers monsoons came, carrying predictable afternoon thunderstorms. Those heavy, pregnant clouds would break and wash the Earth with God's tears. I could never bring myself to release like that. Each successive year crawled forth from the skin of the one before, like the high desert rattlesnakes I also avoided. I kept swelling up, getting heavier and heavier.

I am certain that my life was saved my 15th year, when I somehow mustered enough trust to share my broil pot with another human being. Maybe it was desperation more than trust that drove me. Perhaps that mountain of emotional sludge had no choice but to eventually burst outward, and overwhelmed any need for trust. I released that torrent in one conversation, then again in many others, all to one classmate of mine. In that pivotal season of my life, she came forth as my Saving Grace. Her name was Beckie, a blonde, green-eyed girl who sat behind me in geometry class.

Only days into that fall semester, I started to notice Beckie's presence behind me. Whenever I turned around and glanced at her in the seat behind me, she smiled back so genuinely. The appearance in her eyes was unfamiliar to me.

She had the penetrating gaze of a person who is witnessing the true image of your soul.

I could see in Beckie's eyes and body language and feel in her energy something different, something somehow cleaner. I could always feel people trying to break through the sheath of their negative prejudice or their discomfort and extend me their cleaner heart. Like a hatchling trying to break through its eggshell. In many interactions, the person on the other side was struggling to pierce that layer to some degree or another. The vibration of that person's struggle was like teeth grinding, or sweat building, or a pulse disturbed. Sometimes it was gentler, like the strain of a butterfly achieving flight. But the strain was usually there, even with those who loved me most.

Beckie, though, held me in a truthful light. Her perception of me neither avoided nor got caught in the quagmire of my race. Trust for her came easily to me. We quickly became close friends. The God that I had been praying to was bringing me a loving force into which I could spill my heart. I did, and Beckie received me.

The first time, during one of our long talks, I found myself dissociated from my own body. I was suddenly aware that I was floating above my own form, watching it speak words to Beckie that I had never before let pass through my lips: "It hurts me to be here, here in this world. I don't feel like I belong here. Sometimes the way that wave cuts through me is so powerful it's hard for me to keep a grip on this place. I am so close to letting go and just drifting out there, into whatever. Anywhere but here. This hurts too much. I'm an island. I've never let anyone come all the way onto my shore. Sometimes I think I could exist in total solitude. The sound of that solitude is a silence that soothes me. This place is too loud, no one sees me. No one sees me."

When I realized what was coming out of me, I was already a river flooding my friend. I overflowed 15 years of backed up, smashed down emotion onto poor Beckie. For whatever reason she felt safe to me, so I flooded her. I let her know how close I was to just letting go. I didn't know why she seemed so welcoming of this flood. But she was.

As she listened in that compassionate, empathetic key, a harmony was struck that kept my walls in disintegration mode. Pieces of the castle kept tumbling into the wash. I was baring things that had not seen the sun, and I could not stop. My lungs, having always felt suffocated to the point of near bursting, were now open wide, taking in virgin volumes of air. I surfaced from beneath a lifetime of troubled water no longer holding my breath. Crying was an understatement. My body heaved out of control. *Thank you, God.* There would be no holding back the river.

This was when the dying stopped. My spirit, limp and fading, held fast at the precipice, paused by its notice of this new light. The emotional pressure hissing away, I was no longer the staunch island I had convinced myself I must be. I had topped the peak of my multifaceted self-mutilation and before me the land sloped downward.

This great release happened at a time when I had just begun to mature enough to be able to articulate my troubled feelings. My growth and Beckie's presence met at a crossroads. If not for that meeting, I shudder to imagine the road I may have taken. Beckie's own pain may have allowed her to empathize with what I was trying to express. She seemed grounded in something my other friends did not: some kind of transforming trauma or epiphany. I experienced her as rain and not just water. Maybe her spirit was made to unlock the fortress I had built, to make me flow. I grew emotional roots and a connection with Beckie in a way I had not before. In that persistent, bruised compartment of my Black adopted identity I achieved a surrender that was unprecedented.

This relationship, this sharing, marked the beginning of my coming out of my long familiar shell. Muted recalcitrance faded slowly in the years to come. I had begun the long march toward speaking words to the person I was. My own voice had always sounded strange and foreign to me. Slowly I began to associate its sound with the familiarity of my being.

During the time that Beckie and I grew into friendship, a presence was drifting toward my horizon. I was unaware and unprepared, but it was providence and it had a plan. A monumental change soon would come, one in which Beckie would also play a role. It began with a moment when my skin was on display for thousands. I was on a basketball court, the famous Pit at the University of New Mexico.

The crowd was surging to the solos and combos of two quintets getting after it. I crossed half-court after a timeout was called. A wave of awareness hit me so hard and suddenly I almost fell back. The arena and all sound swirled to a stop. *My mother is here, watching me. My birth mother is here.* It was the first time I had so vividly thought of her. I could almost imagine her face. Scanning the crowd, I trembled, picking out brown faces in the sea. *Is that her? No. Is that her?* Powerful nakedness plucked the hairs on my skin and raised bumps of emergency. Adrenaline puffed up my breathing. *My God, she's here. What do I do? She's seen me.* I had crossed half-court. *Somebody call timeout.*

Even with Beckie's presence and the friendships of Kent, Dean, and others that I was beginning to depend on more for my happiness, peace was far from mine. Complication mounted. Friendship began to be the place in which I took solace and found joy, hastening my emotional drifting away from my family. But these friendships were themselves forged within a maze of emerging challenges to my sense of belonging. My peers and I were steadily growing into complex personalities that had outgrown childhood naiveté and purity. We began to extend into the conflicted haze of adulthood. Our social relationships increasingly were dictated by and constructed upon the hardening cement of our social attitudes.

The constriction now announcing itself across my chest was a thing called conditional love.

I had a feeling my friends were comfortable with me not just because of my friendly disposition. It also had something to do with the fact that as long as I existed there, in mind and spirit with them, I was a safe version of Black. But if I were to venture into the personality territory of most Blacks, I would have, in their eyes, entered a feral state. I would then be an untamed rogue outside of the boundaries of their fence of civility. My smile would not indicate warmth but sinister intent. My body would represent a receptacle of hardly restrained urges—toward sexuality, violence, and revenge.

In the avalanche of sincere caring and true friendship, there were intruders. Smiles and love taps came to me, indicators of acceptance, the popularity Kristin craved. "I like you, John," was the message; even, "I love you, Man," which would have been all a child needed except that most often there was an underground river running beneath that affection and acceptance. It had its own voice. "I love you, Man," . . .

As long as you don't:
play that music
wear your hair that way
walk that way
talk that way
eat that way
hang with them
believe that way
show a glint of anger over
what's been done to your people
blame me for what my ancestors did
hundreds of years ago
[Slavery: 100 years ago=1 lifetime. Segregation: 20 years ago=1 childhood]

My spitfire response:
Your ancestors still are doing it,
through you the past
is up in my face right this very day

And, of course, at this time sexuality was announcing itself all over our bodies and minds. I was now moving through the angst-ridden whitewater of adolescence. I was larger now, and my voice was deepening. Hormonal surges were crafting forth a sexual being, and an adult-sized body was making my emotions a more ominous contention. The air shifted so slightly around me. I was now starting to taste the world of adult relations, including its old and scarred beast of burden: the never-ending tragedy of 'us and them'. . . .

Mirror, mirror on the wall,
who's the . . .
Damn, my lips are too big

Black self-hatred was more than an idea. Its grip suffocated me. I was its whip-struck victim. Long before I had ascended the high ground of a girlfriend and a kiss, I clamped Mom's clothesline clips down on my nose, hoping that would force my nose to become narrower, like most everyone else's. I tightly pursed my lips, tucking them slightly inside my mouth to diminish their volume. Some moments found me staring at my skin, literally wishing it away. It was an all-encompassing scarlet letter, written in hideous hues. If I had had access to a bleaching cream, I would have bathed in it.

Despite the number of Hispanic youth around, some of them with skin darker than mine, I imagined that my skin seemed more offensive to the White people around me. Everything attractive was everything I was not. I only dreamed that any of the girls my age could be attracted to me. I was pathetically frightened around girls and it was obvious.

The few times during middle school and high school when a friend told me that a girl liked me, I wasn't close to believing what I was hearing. My confidence was so low that the girl could have told me herself that she liked me, and I would have spent that whole next night wondering if she could possibly have been telling the truth. *Maybe she has me confused with some other guy.* From the warped perspective of my self-revulsion, the Los Alamos of my childhood was a fairytale ball, with all my peers engaging in adolescent passion that I would never know. I felt myself to be so far out of the ballpark when it came to attractiveness and dating that I could not see somebody's interest in me even when it slapped me in the face.

I was jealous of the attention some of my White male peers received. I longed to have girls attracted to me, wanting me. The idea of a female liking me was such a strong fantasy that race hardly entered the equation of my desire. It wasn't as though I had a racial preference. I had virtually no choice. I was surrounded with White and Hispanic girls. That, along with getting to know them as human beings beyond their race, made it easy, in the flush of hormonal blossom, to find beauty in many of the places I looked. I could have counted on one hand the Black females anywhere near my age in town, with fingers left over to snap.

The fact that some of my friends assumed I would be automatically attracted to those few Black girls was another irritant to my raw social identity. They pointed out the rare sighting of a Black female my age walking by and said: "There's one for you."

"One what?" I bit back. *These people actually think I should be happy to get with any Black female I come across. What are they saying, I'm not good enough to date other girls? That if a girl is Black that should be enough for me to like her? Am I an animal for breeding in their eyes?*

My friends may have only been trying to be sensitive to the possibility that I would be attracted to girls of my own race. That's not how I took it. I was already in a chronic state of alert for signs that I wasn't fully considered a part of the group, a part of the *thing*. The thing the White and even Hispanic youth were blessed with: Belonging. My defensiveness had me reading between every line spoken and unspoken. My net was vast and always on the ready. Sometimes it caught hold of the truth, and left it flopping around in the sunlight, revealed. Sometimes it caught my fears or imagination. Either way, I consumed whatever catch I took in on a particular day.

There's one for you. Those words gave me insight as to how distant and homogeneous the notion of Black people was to my peers. Many of them didn't look at the few Black people they encountered and ever get past the color of their skin to notice how attractive they were or weren't. Or what their eyes said about their soul. Or what their smile or their walk said about their personality. To them, these were just—Black people. Objects drifting at the periphery of their social world. An object being easy to toss together, that is what they did. *You're a Black person, she's a Black person—you two should go together.* Despite a certain amount of validity to the idea, given my need to be related to, I hated that presumption. It set me aside, apart, away from my social group.

My racial self-image was so low that I was far from able to feel good about the few young Black women in town and their appearance. I was attracted to a couple of them at different points through the years. The feeling caused me shame. Shame because I believed that if my classmates knew they would judge me negatively. As if I had revealed my inferiority or difference by being drawn to a person who was a 'Them'.

Around the time of my high school graduation, I heard from a friend that a younger Black student had a crush on me. I didn't know the younger girl well, but she was sweet and attractive. I could not allow myself to cross the line into embracing in such an intimate way something of the Blackness I had spent 16 years learning to neglect and deny. I propelled my heart away from responding to her affection. Mustering up 'being Black' in the eyes of my White social world was a task beyond my shrunken spirit. My sickness was this far down the road. To Rudy, or Anna, or the rest of my family, my skin may have only been a colorful addition to the diversity of the family. It was my code for torment.

It took me five months to work up the courage to kiss my first real girlfriend. I was a senior in high school. She broke up with me after three months, believing I wasn't attracted to her because I had barely held her hand in all the time that we were 'going steady'. I was anything but steady. I was a wobbly, whimpering mess. It had taken an act of God for me to ask her out the first time. Three months later I was still trying to figure out what she saw in me. *Fat lips, broad nose, ugly Afro, skin too dark. What do you want with this? Everybody's going to look at you, like they look at me. Do you really want to be a part of that?* When we graduated, she wrote in my yearbook that I was 'the most handsome guy in the school'. I thought she was clowning me.

When we broke up temporarily following that initial three months, I was crushed just as badly as any first-love puddle of a boy. I assumed she had finally realized I was Black. Either that or she had begun to get hassled for dating me and couldn't deal with it anymore. When a mutual friend of ours told me why she had broken up with me, I went begging back to her, pleading the extent of my love. We got back together, but in the ensuing months the poor woman still had to deal with my extreme shyness.

Her parents were the kindest spirits, but I was still almost halted into idiotic nervousness around them. I feared they might be troubled that their daughter was dating me. My eyes watched their every vibe. I applied my personal litmus test every time we interacted, but I could come up with little evidence to confirm my fears. That situation was a good example of why I was so well mannered. It wasn't so much because I had been raised so well. My manners were rooted in my fear that people were just waiting for me to step wrong and become 'Black in effect', and not just in appearance.

Ecstasy smacked my lips like a lightning bolt one night at a youth dance at the community center. My girlfriend had finally had enough of my act. She threw me up against a post and took things into her own hands. She had me posted up like she was going after the last rebound of the state championship game. I wasn't getting out of this one. Her lips moved toward me with serious intent. *Contact.* I thought I had levitated but my feet were still grounded. *So, this is what everybody else has been up to. I can't believe this woman just kissed me.* Habit had me half-thinking she was going to raise up, offended, and slap me, even though she had been the aggressor.

She just smiled and said, "Finally, huh?"

Yeah, finally.

Sexuality was simple compared to the contradictions of love and racial disconnection I was working to resolve, with much less than success. I was developing ideas, morals, and beliefs about the world that were extensively rooted in my emotional investment in the lives and history of Black people. *How could everyone else possibly relate to the way I feel about life? Why would they care as much as I do about these issues?* I continued to match my values and opinions, in secret, against what my family and friends were expressing. What I noticed was not comforting. It ate at me that race was an off-limit topic in Los Alamos as a whole. I could only assume that people seemed to be so afraid of being labeled racist or prejudiced that they had learned to relate to those subjects as poisons to avoid at all costs.

The thoughts and conversations among my high school classmates were relatively world-wise and increasingly value-laden. And yet life at that moment seemed like it was to some of them a play world, a kind of fantasy enactment where everything on the surface was viewed as a matter of one-dimensional reckoning. Even if they did want to change the world, their identification of the source and the solution to social problems was often generic in a way that disappointed me. "We need to get rid of poverty, homelessness, and violence," someone would assert. But there was no cultural meat to the idea. There was too little exploration of why the problems existed in the first place, what U.S. American values led to the situation, or where those values came from.

Although I almost never spoke out on my thoughts about the issues, I knew which topics were considered an intrusion. Underneath the bland conversation was the ugliness and foul waste of immediate social inequities and prejudiced excuses for that inequity. When any of this was introduced, the reaction was as though someone had sneaked an undesired story line into the script. Too often it was marked out, and moved quickly beyond. I wanted it read.

A classmate in casual lunch-time conversation might express his impression of the difference between people in Los Alamos and Hispanic Americans in the neighboring valley of Española, or people in the Pueblos along the Rio Grande. Sometimes it was a condescending opinion. I wanted all conversation to stop that instant and focus on the underlying attitudes rooted in that comment. *Why the heck do you think they resent us up here in Los Alamos so much? There's a reason behind how they view us. They didn't just arrive at their current economic condition because of their nature. They had plenty of help getting there. Can't you guys see what's going on?*

Many of the students had racial attitudes that were liberal, but which lacked depth. Some were just ignorant and arrogant. Neither brand comforted me much or made me feel a part of this 'student body'. *If they feel this way about Hispanics and Indians, then I don't want to imagine what they really feel about Blacks.* My problem was that I did imagine. I couldn't help myself.

I wanted honest conversation between parents and their children or between my teammates on the basketball team; discussion between anyone about why Black people so often lived at the fringes of society—in poverty, undereducated, criminally engaged, engulfed in violence. All around me was a bizarre conspiracy of silence.

I found it strange how people so often dealt with a Black presence like a ghost in the room. As though it was taboo to verbally acknowledge that presence. The discomfort was a strong indicator to me that for them Blackness itself was not a neutral or natural substance; that they too had been touched by the poison fingers of socialization and made allergic to what they claimed didn't matter. *I don't care if a person is black, white, or purple, they say. I reply: Then why do you keep slipping when you walk across the colored paint?*

It was like having an affliction that no one wanted to bring attention to by mentioning it. *My race is not an affliction, at least it shouldn't be. But maybe in this world it is because I sure do feel afflicted. Why does almost every single one of these people seem completely unable to mention even the word 'race' or the word 'black'? All this emotional constipation and congestion is killing me.*

It wasn't a fear of speaking honestly about opinions they thought might offend or hurt me. I knew what that energy felt like. This was different. I sensed many of them hadn't worked through these issues much at all, even verbally with other White people. Their vibe was vacuous when I approached the subject with them.

It was the same hollow vibe that I would have emanated if someone had tried to engage me in a thoughtful conversation about quantum physics. I wouldn't have even had the language to grasp the concept that would have allowed me to enter the conversation. It was that kind of vacancy. The look a two-year-old gives you when you ask her why she spilled the milk. Blank. The investment just wasn't there. There was little accumulation, barely any residue of the substance that could be scraped from the souls of so many Black people if a spiritual autopsy were ever performed in the afterlife. And yet this was my current life, and I had to find a way to coexist with people I needed to love. People whose love I needed. All while enduring so much empty space.

Yes, I was a serious child. But then, I was swimming in the deep end of a substance for which I had received no mentoring or guidance. This was who I was and what I cared about. I couldn't help it that the way Black and White people, men and women, 'rich' and 'poor', related to each other weighed heavily on me. I didn't choose to be serious about it. Those things were serious all by themselves.

When your house is burning, you tend to think about flames. But for me to speak on those 'flames', that was not acceptable. I rarely mentioned when something had offended or bruised me for fear I would be called obsessive about race. It was like being held underwater and being told that I was obsessive about breathing. It was those who held me underwater who were obsessive about breathing, for they were afraid to let me have my breath. The hand with which they held me underwater was connected to the very fixation they scorned. You have to step through 'race' before you can put it to bed, get beyond it. Their avoidance caused it to bloat and metastasize. It flooded their lymphatic system and became them. In loving them, it became me all over again.

As I moved toward high school graduation, my racial attitudes were growing strident and indignant. This did not mean I was comfortable around Black people, or that I felt positive about being Black. What drove me, even from the clenches of my negative racial self-image, was a passionate anger over the condescending and superior attitudes streaming through the contradictory waters of our national culture.

Insecurities feasted upon me because I had never completely achieved a sense of being a part of 'this': this family, this community, this nation, and this cold humanity. The way Mom related to me at times gave me the impression that as her love for me grew, so did her fear that her dear child was now becoming more like that figure from across the racial fence she knew from her own childhood. That image she repeatedly saw as a schoolgirl in Peoria—that rejected, disdained, and somehow less fully human image. That 'different than', 'other than' being that was 'Them'.

She seemed to intuit what my moods, my anger, and my withdrawn countenance were about. It threatened her because it hurt and frightened her. Maybe it tapped into her own insecurity: *Do I have the right or the ability to raise a Black child, a*

Black young man? Either way, I triggered something in her, often causing her to snap back, not so much at me as at 'It'. It—that separate, forbidden essence.

I didn't understand all of this then, nor did I even have words for the energy I felt coming from her as she struggled to get me to let down my walls and come back to her. *Please, John, let me hold you again, sing to you again. I love you so much. I need you to know that.* What I did understand was that I could feel her nervousness in those moments when I departed too far from standard Los Alamos youth behavior or attitudes—characteristics of Whiteness that no one saw as having to do with their race or culture.

To my family, like most others, our lifestyle was simply 'the way we live'. My wounded translation of that indirect message was, "W*elcome to the way we do things. This is who we are. This is who we expect you to be.*" Usually, though, Mom had no reason to worry about my attitude or behavior, and was more than happy with how I was turning out. By that teen age, I was, in a very rounded way, a 'good' young man—the concept 'good' meaning all kinds of things sweet and soured. But that band holding me to cultural obedience was stretching.

For many reasons, I wanted to gravitate toward the cultural center of my environment. I wanted to be like the people in my family, because being like them meant making them happy. In turn, their pleasure with me was my great reward. The more they were comfortable and pleased with who I was, the fuller was my security and rooting—on one level, at least. The same was true with my mentality for seeking approval in the community. I burned with a desire to be liked.

But my racial essence and the particular cultural orientation toward which I was pulled stretched me like stale, brittle taffy. I began to break. I identified more with being Black by the day, but in order to be like Mom and Dad, or Kristin, Anna, and Rudy meant I had to stretch myself a certain distance to meet them at that point where their values, perceptions, and priorities orbited. I had to settle into that space with them. Sometimes I could do it. I could fall into that family flow that seemed so easy for them. I was able to focus on dinner conversation, trips to the store, watching television together, running into each other around town. I could do that, at times, and fill with the pleasure of it. Just being family. I could exist in that sweet ether for moments, days, and even weeks. Ultimately though, it was a joy I could not sustain.

Spanning that gap between my racial identity and my family and friends' cultural reality took a toll. It was like having my feet tethered to one side of the Grand Canyon, my hands to the other. I managed not thinking about the immense distance between the canyon sides and the canyon floor below for spans of time. Eventually, my mind and emotions would return to that suspension, that vulnerable mid-air position. Then my stomach would drop.

Early on, my parents may not have thought too often about the possibility that, as I aged, I might feel off-key from the note, and off rhythm from the cadence of our family. They may have believed that as long as I bonded well as a baby, the emotional attachment ahead would be a downhill road for me. Maybe they didn't realize that ultimately the attachment would have to be mutual. And that it would rest largely upon their effort and ability to bond with even my evolving racial identity. They seemed unprepared for what I was growing into.

I tried hard but could not get myself to consistently believe that my parents loved me, especially Mom. With the constant backdrop of my Blackness as a blatant reminder that I was not biologically from this family, I repeatedly tested their love. When things were good, they were good; but the moment even slight anger was hurled my way, the bottom fell out from my security.

It frightened me to think that I might never be able to feel attached to anyone, in any relationship. *Maybe that umbilical hernia has done irreparable damage after all.* In the fifth or sixth grade I finally had surgery to repair the hernia I had at birth. By then, I was in that age of the eagle, flying quickly toward my imperfect personhood.

So much of those first 17 years was happiness and brightness. It kept me afloat. I was given uncommon amounts of love and affection from my family and friends as the tonic for a ride some Greater Wisdom knew would be rough. Fissures erupted, shaping the way that I carried myself around the house. The crying, yelling, pouting, and extended silent treatment I doled out were acts of exasperation at not being able to effectively communicate my emotions.

Through my adoption, a new human personality with his own past, spirit, biological inheritance, and higher purpose had entered our family unit. A new family culture needed to have emerged from that injection. From where I stood now, 17 and teetering in a heart storm, one had not. Even with those blessed stability strokes of committed, loving parents under the same roof and generous social popularity, I was anything but stable. Like so many self-absorbed high school seniors before me, I was suffocating and could not wait to fly away. I was ready to leave my room, come out from under the bed and the blankets. The turtle was on the run.

". . . for the black folk thought of one John,
and he was black; and the white folk thought
of another John, and he was white.
And neither world thought the other world's
thought, save with a vague unrest."

(W.E.B. DuBois' *The Souls of Black Folk*. Chapter: Of the Coming of John)

KINSHIP EMBRACE

MY second birth was long and messy. The gestation had taken 17 years. By the time I was fully delivered from the womb of my youth, I would be 27 years old. Childhood is not nearly completed at age 18. Its true completion exists in the way we live out our adult lives—lives spent closing the punctures in our soul left over from early days, years spent riding the wave of blessings childhood so graciously granted us. My first brave and glorious act of 'adulthood' was to run away.

As I tried to decide where I would attend college, I knew two things: I wanted to get far away from New Mexico, and I wanted to go somewhere with more ethnic diversity—on campus and in the local area. I received a flood of brochures from schools around the nation. Plowing eagerly through them, I found myself fixating on a brochure from Florida A&M University in Tallahassee. I was both attracted and intimated by the brown-skinned faces that populated the brochure of this historically Black university. Unfamiliar with Florida, I imagined sunshine, beaches . . . and these brown-skinned faces. *What will they think of me? Will they laugh at the way I talk? How will I even begin to make friends with them?*

Ultimately, I was not ready to immerse myself in Blackness. I wanted that presence, but was afraid it would reject me. I could not take rejection from the other, distant half of my world. Had I been alienated from one half and rejected from the other, my esteem would have taken its final blow. I would be stardust, drifting forever in my solitary orbit. No, I needed a more gradual transition into what I sought. I left the possibility of Florida A&M behind, never knowing how close I had come to following an instinctive trail, like a homing pigeon, back to my biological roots.

I chose a small, liberal arts college in a suburb of Portland, Oregon. My understanding of its 'international' student body, as the school promoted it, was that it promised plenty of cultural diversity. Still, I knew this would be primarily a White environment. I did not wish to admit it, but it was what I felt most comfortable with. I would be able to play collegiate basketball there and not have it dominate my academics. It was a small, intimate campus. I was still a moonflower—retreating into myself in the light of day, daring to open up only under the cover of darkness. This would be a fitting location for my entrée into the broader world.

The labor that led to my second birth began the moment my family dropped me off on the campus of Lewis & Clark College the first day of my freshman year. I found myself in the shadow of another volcano. Mount Saint Helens loomed in the distance, towering over the horizon to the north. I was a socially young 17, but I was anxious to get away from Los Alamos, away from that isolated bubble, and take a breath on my own. I had never been to Portland or even the Northwest. I was excited and hardly intimidated—my mind was focused on this new environment, one in which my peers came from everywhere, and looked like everything.

The first birth contraction occurred when I entered my new dorm room, my family trailing behind me. The scenarios of my life played over in my mind as we approached the dorm building. My parents may have been going through their own parent ideas—whatever those might be when you are leaving your child for the first time to his own affairs a thousand miles away from home. As we entered the dormitory and began climbing the stairs to the third floor, my own thoughts were firmly revolving around one frightening thought. I knew that I would have two roommates, and I assumed that, as was par for my course, they would be White. I wondered, *How are these two roommates going to react when they see that I am Black?* I was sure they were expecting a White roommate.

I located the room at the far end of the hall. The door was open. Somebody was already inside. The hallway seemed to lengthen as we walked—an overture of drama. Life turned into a dream state, slow and separated from me. I swallowed hard and entered the room. Seventeen years of looking into the eyes of White people and processing their varied reactions to me had provided me with a keen sense of nonverbal communication. I could read a soul in much less than a second. My chest was tight. I felt the entire nature of my college experience was riding on this one brief encounter and what it might hold. The wrong response would sour my spirit. What I saw then was the foundation for my next four years.

I saw a young White man, blonde with stark blue eyes, turn and look at me. Our gaze locked into each other. I did not see even a flicker of aversion or discomfort. He may have been surprised to see that a Black person would be his roommate. But there was absolutely nothing in those eyes, in the movement of the muscles of that face that betrayed even a sliver of negative regard for the person he beheld. I had seen his heart. That's when I took my first breath. The dream state dissipated back into real time. My parents didn't even have to stay around any longer. I had just lost my need for their reassuring presence.

Eric Stone and I shook hands and introduced. His mother and stepfather, Patty and Vince Wixon, were also in the room and my attention turned to them as we shared our greetings. I looked with the same purpose into their eyes and faces, and found the same response. Eric's family and mine fell into the easy banter of two families meeting for the first time. Two families with the words, *These seem like nice people*, a calming refrain passing through their heads.

Later that day I met my other roommate, Matt Roth. I went through that same slow-motion moment with him, seeking the truth in his eyes. He showed me the same human embrace as had Eric. I knew this college thing was going to be all right. I had something here that I was very familiar with—living in an intimate space with White people who regarded me at least as a person beyond the fact of my race. So, the first reassuring step on the journey to my Black heritage occurred when I was sure my two White roommates accepted me.

Eric, Matt, and I quickly became the kind of friends who loved each other deeply, and genuinely sought out each other's company. Eric Stone—the actor/artist from Ashland, a small theatre town high in the clean mountain air of southern Oregon; and Matt Roth—the gifted and intensely competitive swimmer from Boring, Oregon, east of Portland.

That's right: Boring. Boring was a down-home kind of community. They held an annual bed race in the area. They actually raced beds down the street! I have to admit I even competed one time. In yet another of the surreal scenes of my life, there I was in a team, pushing a complete bed set on wheels down a street in the shadow of Mount Hood. The street was lined on both sides with a throng of cheering townspeople, just about every one of them White. In the middle of Every Town, USA, the only Black guy on the street was making like a member of the first Jamaican Olympic bobsled team. I felt just as out of place as the Jamaicans must have, and, like them, I enjoyed every moment of it.

Those were my roommates—Eric and Matt. Then there was me, the Black kid from a town over 7,000 feet above sea level, but still not high enough for me to touch the sky of my happiness. On a campus of 2,000 students we were a visible threesome—from the cafeteria to the dorm and everywhere in between. The relationship we formed was the nest that gave me strength to grow into myself, even as I found my roots in the arms of the scattered few Black students on campus.

I was still shy in those college years and, early on, I was noticeably quiet as I strained to gather my esteem in this new environment. The tonic for this was a campus life filled with friendly students, being a part of the basketball team, and drinking in my heritage from the other Black students with the desperation of a longhaired puppy rescued from the desert. Similar to my earlier years, I could count the number of Black students on campus almost with my two hands. For the most part, we sought each other out—subtle glances and greetings stuffed with recognition of our isolated circumstance.

At first, I was overrun with anxious anticipation each time I passed by or interacted with other Black students. *They're going to smell the scent of my background on me.* It meant the world to me that they accept me. I tried on so many variations of speech, walking style, and body language; it was a sad identity dance. I needed some way of being that fit. *Something Black enough to be accepted.* Something familiar enough that I could carry it off as natural to me. I found my entire rhythm evolving—my manner of movement, my attitude of being. It was like going through adolescence again. My mannerisms and clothing were inconsistent and ungrounded. I was auditioning forms of the Blackness that I would adopt.

I sensed a connective force leading the other Black students to gravitate toward me, despite my obvious social awkwardness. I felt taken in. A kinship circle was sensing my needs and responding. Their embrace felt like a reflexive response to support 'one of their kind'.

It helped that by self-selection, I had placed myself in the company of people who had a certain kind of background and personality. Though most of them had not been as racially isolated as I was growing up, most of these few Black students had experienced a significant amount of exposure to White culture and environments. It took that plus a particular kind of personality to exist and thrive at a school like this over the course of four years.

While I was at Lewis & Clark, we created an African American student group, which was to become an influential experience in the continuing evolution of my identity. Being able to sit around a table with those 8 to 10 people, freely talking about the issues that concerned us as African Americans on that campus was revolutionary for me. The campus events we organized and held, the speakers we brought in, the discussions—all of that was as pioneering to me as if I had landed on the moon. I began to give myself permission to think about and care about the issues that I had always suppressed.

You couldn't have found 10 personalities more distinct than the ones in our student group, but we were bonded by the bold and undeniable way we stood out in that campus community. We fed off each other with a palpable need, drawing strength from a group dynamic that made us feel that we had the right to be who we were. Even through all the arguments and personal conflicts we endured, we fed each other the sustenance of simply being able to relate to that one ominous part of our being.

My sophomore year, a tall, lanky African American freshman from Davis, California, enrolled at Lewis & Clark, and joined me on the otherwise White basketball team. Kevin Schultz also came from a White adoptive family, though our parallels stretched much further than that. Kevin's personality was eerily similar to mine. He was deeply sensitive, pensive, and passionately philosophical. He was a walking spirit, wounded, gifted, full of life and love. Our recognition of similar experience and nature in each other was immediate. Kevin and I became that constant mirror image reminder to each other, much like Greg and I had been all those years.

Our friendship was very unique among the relationships we developed at Lewis & Clark. Intimacy born of insight bonded us whether or not we wished it to be so. As we shared our responses to group conversations or different situations during the day, all it took was a glance from me, or an expression from him, and the other understood in an instant. The mirror we formed for one another was clean and clear.

That kind of intimacy can breed unease between two people as much as it can bring comfort. Just as with Greg, I spent much of the next three years catering to the dissonance I felt about Kevin. I basked in the reassurance of his presence in my life, on campus and on the basketball team. I also hurt for him, because his pain was as evident for me as the skin on his body. His hurt in turn recalled my own. Kevin was my joy and pain. The joy lay in the fact that he was the one person around who could understand, even among the other Black students. The pain came from the fact that . . . he was the one person who could understand. This left me naked in his eyes, which was new for me. Other than with Greg, I was unaccustomed to anyone being able to feel my vulnerability. To Kevin I must have been that small child desperate to feel good about being Black, just as I saw the same in him.

Being Black in a White environment is a never-ending audition, conducted mostly in obscurity. There is so much to express; so little encouragement to do so. Kevin and I told our stories to each other mostly through osmosis and nonverbal repartee. We carried each other through those years. All along the way, Kevin was backdrop to my brooding, foreground to my emotional ripening. My path from 17-year-old to senior took me steadily further from the person I had been.

Mundane moments were the most meaningful strokes of all. I had no car, so usually I was stranded on campus, away from the city of Portland. One of my friends, Lamont, from Southern California, began taking me into Northeast Portland with him to his barber. Northeast was the one certifiable Black community in the Portland area. His barber's name was Joe, and he was good people. I liked him right off because I learned that he was a boxer. Like Kevin, Joe was sensitive and philosophical. He filled his customers' ears from start to finish with his reflections on everything under the sun, especially those things race-related. Joe must have been about 30 at the time, and though he spoke with a manner many associate with the uneducated Black inner city, he came to be my prized professor and ebony wisdom tree.

I was a freshman at that time, and still a verifiable virgin to African American culture and personalities. I was intimidated and unsure when I first started going to Joe's shop. But I needed that experience. I needed to go into that neighborhood, step into that shop, and smell its distinctive scents. I yearned to bathe in the ebb and flow of conversation. Joe easily fell into a mentoring persona with Lamont and me. He always asked us how school was going and what we were into. I was shy, quiet, and caught in the glare of this new cultural flavor, but over time I gained ease and enjoyed stepping into those conversations with Joe.

Anybody who argued that there weren't distinct cultural pattern differences between White Americans and African Americans wasn't living in the society I knew. I quickly came to know the culture of Black barbershops well. It was a whole different ball game from the White ones I had known. Going to that barbershop in Northeast Portland wasn't just about hygiene, though the ease with which he cut my hair was a sweet and affirming change. *My hair is normal for this man. Free at last.* But more than hair care, spending time in Joe's shop was for me and the other customers about self-esteem as a Black man, working out frustrations, and bouncing your emotions off people who could relate. You went there to heal, to feel good about yourself, because when you went back out that door, you were back to the battle.

I had just come from dying of thirst in the desert. I needed Joe and I needed that barbershop, those people, that flavor. I learned years later that Joe had passed on. The sense of loss that came over me was bittersweet. My memories were of a Black man, doing what he loved, doing up hair proper for his people, swapping stories around the shop. And dropping knowledge all the way.

Throughout college, I was overjoyed any time I found out a woman was attracted to me. Mostly, I dated whoever took the initiative with me. I wasn't going to approach too many women; I was scared to death. College was my coming-out party in terms of dating, because it was then that I began to realize that *Maybe I'm not so ugly. Maybe some women could be attracted to me.* In the light of this dawning, it did not occur to me to discriminate over the 'kind' of women they were. But even in that season of ethnically diverse dating, an important root was taking hold.

For four full years at Lewis & Clark, I fantasized over and worshipped a beautiful, mysterious African American woman who played on the volleyball team. I tortured my friend, Char, endlessly, proclaiming my love for this God-woman I lusted for. Black beauty sashayed. I drooled and prayed. *Even angels, in their sleep, must dream and creep, through the forest where I clamber pines to seek the sky. Maybe she will lose her way and stumble upon me. Maybe in the dark she won't notice I am black and bruised. In that moonlight, I just might . . . occur to her as something beautiful.*

I was a stumbling, bumbling fool, brimming with hormone and longing, too frightened to even approach this woman, much less speak to her. Char was a true friend because I badgered her with my desires, needing her encouragement to go after the object of my obsession. I knew very little about this woman's personality and truly cared very little. I romanticized over her Black beauty. I watched her move around on the volleyball court, entranced by the sight of her rich brown skin, moving over taut muscles. She could leap out of the gymnasium—her athleticism was stunning. I was in love with her portrayal of my ideal of Blackness, which was more than enough for me at that stage.

It took alcohol, the darkness of a dorm basement party, and four year's worth of exasperation and arousal to bring me to approach her. I was Jell-O in her presence, except I lacked even that solidity. As I struggled for conversation like an eighth grader in over my head, she saved me from ultimate humiliation by taking the lead. "I like the way you move on the basketball court," she told me. The clouds parted in my sky. We danced. She was a bouquet in peak blossom against my chest. I was beyond heaven. I had scaled Everest. My head above the crowd, I surveyed my domain. Privately, I pounded my chest like a silverback gorilla. The dance floor was hot and tight, soaked bodies throbbing to stale house music. Black night crept into that basement room through a ground-level window and birthed indigo children. Though we were dozens dancing, cloaked in darkness, an illusion of similarity, it was a rare moment when I reveled in the splendor of my distinction.

Consummation? The moment on the dance floor was to be that for me. It was all I needed. My friends never heard the end of it. I remained too shy, insecure, and unconfident to pursue her further, but she remained in future years a dazzling symbol of my earnest entrance into the wonderland of the African American woman.

One factor in the change in my dating habits was the increased health of my self-image and self-esteem. I had slowly and deliberately constructed a positive view of my racial self through hard work once I stepped chilled and dripping from my long and ivory bath. I took on increasingly positive feelings about Black people. Along with that came a steadily more appreciative and attractive view of Black women.

I found hold in a proud river running within me, a certain nature that these women and I shared. My eyes opened to an incredible physical and spiritual beauty in these women. Awakened in me were memories from our shared distant past. Memories passed down to us through a spiritual ladder that spanned generations and bridged the existence of our people on varied shores. I was in awe of this memory. It shook me daily from the slumber of present time, and forced me to recall my ancestral past.

The more that I was surrounded by Black women, the more they became normal to me. From normalcy, they evolved into beauty. I had to graduate them up the rungs of my self-rejection. As they ascended, the rungs themselves disappeared. My attraction to Blackness in others was seed for loving my own self, long before I realized it. On the momentum of that boomerang, I waded in.

Few Black women were on campus at Lewis & Clark, but many more than in my hometown. More Black women lived in the city of Portland. Still not enough, but more than I was used to. This trend would continue later, in California, and eventually in Washington, D.C. By the time I finished graduate school and moved back to Portland for a year, I was not only living in a distinctively Black community for the first time, but was also socializing almost exclusively with Black women. Not because of any political agenda or prejudiced selectivity, but because after all those years, it was something I needed desperately. I had reached that line. *I can't take it any longer, explaining basic emotions to people who look at me from across transparent panes and wonder what my problem is.*

In the years to come, I would finally feel like I was not being deprived of the rightful opportunity to be around a plentiful number of Black people. The White people I had known were almost exclusively themselves immersed in communities of White people. I had granted to them that this was a positive, natural circumstance. They rarely stopped to realize how they had consciously and subconsciously led themselves to such environments, places where a significant number of people appear, behave, and believe like them.

I was disappointed to witness in some of my college friends an awkward silence, and a few critical behind-the-back comments about how "He's hanging around Black people now." I was hurt and angered as these friends indignantly took my social drift as an act of betrayal. They could not stop seeing me as they wanted me to be: a person who was not like other Black people, who, on the inside, saw and experienced life just like them. Their reactions to my daring to form relationships with Black people told me all I needed to know about the conditional acceptance I had previously received from them.

My pleasure in having Black women around me was far from restrained to the dimension of dating and romantic intimacy. An intense current ran through me; I was able to look around me and see Black mothers, grandmothers, and little girls. Generations loving, arguing, and caught up in a melody: rhythmic, unbound, and unpredictable. That current stroked something long unattended inside me as I witnessed young and old, Black women living . . . just living. The opportunity to be among Black people living as people, and not having to imagine them as one-dimensional images from afar was not lost on me. I didn't take it for granted, though I knew many of those very same Black people took it for granted. How could they not? It was all they had known. I was envious of that kind of unquestioned oneness—Black folk just living. What a fantasy churned inside of me.

There was another cause for my attraction to Black women when it came to relationships. After so many years of being the distinctive 'Black guy' in White environments, I was tired to my bones of living like that. I realized that in a thing so meaningful as a relationship with a woman, I needed to have that person relate to me on at least that one level that caused me so much pain. A Black woman would not automatically understand every aspect of my Blackness as it had affected me. But, at least there was a level of shared reality in the racial dimension. I needed that as I moved forward in my life. I was tired and through with being the token.

My junior year at Lewis & Clark some kind of madness got into my soul and I decided I would register for a particular overseas study program. Lewis & Clark was a school esteemed for its international study programs. About 60% of undergraduates went abroad for a semester or two. Many of my colleagues were taking trips to countries populated mostly by White persons—European locales, Australia, England, etc. I had long since had my share of that cultural persuasion and made it known to whoever was in earshot. All I knew was that I wanted to travel to a place as culturally different from the U.S. as possible. I sought a place where I could blend into the local brown skin. The small and unassuming nation of Nepal would be that destination.

Nepal is a country distinguished by having Mt. Everest and the rest of the Himalayan mountain range as its northern border. Kathmandu is its capital and by far the largest 'metropolitan' area within the national borders. Nepal is an Asian cultural society, located as a little brother between the giants—China to the north and India to the south. I looked forward to experiencing the country's mix of Hindu, Buddhist, Christian, and Muslim cultures and communities. Another attraction for me was that Nepal was located directly on the other side of the globe from the U.S., with a distinct language not at all related to any Latin-descended language. I wanted to get as far away as possible—in both distance and culture, and this filled the prescription.

I showed up for the first orientation of the student group that would spend 1988 in Nepal. The group consisted of 25 students, plus a professor and his wife. *Surprise, surprise, I'm the only person here who isn't White.* I was struck by a private pleasure when I realized that when this group made its way over to Nepal, roles would be reversed. For the first time, these 24 persons traveling with me would be in the color minority. I would finally represent the color norm. Mischief, emotional wounds, and curiosity left me anxious to see how my travel mates would deal with extreme racial isolation.

Our plane arrived in Kathmandu safely, but it quickly became clear to me that my social experiment would not get off the ground. In the streets of Kathmandu, my brown skin easily blended in. That was the only thing about me that did. Moving through those crowded streets, my colleagues and I were swallowed into a mass of human activity. The March air was thick, warm, and wet. But the bath I in particular took astounded me. There we were, 24 White people and me, in a sea of brown, and who was the target of all those staring Nepalese eyes? Some things never change.

Walking those dusty, swarming streets, I was engulfed in attention. The moment I paused at a market stand, a crowd of 30 people converged tight around me. They stared up at me, not a twitch of evasion in their gaze. This was like a celebrity crowd reaction, except these people had no idea who I was. It didn't help things too much that I stood two heads taller than most of them. These were short people and I loomed over them like a high-rise. They were also built small. My body was built up from playing college ball, so comparatively I looked swollen and freakish beside these small-boned, slender folks. But my size alone was not responsible for this amazing reaction.

My colleagues were just as taken as I was by what was happening. They couldn't fail to notice it—the crowd moved toward me in droves, buzzing with commentary to each other. The familiar explanations came from my companions: "They're probably just fascinated by your size." This was obviously not the deciding factor. Another student on this trip was about the same size as me. He hardly received a passing notice. The professor supervising us, Matt Roth's swim coach, Gary Emblen, was easily taller than I was, but he too drew minimal response. That first day in Nepal, in the Hindu Kingdom on the other side of the Earth from home, I knew I was in for an experience. Now, I wasn't sure what kind.

A group of local teachers spent six hours a day, six days a week with us the first six weeks of our visit, teaching us the Nepali language. They gave each of us a Nepali name after a period of observing our personalities. The name they gave me was 'Jivan', which means, *Life*. The name was a part of the warm embrace I felt coming from these gracious people. I quickly grew into the name. "Jivan Dai! *(Big Brother Jivan)"* became a familiar announcement and beckoning.

As the weeks mounted into months, the reaction of the Nepalese to me became clear and understandable. The first thing I noticed was that Kathmandu was host to a steady throng of hundreds of White Europeans and American tourists. Many were trekkers based in Kathmandu, either headed to conquer the Himalayas or the mountain ranges to the west, or returning from those journeys and on their way home. The people of Kathmandu, if not broader Nepal, were well acquainted with Caucasian skin and Western ways. Out in the country villages we visited, folks were less accustomed to seeing White people, but many of the trekking trails curled near to these villages, so such sightings weren't unprecedented.

I was the alien presence. The Nepalese had almost never seen African Americans before in their country. The only Black persons who came through Kathmandu had been Africans, and there hadn't been many of them. My size, clothing, footwear, and manners sufficiently indicated my U.S. American background versus an African one, based on the locals' comments. The only African Americans they could associate me with were transcendent personalities, covering the thousands of miles and the continents and waters to Nepal on the transport of mass media. The locals' gleeful pride in being American-hip was evident as they called out to me, "Michael Jackson!" "Mike Tyson!" "Michael Jordan!" These three pop culture figures represented the Black America they knew, and this was their way of reaching out to me. Riding along like a behemoth on my undersized Indian-made bicycle, I happily caught the peculiar welcome they threw.

The attention I received was far from subtle. People literally blocked my path and stood up against me, staring up in deep eye lock. They brushed their fingers along my skin, commenting humorously to each other. Whenever I was sitting or bent down to their level, their hands found my hair. They played with it like an astronaut examining an alien substance on a distant planet. When our student group was out trekking in the countryside, we ate our dinner together in a large tent. The local children came around reliably during our meals, plastering themselves like ghouls to the outside of the tent, looking in at this strange scene of Westerners devouring masses of food the children might have subsisted on for weeks. The children poked at my head through the tent screen, laughed, pointed, and danced around me. This was virtually nonstop.

I learned a great lesson about the nature of human relations as I continued my daily washing in social scrutiny. The energy behind the attention I was receiving in Nepal was at least as strong and often more intense than the energy I knew like my own skin back in the States. Both energies had everything to do with my physical image and the inner qualities that Blackness suggested. But, life had brought me here to Nepal for more reasons than curiosity. One was revelation.

It became apparent that the energy these small, humble people directed my way was one of fascination laced with an inherent allowance for my human dignity. These people granted me my full humanness. I could feel it in their vibration. It resounded in the hum of their spirit. They were fascinated with me, nothing more. They were blessed to not carry the burden of having been racially socialized in my home country. This was Nepal, a country landlocked by China and India— with little influx of negative European or American attitudes concerning Black persons. These Nepalese had no Black-specific prejudice to stand on.

My Blackness activated only a healthy curiosity. The difference between their energy and the energy I was familiar with in my country, friends, and family was as clear as the air on Mt. Everest. I sensed this distinction immediately, but as its origin dawned on me, my lungs opened up. I felt a freedom I had never tasted before. This was verification for what I had already known throughout the previous two decades of my life. There is a perceivable difference between attention received from the mouth of racially-based social illness, and attention received from a source void of prejudice. This would be a daily bath I took the rest of my days in the Himalayan kingdom.

While in Nepal that year, each of us lived separately in the home of a host family. Within the walls of my hosts' home, the Great Spirit continued my lesson. My host family was the Lamas, a people of Buddhist heritage and Tibetan roots. Their family culture seemed to be an understated combination of the region's diverse religiosity. The Lamas were a household more educated and internationally exposed than most of their community. They had previously hosted students and teachers from abroad. Their widened perspective was evident.

The first day I showed up at my host family's door, the old fears flooded me. I felt like King Kong as I stood before a door-frame meant for smaller humans. *I know these people couldn't have expected a Black person to be their visitor from the U.S.* The months ahead would be long indeed if I detected any kind of negative reaction when they met me. I took a deep breath. My auntie, Dolma Lama, greeted me at the door. Familiarity swept me back to the Pueblo Indian communities I grew up around. Dolma could have passed easily as a Pueblo woman. Her sweet demeanor revealed itself immediately in her cherubic face and friendly smile. I let out my breath.

My host brother, Gopal, was near my age, and had a brilliant mind. He was a student at the university and was full of fascination with the world. He spoke English very well, and our conversations were broad, searching, and passionate. Gopal lived in the home with Dolma, his auntie, and her husband, Kancha. Also residing there were their children Chenjum, Dorjee (now there is also Sonam, the youngest), and Gopal's cousin, Lucky. Two sisters from India, Tara, 20, and Purnima, 17, also lived with the family and Dolma's brother, Purna, was a frequent presence.

I never did lose the sense that I was a giant roaming through that house that fit me like an undersized and wash-shrunken T-shirt. But over the months, my host family's love grew into me. It became encompassing enough that I believed in it. From the first moment, the only hesitancy I detected in them was one for a stranger. My childhood shyness reemerged in their presence. I was a quiet figure around the house, especially since I hadn't fully grasped their Nepali language.

Their approach to me was matter of fact. I settled into their comforting greeting: "Jivan Dai! Dhal bhat kaanus? (Big Brother, Jivan! Do you want to eat some lentils and rice?)" Something about being asked to come and eat so lovingly touched an old place in me: *Mom's calling.* They were obviously aware I was Black, but they seemed less discomforted by it than those close to me, back home. To the Lamas, my Blackness was just a part of me. They didn't try to avoid seeing it or dance around it. They shook hands with it as they embraced me whole. This allowed me to develop a strong attachment to them in a brief period of time. They became a part of me, a family to me, and we are family to this day.

In Nepal, I stood on this world's tallest mountain, Everest, and breathed an air so pure it sent me soaring. Spirit vision took over as I looked down from 18,000 feet in altitude at the clouds ringing Everest. I had communed with Buddhist monks high in their mountain monasteries, walked on perilously narrow cliff-side paths, and played with some of the most materially indigent children in this world. I rode on elephants through subtropical jungle near India's border and camped in snowstorms on glacial mountain paths. Now I stood on Everest and saw my own nation from a bird's eye view. I had known spiritual richness here in Nepal's material abyss. From that vantage, my homeland paraded before me a masquerade of empty souls. We had given much of our humanity away.

My greatest gift from that passage was the confirmation that there truly is a difference between energy received from a prejudiced heart and a prejudice-free heart. I knew now that my life had been not an imagination of paranoia, but a portrait painted by the Divine voice within. I was supposed to feel the way I felt about my experiences. *There had been a purpose in it.*

I had stood on the Earth's rooftop on the soil of Everest and felt Great God brush my face from six inches above with permission *to be.* This was the souvenir I took home to the . . . *land where my fathers died, land of the pilgrim's pride.* When I returned to the U.S., depression ran through me for months over the loss of the particular purity Nepal had granted. I was shamed and saddened at my reunion with the sour rankle my entire society shared as victims of a nation's racial tyranny.

College ended. The degree I held in psychology was not nearly so meaningful as the certificate I had acquired in self-esteem. Through relationships with people who told stories of their own struggles, I learned that I was not oversensitive, but rather that I had been previously under-buttressed as I faced the stench of prejudice. So much of the piercing emotion that swept through me almost daily as a child had been a natural life blossom mutated by my isolation. Connected now with a tangible, touchable circle of Black kinship and White persons who explicitly honored that bruised Black part of me inflated my self-righteousness. I was emboldened. My usual passive response to periodic racial ignorance was a relic of the past life. Now I had soldiers at my back, friends at my side, confidence that I was not alone. Racial incidents ceased to crush me, leaving me ashamed of what I was. Instead, they strengthened my resolve to live as a dignified human being.

My journey continued, south of Oregon. On my first day of graduate school at the University of California, Santa Cruz, in 1990, I met a rare spirit who would become a brother to me, Virgil Adams, and a great mentor in my blossoming years, my advisor, Dr. Thomas Pettigrew. Both would play strong solos in the jazz riff that was my mad dash into a new identity. That first day, I had just met Tom when I turned and looked toward his office door. Walking in, framed by the August light, was the large, powerful figure of Virgil Adams. "Hey, Man," Virgil grinned the words in his warm style. Tom introduced us to each other as incoming students. We also would both be blessed with Tom as our advisor.

Virgil and I had both broken into grins when we saw each other. "Man, I thought I was going to be the only African American in this program," Virgil sighed in relief.

"Yeah, I was thinking the same thing." I was swollen with optimism. Our grins were not the forced smiles of polite protocol. They were the ecstasy of our spirits. We knew in that moment that we would not be alone. After those introductions, Virgil and I went downstairs into the graduate student offices. We dove into excited conversation about who we were and what we expected out of this new experience. In that first moment of graduate school, with classes, research, dissertations, presentations, exams, and who knew what else before us, Virgil and I were completely consumed with the fact that we were not going to be alone in our Blackness. This was the power of racial isolation in a race-ill nation.

During that first conversation, Virgil and I made a pact. "Let's finish this program and earn our doctorate degrees within four years," Virgil said. I would very soon become familiar with his bold, defiant streak, his dreamer's mentality.

"Yeah, we can do this. We'll have to push each other," I responded. The objective of the pact itself was not so striking as the one that underlay it. We were driven to show all the students and professors around us that we were as intelligent, disciplined, and capable as they were. That motivation burned like rocket fuel in our breasts for the next four years.

Virgil's life had been a very different story than mine. Though he had lived and been schooled in some predominantly White environments, consequently being shaped in ways similar to me, he was raised within his biological family. In fact, he had been immersed in a very strong, broad extended Black family in Sacramento, California, very near the area where my friend Kevin had grown up. Virgil knew the streets well and, in stepping up to the challenge of graduate school after time away from the academic world, was going through his own transformation. He was a few years older than I was, and wiser to the world. We eventually became roommates, but even more quickly became brothers.

Virgil had a spirit like Muhammad Ali's in that his love for his Black self and his people was strong and unabashed. He had a passion for making African American lives better. I hoarded scraps of Virgil's essence and soaked in the waves of his self-security. I felt blessed to have his huge heart in my life—he had no idea how much his presence bolstered my growth into a healthy African American identity, and therefore into a healthy overall state of being.

Even during those graduate school years, I was still that frightened child, needing more than anything to be able to talk through and emote over those things in life that mattered most to me. It was a need my brother Greg and I both shared. But having been children, we weren't able to achieve it with each other. My relationship with Virgil gave me that opportunity. Now, armed with the power of articulation, I vacuumed Virgil into my private heart and commenced to flood him with my passions both bright and darkly blue. He stayed there with me in that place, and flooded me right back with his own brilliant storm. *Greg, how I wish you could know this joy.*

Virgil's extended family was highly educated, with numerous relatives having earned graduate degrees. I had the opportunity to meet one of those relatives once, and the experience changed me. Virgil took a friend of ours and me to Sacramento to visit his uncle, Harold Adams. Uncle Harold had been a father figure to Virgil since Virgil's father— Harold's brother—had passed away in an automobile accident when Virgil was eight. I didn't know what I was in for. We arrived, thick hot Sacramento air collaring our necks, bringing out a helmet of perspiration on our heads. Entering the humble house, I felt the air shift into a kind of stillness. Then, the Sankofa bird swept me into my past. A small man, facial skin weathered and dark, hands five-fingered parchment paper, greeted Virgil with a love astounding between men. We sat.

The moment Harold's eyes held me in their grasp, I knew Virgil to the core. Here was the source of the words, the philosophies, and the mannerisms that I had come to know in Virgil. Virgil's love of his uncle was evident in his very being, and it seeped through his pores.

I loomed large over Uncle Harold as I sat next to him, but he dwarfed me. He was a giant soul, a towering spirit. And those eyes . . . huge orbs aged gray that looked through you as though they were fixed on some heated conversation of grumpy elders in an African village long gone away. I do not recall what we spoke of, only that we communed with an intense and emotional passion, and Uncle Harold's gaze remained always on one of the three of us—unrelenting. In those few hours we were in that home, the small man with the large eyes and the bursting heart lowered me down into the depths of my own soul, and had me drinking from the mixed brew of my own love and pain.

I fell in love with Uncle Harold that day. He loved me back. I was amazed. His pure, instinctive, and immediate love for me made me love my Blackness, made me love it like nothing alive. I felt the vast and old Black pain cascading down Uncle Harold's skin, onto the floor, and over to me in a pool. I drowned in that pool, and when the time came, I did not want to leave. In those moments of splendor, in the midst of a surging heart, I wished so deeply that this 'Uncle Harold' had been my uncle, too. I ached that he could have been the Black anchor, strength, and root that I needed. We drove back to Santa Cruz overwhelmed and in silence. Except for Virgil. His knowing smile decorated a mouth that talked all the way home.

Tom Pettigrew changed my life more than his razor-sharp mind will ever imagine. In presenting me with Tom as my graduate advisor, the Great Spirit Life wielded its sense of irony and surrealism. It brought me a short, bald, passionate fireplug of a Scotsman raised largely by a Black housekeeper in Richmond, Virginia, to shepherd me on my way.

Tom recalled frequently to us during those years how he still called that woman, Mildred Adams, then in her 80s, every Sunday. His love for her and her nurturing of him were central in the molding of a White man extremely set apart from his racial flock. Virgil commented that, "Tom is a White man that honestly knows more about Black people than I do. That blows me away." We were both blown away. Tom is one of the world's foremost social scientists of race relations. The reasons almost instantly became apparent to us.

Tom might claim his impressive storytelling skills to be a part of his barstool-centered Scottish heritage. His voice was that of a raspy, road-worn blues musician with a thousand gigs under his belt and a passel of yarns to show for it. He spoke like one, too. "That Cat was absolutely ignorant, man," Tom would drawl in a cool cadence. He dazzled Virgil and me with his tales of being kicked out of South Africa during the apartheid era for stirring up trouble by agitating Afrikaners as he brazenly stuffed their racism in their faces. I admired his story of going door to door in the 1950s in the Deep South, asking less-than-welcoming White folk about their racial attitudes as part of his doctoral dissertation.

His stories about friendly encounters with Malcolm X and Dr. King, less favorable interactions with Robert and John Kennedy, and crossing paths with other notable historical figures enraptured me. This man lived and breathed the work of race relations from the marrow of his bones. I wished more people had his genuine conviction for unruly, unpredictable, painful but necessary racial progress; and that fewer had the surface commitment of living to simply keep things smooth.

I had never known a White person as indignant about the racial attitudes and destructive legacy of White people as a cultural body as Tom Pettigrew. He would shout it from a bell tower if given a chance. The man had no fear in that regard. As a seventh grader he had been expelled from school for calling his history teacher a bigot for the teacher's derogatory 'nomenclature' for Negroes and praise of Hitler's anti-Semitic fervor. This was a White southern boy chastising a White southern adult in 1943!

I saw that White people so often turned to Black folk to do something to improve race relations, as though if we just 'got over' our issues we could all be holding hands living as a common American (*White*) culture by now. Tom Pettigrew blasted White people to find the courage to face themselves and their blatant and subtle, culturally rooted flaws in relating to the rest of the world. I loved him for that, and wished he could be duplicated in the millions, for I found the lack of that kind of self-reckoning to be at the core of our racial conflict. My heroes had not been defined so much by the skin they wore. I had never been afforded that level of simplicity. My heroes instead had been defined more by the conviction of their hearts to embrace even the most difficult, conformity-silencing truths and demand better of us all.

Tom Pettigrew was a kick in the rear end for me. I realized that if a White man could be this dedicated, this unafraid to speak out and to risk social and personal censorship, then I had better step it up a gear. Knowing Tom Pettigrew and being his student was as racially liberating for me as reading about the lives of Malcolm X, Dr. King, Steve Biko, and Mohandas Gandhi all in one. I was in my mid-20s. My spirit was rising.

Tom was like a photo negative of my life's color image: White man touched by an intimate family relationship with a Black woman. Even from across the country, on the shores of California, this man in his 60s still was pulled powerfully to the nurturing lap of a woman who made such a human impression upon him when he was a small boy. That is the power of honest intimacy to affect the heart of a man.

One of the ideas Tom promoted often to Virgil and me was that the strongest determinant of a person's racial attitudes is the degree to which that person has intimate family and friendship relations with people of that particular race. Tom's love for African Americans was sincere to the point of it not being a choice or manipulation of his adult attitudes. His love was real because he had no choice. He had been immersed in a family environment in which a Black woman played a central role. Tom grew to know Mildred Adams as a human being, in that season of his life when his own personal attitudes about the world were being seeded. Mildred's race could not be the determining factor in Tom's emotional relation to her, because daily he had to live with the full span of her human qualities—her imperfections, flaws, beauty, and intelligence.

I had been gifted in a way similar to Tom, by being endowed with a White family and a White childhood environment. Whether I wished for it or not, this was my world, and knowing the people in it forced me to know their human essence. It was not easy for an African American of the personality I was—sensitive, open-eyed, deep-hearted, and fully aware of the legacy and continuing reality of White racial dehumanization—to remain free, free in the heart from prejudice toward White persons.

That endeavor was a struggle for me. I had been given plenty of reasons to hate, scorn, turn bitter, and burn my spirit bridge to those humans in my Greater Being who were racially White. I had endured things up close and personal from White minds, hearts, and bodies that other African Americans only imagined from afar. But I also had known the beauty of many friends, family, and strangers—some of them the same persons who harbored the poison seed of prejudice. My face had been pushed deep into the mud of their humanity, leaving me smattered with the undeniable remains of their being. I could not make a clean categorical judgment out of that. Recognizing this as a blessing preceded my dawning realization of the Divine purpose of my life.

I kept walking toward myself. Malcolm X, Alex Haley, and Martin Luther King embraced me in kinship from the other side of the Great River as I read about their lives in *The Autobiography of Malcolm*, *Roots*, and other books and articles. Mohandas Gandhi pulled me to him in the same way through his *An Autobiography, or, The Story of My Experiments with Truth*. I had found and read this book repeatedly while I was in Nepal. Though Gandhi was not African, he was fierce in his determination that his own oppressed people hold themselves in dignity, and that they be regarded with dignity. He was so small yet so large in his will. I could not help but break into tears at the example his life was to me. A diminutive Hindu Indian who wore the self-spun clothing of a peasant pushed me down my African path.

I was moving toward the mid-stretch of my twenties now, feeling my oats. Like most that age, I was starting to think I knew something. An arrogance of intelligence had me thinking that I knew things the world had not yet clued in on. In fact, my knowledge was only the aftertaste of a crumb of wisdom left behind by my elders. Still, I was eager and spry. I began to seek out myself in distant Blackness through literature. As I did, my striving became adroit and limber.

Langston Hughes was a snow-covered hillside I topped then sledded down, racing toward my Self. John Edgar Wideman was an ice pond I skated over in my bare feet, reaching the other side bloodied underfoot and halfway toward hypothermia. But at least I reached the other side. I had skated that much closer to myself. I maneuvered through and across terrain composed of names my family and friends were likely to have never heard: names like Baldwin, Robeson, Dunbar-Nelson, Audre Lorde, and Ntozake Shange.

My chest, on the other hand, was a constant container of drum beat rebellion and uprising. Boom, boom, boom—things were bouncing off the inside walls of the cavern sheltering my heart. They were weary things (Ellison), their hands beating on goatskin with lasting ennui. They were enigmatic things (Zora

Neale), daring to make the drum weep 400 Sun trips worth of sorrow songs. They were things serendipitous and stolen. My retrieval was ravenous.

I was learning the value of anchoring myself in something larger—something preceding me that I knew would understand me and feel comfortable with my Blackness. I knew that to withstand hostility, subtle negativity, or even just social isolation, it not only mattered who my ancestors were, but also that I keep them alive in me. Another concept was dawning in me as well, a value I had long heard spoken from the pueblos and the reservations: Each of us must, in our living, honor the seven generations before us and after us. I was learning that it was important for me to identify with even the aspects of my heritage that I judged as negative. I saw that even with negative truths, I could develop a positive relationship that would grant me insight and growth.

One of the negative truths I learned about as I stepped into the African kinship circle was that African Americans were just as frequently driven and blinded by prejudice as were White Americans. Though Black prejudice was essentially a wounded one while White prejudice was overwhelmingly a condescending one, the endpoints of both energies were the same poisonous distillation. My heart broke as I stood within Black social circles and listened to the very same prejudiced mentalities come spilling out of certain mouths.

If only these people could hear themselves talking. Don't they know they sound just like the White people that crushed my spirit with their words all those years? Don't they know their absolute judgment of all White people includes the very people who raised this Black person? Don't they know their slings tear the hearts of my White mother, father, sisters, brother, and friends? White people are just as varied as y'all know Black folk to be. How could you become the very thing that has decimated us? I am so tired of this sickness. My disdain for prejudice of any kind hardened into a cold, gray sinkhole. Much of my hope for peace on this Earth perished down that drain.

With each experience and each relationship I became more convinced that the true enemy, my enemy, was a kinetic force stowed away in whatever hue of skin it chose to inhabit. It entered through the openings left in torn hearts, infecting with a quick-growing malignancy. I thought about Los Alamos, Illinois, Oregon, California, everywhere I had been and lived. I saw how social integration was a greatly deceiving surface dance. I knew that diversity was a wasteland so long as individuals did not value those they 'diversified' with. Emancipation, desegregation, affirmative action, multicultural education, transracial adoption: These were all processes that society had mistaken for spiritual transformation. But I knew Black lives still weighed less than White lives when placed on the scale of value and worth. Only a great and raw spiritual bleeding would change that.

My identity was not stabilizing as much as it was sloughing off dead cells. Exfoliated, sunlight reached it and it became energized. I beheld all things with newness. In my lifetime, I had been embraced by all manners of people. That embrace was characterized by a variety of energy and attitude I was driven to comprehend. The idea of kinship was part of that. In relation to my race, I had known kinship and its imposter. The true force was an embrace that valued and honored my racial characteristic. The imposter force was another creature. For it, my race was a thing to contend with. What made the whole thing untidy was that I had many times encountered both true kinship and the imposter in the same individual.

I returned to Los Alamos for visits. The psychological stretch necessary to connect with my family and old friends broadened. I had moved further away on the continuum of culture. My tolerance for violations to my dignity had shrunken. My willingness to stand up for impulses and ideas had sprouted. Mom took much of my personality change as evidence that I had gotten full of myself because I had gained a higher education; that I thought I was better than they were. With the resistant attitude I carried with me on those visits back home, I might have tapped an insecurity or sore spot within her. She had not attended college, and had spent all those years in a college-educated town like Los Alamos. I didn't think I was better than the rest of my family. I was just increasingly foreign to them and them to me—and was venting resentment in steam.

A fantasy of mine and I met one day on the physical plane, as the African kinship circle began to show off, reclaiming me. I encountered the man who had touched me through the television in an earlier season, when I was small and the world was my bully. His body was seated, his hands shaking. I was underwater, though we were on dry ground. Sound of the crowd around me was muffled. Slow movement toward him. Kneeling to his seated level. His face rigid; eyes soulful.

No greeting from my mouth, just: "I want to give you something." A change comes over the eyes—surprise. *Relief?* I am not another of the millions who have wanted. But one of the millions who have loved him in the way he wishes they would love one another. I extend the envelope containing the poem, containing the pride and the pain, emotions harboring the need so deep . . . the need for him.

He takes from me in his hand the gift I took from him in the first place. He stands to *touch me*. We are eye to eye. Playful, mischievous spirit conquers his facial rigidity for a flash. Fists threatening. We shadow box toward but not at each other. Even in our jest, the shadows we jab and hook at are long ago private monsters—for each of us, our own. Flashbulbs intrude with their lightning into our peace. Who knows how much time has passed. "You a bad man," he whispers.

I have no words, only the love in my eyes that he is endlessly showered with. I pray osmosis carries that emotion to him. He grasps my hand, *soft grip*. I place my arm around his shoulders. Even now, he is large and strong. I am reminded of when I napped in the lap of my private Daddy mountain range.

I feel I have somehow come closer again to that particular man-love. Like so many others, I struggle to release my hand from his. I have been touching something magical and have been transported. A deep breath and I am capable of letting go. Somehow, in the presence of this man who I fantasized as being my Black father, I am closer to Dad. I realize they share the same soulful lake quality in their eyes. They both occupy their own unique, special worlds, so far from normal.

Muhammad Ali turns to the horde of children waiting for him. He is back in that familiar space; shuffling cards, towering over little people, a giant trickster; a magician who has yet to reveal the secret of his mystical touch.

We call people great, though my spirit holds that there is no greatness but God. We simple humans achieve some measure of greatness by virtue of the degree to which we access That Which Is Great. The great ones we love are all imperfect persons who have accessed many things in their lives, some disappointing to us, some sun-splashed with a magnificence that carves grooves in our lasting emotional portraiture. In that those people have accessed some measure of Greatness, we call them great. Those people. That man.

As I walk home, the tingle is still in my hand. I realize that what Muhammad Ali has accessed is a bottomless reservoir of love. I remember the desire he has so fervently expressed: that people would love one another as much as they profess to love him. I am reminded of the long ago carpenter who gave of his life, led by the same unbending desire. I think of the millions of Black souls who have not received that same glow of affection. The glow that held me as my footprints grew. The thoughts trail me back to my apartment like a wisp of dignity orphaned. Foreshadow speaks to me: *Show me that you love my people.*

What is born in the sea
even if carried deep into
the breast of land
made dry in the desert
sage in the mountains
or sweetened in the orchards
shall yet and always carry that
old and familiar salt

MOTHER & CHILD REUNION

Silent Reunion

By Mary E. Woods, December 8, 1983

The time had finally arrived! I was tensely nestled beneath the thinly woven blanket, eager for a few winks to relax my nerves. Tonight I was going to see my son for the first time since his debut into life. Anxiety was high, likewise my fears. For coupled with the weeks of anticipation of this moment was the stark realization that he was not legally my son. He belonged to someone else.

As I lay there, the pounding of my heart punctuated the fear that gnawed within me. What if he weren't there? What if I fainted at the sight of him? My mind was running wild with negative thoughts. Eventually the pounding subsided as I drifted off into a short period of sleep.

Sixteen years had passed since I made the dreadful decision to relinquish my newborn son to the methodological process of adoption. But this baby had become a part of me, and the thought of having to give him up was almost unbearable.

They gave me no other choice. I was recently divorced and depended greatly on my sister and my brother-in-law for the livelihood of myself and my two sons. The doctors could not predict the length of preexisting illnesses that were draining me physically. So, unwillingly and almost in a state of oblivion, I relinquished all legal rights to the child a few hours after his birth.

The hospital labeled my delivery as a "Do-Not-Announce" case; I never saw the baby. I only knew that he weighed seven pounds and two ounces. The experience of witnessing his first cry was not mine to have. Rather, I returned home empty-handed, recalling the sadness that engulfed me when my nine-year-old son had responded earlier to the news that I was giving up his baby brother. His young, heart-rending plea was still resounding in my heart—"Mother, don't give him away; please keep him." I couldn't tell him why I had to give him up. He was too young to understand all that.

Despair gripped my spirit as I reflected on the months preceding the birth of my baby. The embryonic fluttering of that tiny form of humanity had aroused my motherly instincts. At one juncture, there had been the threat of abortion. But the fetus clung on to life and grew closer to my heart. Once an airplane flew overhead and he leaped boldly in my womb, from an apparent restful state.

But I would not know the joy of motherhood with this particular child. I would never nestle him close to my breasts and share the greatest moments of an infant-mother relationship.

My body had calmed when I awakened shortly before departure time for the long-awaited event. No longer was there fear of seeing him and reacting irrationally. I was ready for the encounter. A friend of mine accompanied me to the meeting place.

As I beheld him, a striking image of my younger son, there were no emotional outbursts—only silence. The silence was between the two of us. He did not know me nor was he aware of my presence. Due to the circumstances, I could not reveal myself to him. I was forced to subdue my feelings.

There were many others at the meeting place, but I was oblivious to everyone except the sight of my biological son in the flesh. I longed to hold him, to cry out and express my love for him. But only an unspoken sentiment passed between us as I devoured his every feature and watched his every move. Ecstasy overcame me, yet I remained silent. Years must pass before I can reveal my identity to him. This will certainly affect me psychologically, but it will be worth the wait to be able one day to share in his life.

Tonight I experienced a miracle. Tomorrow will bring its uncertainties. Nothing can erase the impressions of this memorable occasion. My son is an energetic, strapping Black teenager. His parents are wonderful, caring people—and they are white. This should bear out his knowledge of being adopted and probably that he wants to know his real identity. One day I hope to share that truth with him.

Until then, I will keep praying that this silent reunion will some day evolve into a meaningful relationship between him and me, as well as between his parents and me.

Mary E. Woods

THE ocean rose within me early in my 18th year. I nearly drowned in my own water. The moment was a dream state. I walked down the stairs from the campus cafeteria one winter evening during my freshman year of college. As I reached the floor and turned to the mailboxes stretched out as a gray metal wall, a change came over me. A foreboding wave was creeping through my insides. The hallway was completely empty, which was rare and ominous. The air turned still, I felt my body launch on a tremor into a noticeably different level of vibration. As I moved toward my mailbox—the number, 2160, I remember even now—I felt increasingly as though I were floating. All was silence and stillness.

I turned the combination of the lock and opened the mailbox door. I had already seen through the small glass window that a single envelope lay inside. My heart knocked hard on my chest. When I took hold of that envelope, a current of electricity passed into my right hand and up my arm. I suddenly knew in some indescribable way what I was holding.

I immediately dropped that envelope onto the ground, and gasped. The reality I had known was about to be gone forever.

I picked up the envelope, thin and carrying a 22-cent buffalo stamp. It was postmarked January 8 of 1986, and was addressed simply, with no zip code for me, nor name or address for the sender. I slowly and nervously opened the flap and touched the letter that would call forth the flood. I unfolded the paper and forced myself to read. The letter was written lightly in blue ink with a left-handed lean and read:

John:

Your real mother lives in Albuquerque.

She loves you very much, but is afraid to contact you because of your parents. She located you in 1983 and wrote them, but they wouldn't reply.

I am a friend of hers. She doesn't know I'm writing you. But I feel you should know she is a good woman and she didn't give you away voluntarily. She has suffered a lot from this. She has newspaper clippings of you and she has watched you play basketball in the Pit [University of New Mexico Arena].

It would make her happy if you would contact her. I can't give you her telephone number because she would know I wrote. But you can call a lady in Albuquerque. Her name is [name withheld]. She can get in touch with your mother for you. Her # is [number withheld].

I don't mean to upset you, John. But I know how much this means to your mother. Nobody knows about this letter.

A Friend

By the end of the first sentence the river was rushing into my eyes, warm and furious. I staggered on instinct back to my dorm room, where my roommates, Eric and Matt, saw the look on my face and must have been alarmed. I gave them no immediate relief, because for the next few months I literally could not speak of what had happened. For the next two years, when I did speak of it, the magnitude of it caused me to stutter. An ocean of emotion swept through me in that first moment and continued to build and cascade through the walls of my identity, peeling off layers of the ideas in life I had always attached myself to, found myself by, oriented to.

My North Star, the identity that had served as my compass for so long, in one brisk reading had vanished and everything that I knew of myself now dangled uncertainly in that space where we cultivate our reality. I could not discern negative emotion from positive. I was still a teenager, just adjusting to a new, broader world in college and now the pillar of my sense of self, my family connection, had just loosed itself from its moor and floated downstream. I was not suffering. I was swimming, wet and washed over.

A few months later, in April, my biological mother, Mary Elizabeth Woods, communicated with me for the first time with a letter of her own. She included the essay she had written in 1983 about her imagined reunion with me. My brother Arnold first contacted me with a birthday card that October. That fall, Mary sent me a photograph of herself. Holding that picture, front image turned down in my hands, was the kind of moment in which everything else in the world ceases to exist. God had pressed pause. Knowing that on the other side of the photo was the image of my own mother whom I had never seen, I struggled to remain standing. *I have the power to turn this picture over and see my mother's face.* People who had seen their own image in the faces around them all their lives could never glimpse the magnitude of my mystification.

I was intimidated, excited, and awed that I held in my hands an image of the root I had come from, an image of my origin and composition. *Just how am I supposed to look at my own face in another? I don't know how to do this.* I had that photograph for two weeks before I finally took a deep breath and turned it over. Time slowed again, I watched my trembling left hand turn the photo over. I saw . . . myself, and the river rushed again. The woman in that photograph looked eerily like me. And while that included a physical likeness, it was the spirit beneath her skin and bones, the essence that leaked out through her eyes, that was strikingly familiar. It was my own.

Mary must have been around 50 in that first photograph. Her skin was smooth, without a single wrinkle. Her bone structure, especially her cheekbones, told the facial story of the American Indian woman that was prominent in her spirit's heritage. Her great, great grandmother had been, in 'The People's' way of stating it, "born for the Blackfoot clan." Her grandfather, Joseph Henderson, was born for the Cherokee clan. *That was my great grandfather wearing sepia moons for eyes in Santa Fe's Old Town Plaza. That was my distant grandmother, Blackfoot woman looking back at me.*

Mary's skin complexion was light brown, similar to mine. Auburn hair in a relaxed styling framed her face. Perfect white teeth showed through a slight, kind smile. Her eyes portrayed the truth of her life. All the miles crossed, the lives lost, the love shared, and the pain bared. She was beautiful, dignified. She carried the story of her life strains almost as foundation over her facial skin. Her image was shown from the chest up, drifting within a black background as if appearing to me in a dream. She wore a black turtleneck underneath a sharp ivory white jacket with large seventies-style lapels. Her mind seemed almost lost in another dimension, as if she were listening to an ancient conversation among distant elders.

This was my birth mother, my first external sighting of *me.* I wasn't sure it was real. I stared at that image a few hundred times over months before I began to believe in it. The next few years this new truth settled in and became a part of me.

As I gained the ability to speak about my adoptive background to others, many Black people reacted with something close to horror. It wasn't hard for them to imagine my painful struggle—regardless of how popular or well received I was, or how wonderful my family was. More than a few times a Black person told me, "I can't even imagine how hard that must have been for you." After all those years it was euphoria to hear people say they could understand, that they could relate. Each time I heard that, I let go of another one of the dismissals of my experience I had received before.

The infusion of Black people into my life brought regrets about my yesteryears. The flip side of my racial isolation had been my family's racial comfort. Los Alamos' racial landscape, and therefore cultural tendencies, represented them to a far greater degree than it represented me. I always wondered why I was consistently tired when I was younger. Other children seemed to have boundless energy. I felt like an old man crawling out of bed in the morning, and often carried the same lethargy during the day.

I worried then that something was seriously wrong with me. Something was. Now I realized that all those years, a great amount of energy had seeped from me. It was from the strain of being Black in a world to which I largely was an allergen. It took energy to be an allergen. The emotional deviations from 'belongingness' left me standing in the middle of nowhere harboring soul water quickly growing putrid. Having nowhere else to put it, I put it on layaway in my chest and let it take on mold in the darkness. I paid it off in coins of a peace departed.

Now though, I had deep wishes. I wished my parents had known more Black people, anywhere, so that we could have more naturally interacted with them instead of having to rely on awkwardly going up to strangers and in effect saying, "Can my sons spend some time with you, because they're Black and you're Black?"

I wished that when our family went back to Illinois to visit relatives that Greg and I were allowed to go out and play with the Black children. I had that desire and curiosity, and there were plenty of children. Instead, I remember those few times I heard Mom's nervous and concerned voice warning us not to go around "those people." She never mentioned why we should avoid them, nor did she specifically identify or describe "those people" as Black. She may have been referring as much to their poverty as their race, but I doubted that the two were not intertwined for her.

Quite correctly, she was warning us about being careful around strangers, especially since Peoria was a big city, and we had the trusting naiveté that comes with living in an isolated small town. But there was something more to that tone Mom used. Perhaps in her mind as a girl, she had confused what was being told to her about particular Black individuals on Peoria's streets with the concept of Black people as a whole.

She surely had been as vulnerable to this as any child, coming to associate negative characteristics with entire groups of people, from nothing more than loose generalizations spoken by adults as "they" "those" and "them." Those words, when combined with that potent word, 'always', without qualification, created lessons intended and unintended for children eager to learn about the rules of life and people. I had been the recipient subject of the "they" and the "always" too often, and grew an early disgust for that careless language.

Now I understood that it was her girlhood lessons that I had heard in Mom's voice when she shepherded us away from 'them'. She, like anyone else raised in that environment of racial attitudes, may have had a heart of gold, but it still could be laced with a regard for Black folk as something 'other', something separate, and even less than equal. I wished I could have gone back to the 1940s and taken that girl who would become Mom to me and transported her to an imaginary world of my making. A place that would have taught her the kind of lessons more consistent with the nature of her loving heart.

I wasn't a different species from the rest of my family. But I did have risks to my emotional development, risks that were not the same as those for Kristin, Anna, and Rudy. Dad's career was rooted in Los Alamos, and there weren't many places like the Laboratory, so the opportunities for moving to another community weren't great. But any accommodations my family might have made to alleviate the racial isolation, or at least the effects of it, would have provided me reason to believe I was truly a part of my family.

Perhaps most of all, I wished I had known, all along, the ways in which my parents had in fact tried to make me feel loved and secure in the midst of Whiteness. Like when they took Greg and me to visit a custodian at JC Penney's in Santa Fe, who was also a preacher and had been friendly to Mom and Dad. They did this with the explicit desire to have me meet someone who looked like me. Then there was Red Jackson, who worked rigging heavy machinery at the Laboratory. He lived a couple of doors away from the house we lived in during the summer of 1969. He was always interested in how Greg and I were doing, and never failed to say hello when our family saw him. Though Mom and Dad made periodic efforts, however awkward, to address our Black identities, I could not have known, because we never spoke of such things.

One day I read a newspaper article about a White man who had adopted a Black son. In the story, he related how social workers and Black America in general approached him and other such White families with a skeptical attitude. He resented this attitude and his sarcastic response amounted to: "What did they want me to do, subscribe to *Ebony Magazine*? Learn to cook soul food? What are we supposed to do, fly the African liberation flag in our house?" I read those words and felt belittled, demeaned, and devalued. The insult fell at my feet like heavy, wet leaves in autumn.

Certain things may seem trivial or insignificant to an adult, but they can be huge to a child. And when that adult is White and the 'trivial' things have to do with making a racially isolated Black child feel less like an alien, then maybe the child's judgment of what matters should be honored. The frustrations in my mind took up words again:

Maybe if. Maybe if the faces on every dollar bill were Black, and every president was Black and Jesus were portrayed as Black. Maybe if 'skin-colored' Band-Aids were brown and not pink, and mainstream, middle-class, and upper-class society were all highly associated with Black people, and the most powerful arenas of society—medicine, politics, banking, real estate, business, law, etc.—brought Black faces to mind. Maybe if history were Blackwashed, and White contributions were Whitened out. Maybe if White people had been enslaved, segregated, ridiculed, ostracized, and forced to 'act Black' in order to be considered five-fifths human. And maybe if most of the people in the U.S. were Black, then just maybe some White people wouldn't make such smug comments about how trivial the little artifacts of culture and symbols of the self are. Because they would be too busy hunting down portraits of White Jesus at flea markets, and looking for those rare books with White people in them, so their children could feel good about themselves . . . at least for a moment in time.

In July of 1989, shortly after graduating from college, I was ready to meet Mary. I drove with my close friend, Beckie, up to Denver, where Mary was living at the time. The friendship I shared with Beckie, born in a revelation of pain, had come to this grand moment in which I would meet my birth mother. We talked along the way about what we were heading toward, both of us nervous and excited. I don't know how I would have survived if Beckie had not been there with me. She and I spent the night before at the home of another high school friend of ours, in Denver. I would meet my birth mother the next morning. Of course, sleep stayed far away that night.

Her heart was gobbling up two beats for every one it should have taken. She was afraid and the fear coated her in a cold sweat. *How is my son going to respond to me after all these years?* She tried to relax, but the current strain of her seminary training and the years of separation from this child, this young man, proved to be too much a thing for peace to find her then.

She cooked with the nervousness of the moment. What meal had she ever cooked that would mean this much? This was her first meal served to this son . . . *this son. I can't believe he's coming. Is this child going to like my cooking? What have his parents been feeding him all his life? Is he going to reject my food* (my love)? *Is he going to eat all of this? But he must be starving* (he had been starving). *I need to make more food.*

In the morning, I gathered my courage and Beckie and I headed over to where Mary was living. We pulled up to the curb across the street from her apartment. I was afraid to even glance in that direction. Beckie saw a woman standing outside and thought it might be Mary. Suddenly I was a small child standing before a storm. I was terrified. I finally got out of the car, paused for what seemed like an hour, then turned and faced my lifelong idea in the flesh of a person. After 21 years, I was returning to the arms of the woman through whose womb I had come to this world.

"Oh, Lord," Mary said, her words muffled against my shoulder. Neither one of us could gracefully contain what passed between us during that first embrace. Beckie left us to our moment, and drove back to our friend's place. Mary and I went inside her apartment. I remember it being beneath ground level, and somewhat dark. I quickly was basking in the amazing scents of down home, deep south, soul food cooking. It was a shower of aroma I had been waiting for since I had left that foster home. I don't know how long she had been cooking but Mary had put my lifetime worth of her passion into that layout. The kitchen table, side tables, and other available surfaces were loaded with every dish I might have been able to imagine, and then some.

Strong smelling collard greens, brown sugar-candied yams, corn bread, fried chicken, turkey, ham, potato salad, dinner rolls, and sweet tea. As Mary continued to prepare the feast, I drooled on the inside. I was quiet, shy, and overcome. Mary did most of the talking, propelled by her own nerves. She saw that I was drained, so she let me lie down for a while and take a nap while she finished up with the cooking. I went into a deep sleep, as much from a need to escape my anxiety as from a function of being taxed by the moment. The food's aroma carried me into my resting state like a comforting blanket. But there was something more. I was pulled into that sleep by a force that was magnetic and overpowering, like I had been drugged. I felt helpless and small in that corridor that carried me into unconsciousness. Small like an embryo.

When I woke it was her food that spoke. She kept encouraging me to eat. I kept acquiescing. *Eat plenty. Eat plenty.* The denouement was the sweet potato pies. She must have baked 12 of those things, and I ate two of them that afternoon. Mary gave me a couple of them to take home with me. We talked some more, and I tried to stay afloat on my sea of emotions. Come early evening, I had enough for one swallow and I called Beckie to ask her to come get me. Mary and I said our goodbye, and squeezed each other with a strength that sought to recapture the years.

That was the reunion. In the years to come, we would write, speak by phone, and visit in person, slowly building our relationship. I would meet my brothers, Arnold and Allan, at Arnold's home in Albuquerque, amazed at the opportunity to see my own blood so up close. We all were overcome with each other. I eagerly noted their personal qualities. Arnold was the talented cook, athletic, sensitive, and, yes, soft spoken. I celebrated especially that. Allan had legs that went up to the roof, making him appear even taller than his six-and-a-half feet. Intelligence overran his cup and took his thoughts all over the universe. He was awesomely gifted with writing, and he too had a solitary quality.

Later I met Mary's twin sister, Martha, and her husband, James, at their home in Colorado. That visit took me so close to my limit it was near to a haunting. I had gone more than 20 years without holding the image of my biological mother in my eyes. Now, in Martha, I was looking at a second helping of that same image. I met one of Martha and James' children, my cousin Greg, and heard about Greg's siblings, my cousins

James and Faye. I was accumulating my people rapidly. Down the line, I would meet Patrice, Allan's youngest sister by his father. Through Patrice, I would connect in spirit with her five sisters down in Alabama, Clarissa, Sharon, Diane, and the twins Lorraine and Elaine. They humbled me, adopting me immediately as a brother. I reciprocated without a pause. After all these years, I wasn't about to leave anybody out of my circle.

The more I learned of Mary, the more I was impressed with her spirit and determination. I was being granted vision into my own nature. The peace Mary gained from locating and reconnecting with me liberated her toward fulfilling her larger purpose. Shedding all the negativity and separations of her own childhood, and a host of chronic health challenges, she returned to college bent on heeding the call of her inspiration. She graduated magna cum laude in English and Religious Studies from the University of New Mexico in Albuquerque in 1988, at the age of 53, one year before my own college graduation. She was on a mission.

The strength of the spiritual voice within her was clear. And it was familiar to me. It left her passionate and driven. She was ordained as a United Methodist minister in 1992, from the Iliff School of Theology in Denver, Colorado, and achieved her Master of Divinity degree there as well. Eventually, her mission would lead her to chaplaincy certification and service as a chaplain in the Laurel Healthcare System. God talks loudly in some human vessels, which is not always an easy thing to endure. As I listened to Mary, I understood that much of the physical and mental struggles she had contended with were the result of a profound spiritual sensitivity. It was amazing for me to be in her presence, covered in the mist of her persona, catching up for the years.

Some women carry their babies low and heavy. Some people carry their Blackness the same way. A great realization for me came when I understood that much of the weight upon me was not from my place in a White family and environment. It was simply that ages-old weight of being Black. Like the natural elements, everything in the universe has a certain weight to it. And on the table of elements, Blackness as manifest within many would carry an atomic weight so extreme it would fall far off the chart. For Mary, I soon learned that she carried her Blackness like a coal miner. Like Harriet Tubman, she stubbornly and unfailingly reached far inside that dangerous place where most did not go. That place was truth, and Mary kept returning there, pulling it out into the open air of conversation.

She spoke with a passion about racial justice and spiritual dignity. It was an intense, driven flame that was familiar to me. I realized it was my flame. As she spoke, I was witness to a source of my burning. Her absolute disdain for destructive racial attitudes, her surging concern for the well-being of Black people in a hostile land, and for all people in a hostile world— these were what I had inherited. She spoke. I reveled in this rare permission to talk about these things. She bled and hurt, and I thought, *yes, this is who I am.* She raged in that dark mine shaft of prejudice for a spark of love and respect. I swooned: *You do not know how deeply I feel what you feel.* Like twins, our opinions on the state of the world and the nature of things both spiritual and void of spirit came forth with startling synchronicity. In this sense, we saw reality in a very similar manner. That alone was very new to me.

Her spirituality was so purely contracted that she violated the boundaries of religious doctrine. It was clear that her beliefs were not descended solely from words on the page or from men of the cloth, but were largely direct inspiration from Above that she grasped faithfully in making sense of the world.

Mary's diction was strewn with colorful, southern splashes of "My worrrd," and "Dear Lorrrd," and "That's just about the craziest thing I've ever heard." Her humor was deft and dazzling—I was taken aback by the skill of it. I thought she could have been a comic. Eventually I understood that her comic gift, like my brother Allan's, was a byproduct of keen 'life vision', more plainly understood as perceptiveness. Mary spoke in her rural Alabama accent of the fey inheritance of those in her family line, the 'touched' souls. The clairvoyant ones who in their overwhelmed struggle to realize, understand, and harness their extreme sensitivity and vision, wavered between health and illness. She was speaking of others, but to me she was speaking of herself. I could see the struggle in her—she was a reflection pond through which I could see the same lifelong struggle in my own being.

I learned about my own emotional and psychological tendencies by observing them in her. Strangers could not help noticing the peculiar energy of our conversations those many times we sat in Albuquerque restaurants eating lunch. That peculiar energy was self-discovery long deferred. It was energy of absolute appreciation, an anxious rush to absorb. Mary shared with me her medical history, a long, disquieted passage that served to me as both insight and warning. With every visit and conversation, I understood more clearly that I would need to gain balance with and control of my bottomless capacity to absorb emotional pain from the world around me. I would have to resist the strong reflex to wallow in and shape myself to the contour of that pain.

My physical, emotional, and spiritual health was a system made more vulnerable by my nature. The same nature Mary exhibited before me. I marveled at how much I was gaining knowledge of, just by witnessing another person 'be' in front of me. This was the power, the purpose, and the relevance of biological connection. The same connection everyone and everything in my life had implicitly encouraged me to believe did not matter. Every moment that passed knowing Mary did matter; I was becoming familiar with myself.

I was conscious that Mom and Dad were concerned about what might loom ahead for me in knowing Mary. We both knew that adopted children don't always find the rainbow waiting for them when they make their way toward their origins. I knew they feared for my heart, and hoped I would not find rejection or hurt in my reunion with a woman and other relatives they did not know. The human part of my parents must also have been insecure about the idea of somehow losing me to my biological family. A family that presented me with certain intangibles they were aware they could never provide.

Counter to Mom and Dad's concerns, my relationship with them was gaining auburn fertility from the roots I was planting in my biology. In being made more whole, I gained a security that allowed me to appreciate Mom and Dad and strengthen my tie to them. In the period of years following my reconnection with Mary, I tried to reassure my parents that my relationship with my biological family would not diminish my relationship with them.

This message may have been occluded in the ugly emotional upheaval I passed through in my early 20s. Much of that insurgency I directed at Mom and Dad. All the pain and frustration and fear of my childhood came to a head during that time. I introduced our family to the power of clouds. Relating to me was akin to walking a minefield. Any action, word, or circumstance might trigger my raw emotions and light the fuse. I had not yet been able to express myself productively to my parents regarding my pain, so all that pressure kept building and venting, building and venting.

My parents endured my substantial growing pains, though for a few years while I was in graduate school there was a painful distance between us. My process of reuniting with biological family added a discomforting and uncertain mix to the turmoil. Accommodating such different racial, cultural, and personality realities, represented by the parts of my total family, was a challenge for me. I felt pulled, as if tethered to three planets moving outward of their own accord. All along, I had a fear of these three planets colliding, resulting in an explosion of race and anxiety. I also had a deeper need for exactly that to happen—that joining, that closing of my canyon expanse, even if friction were to be its unavoidable accompaniment.

A licorice-colored walking stick sat next to Storyteller like an obedient pet.

"Where'd you get that stick?" I asked.

"Where'd you get that big head?" she responded.

"You got jokes."

"You got a big head."

She broke her deadpan, laughing with a brief rasp. "This here's endangered Tanzanian ebony wood, boy. Keeps me upright. Come here and touch on it. Come on now."

I wrapped my hand around the stick. Gone. Down an alleyway, gray black, rainwater left over in puddles. I was walking toward a dead end, centered by a stoop that led to no door. On the stoop, an old man sat, blue gray eyes, burnt mahogany skin, sporting a beat-down brown derby. His elbows perched on skeletal knees so sharp I thought they'd eventually tear through his slacks. His slacks . . . paper thin, worn, poor excuses for clothing. Black Stacy Adams shoes on his feet. They had more lines and marks than his topographical face. His right foot hung down over the stoop's edge, tapping up splashes of rainwater as he kept beat with the saxophone to which his lips made love. The offspring was a sound that walked a line between wail and . . . angels in chorus.

He stopped playing upon my approach and nibbled at his lips like Miles Davis, getting a feel for the flesh of his body's instrument. Grinning, he spoke—his voice a sandpaper victim of an endless succession of juke joint smoke clouds. "Out of the darkness, into the dawn. What once was a shy word, becomes a proud song." I was lost to his Bundini Brown-type rhymed exclamation.

On cue, he explained. "I can see you 'bout to break out. Gotta let that last bit come on out, though. You can't pull one over on me. I know you're a turtle; carried the whole world on your back all your life, used that shell as a shield. Bet you didn't know the nature of your own spirit animal. Yeah, a turtle protects its feelings and withdraws into itself. But what's important is that a turtle embodies Mother Earth. Turtles let their stuff ripen before sharing it. Just like the flesh of the peach, the pearl of the oyster. The universe broils in you, son."

Then he inexplicably switched tracks, saying, "Son, Blacks are bruised like bruises are black. You can't erase that; you can't put it back. I'll tell you another thing, if you aren't at peace with how things are for Black folks in this country, don't lie about it. Don't betray it. And never be afraid to claim pride in being Black. You know what peace is, son? Peace is when you've made your spirit a thing that can't be carved, like Rafoko stone from over there'n Zimbabwe. You can't hardly carve that stuff. It loves itself that much, unwilling to give up its essence. Be like Rafoko, so's nobody can bend you to betray your truth.

"You want you some peace? A'right then, you can't never grin in the place that you grieve. And you can't never shame in the place that you celebrate. You manage to pull that off, and peace will meet you piece'away, I guarantee you that.

"Yessir," he concluded, "Out of the darkness, into the dawn . . ." Nibbling his lips, he took to kissing on his reed again, and on the airwaves of his first notes, he himself turned to darkness and was gone.

That there child
is the delta of many rivers
Who comes after him
shall be a new people

MY NAME IS JAIYA

MY life in the season of my 20s provided me with a sense of permission. Not only to be my core self, but to express it and demand to be respected for it. I had come miles already, and for the first time, my esteem had risen to a level that allowed me to step out and mentor younger African Americans. I was amazed to see in them the same impulse to 'be', coupled with that familiar stifling fear of 'being'. Only now could I begin to see beyond my own walls clearly and consistently enough to see that I was needed by others. This was a rampart to my conscious movement toward a healthy self-regard. My growth was not entirely smooth, though. It wasn't smooth at all.

The tension between being a Potter family member and being my Black self was no small thing for me. As I increasingly filled out the subtle corners and sophisticated workings of my Black identity, there was strain. I saw how my parents, more so than my brothers and sisters, sometimes reacted to me more curiously than familiarly. It must have been hard for them to chart the course of my growth apart from their cultural world, across the physical distance that usually separated us now that I had moved away.

I often wondered how my family saw the evolving me. I knew they were witnessing a transformation. *What do they think of how my speech is changing? How do they feel about the attitudes I express about race? About the people with whom I socialize, the women I date?* They were aware that I did not feel comfortable with Los Alamos when I visited, even if I felt strongly about a number of people I knew there. But Los Alamos was home for much of my family. Home felt good to them. I wondered whether it hurt them that home didn't feel good to me in the same way.

It would have taken a miraculous self-contortion at that age to feel well-attached to my parents, given their cultural reality, and at the same time feel good about being Black. The distance between those two polarities was a recipe for bread that could never rise. My need to feel good about myself drove me to continue to find a way to gain racial pride. I searched hard for positive, meaningful relationships with other Black people. The further I stretched my spirit, the more I drew tension in the line connecting my family and me. They were not coming with me on that voyage into Blackness, not at all.

Mom and Dad's unconventional decision to adopt Greg and me, given their cultural lifestyle and backgrounds, cued my curiosity about that decision. Though I had never directly asked them about it previously, I had needed all along to understand their rationale. I was now in an indignant poise with my Black identity—angry and offended at our history in this society. When I realized that Mom and Dad had not once ever said a word to me about my adoption, I was dismayed and suspicious. It disturbed me that the beginning of my life had been so totally wiped from existence. It was almost as though a secret was being kept from me.

In my mind, my parents weren't the most likely candidates to adopt two Black children. I recounted their profile. They weren't West Coast liberalism. They weren't a young couple inflamed with a passion for contributing to the Civil Rights Movement. They had been raised in the heartland, in racially segregated and socially conservative Peoria, Illinois. They had virtually no meaningful, lasting relationships with Black persons and were squarely the products of White cultural heritage. They were acutely *not* the prototypical White family to adopt two Black children in the late 1960s, but they did. I could not stop feeling as though there were missing pieces to the story. Conversations left out. Hurtful truths hidden away.

No extended family is pure with perfection, and prejudices of a thousand flavors have a way of drifting toward children from their relatives, so this was not a reason for my parents to not adopt us. Still, I wondered to what degree Mom and Dad considered the implications of adopting Black children into their larger family culture. My curiosity wished to hear any of those conversations or private thoughts. *What went on? What's being kept from me?* The pervasive mystery cloud had kept me off balance throughout the years.

I finally pushed Mom on the subject of her family upbringing. She explained to me that her father's and even her own racial attitudes and perspectives were largely the consequence of living close to a large, poor Black community as a child. She was pained to tell me, "Yes, John, when I was growing up, we were taught that Black people were dirty and unclean. It's just how it was then."

I understood that kind of socialization. What perplexed me was the extreme contradiction of her childhood teachings with her decision to adopt Black children. *Has she ever spent time soul-searching and questioning what she was taught about Black people, once she invested in adopting one?*

Later, Dad would tell me a story. He and Mom attended a picnic held by the Council on Adoptable Children, whose mission was to promote adoption of hard-to-place children. This was back in Illinois when my parents were living in Champaign-Urbana while Dad finished his doctorate degree. They had just adopted me. The picnic was held to introduce families who were interested in adoption to those who had already adopted. Dad got into a lengthy conversation with an African American man. Concerned, the man asked Dad, "How are y'all going to teach this child all of the things that a Black child needs to know to grow up in a society so strongly aversive to Black people?"

The essence of Dad's response was his typical, sincere, understated retort. He said, "I probably cannot do a good job of that because of my ignorance and limited life perspective.

All I can do is try to teach him what my father taught me, and hopefully that will provide him the tools and the strength of character to figure out the rest on his own."

When I heard this story, I ached with both fulfillment and regret. *Why couldn't I have heard exactly this kind of story as a child? I needed to know that you and Mom were confronted with difficult questions, that you were forced to think through the implications. My life was way too complicated for me to be okay with the idea that your only thoughts about adopting us were as simple as discussing the weather.*

Dad's willingness to acknowledge his lack of insight into aspects of my necessary development was an important trait for a parent like him to have. But, I thought, *How exactly was I supposed to 'figure the rest out on my own'?* I had been lost in a racial hinterland. It was not enough, for me, that my parents simply related to me as they had been related to by their parents. Something in our relationship had needed to stretch and elevate itself out of their cradle and into mine.

Reviewing my childhood, a pattern emerged. I had been the subject of a collective and benevolent agenda. Many people were on some level aware that I might not feel as though I fit in. This bothered them. Their response to this was to actively encourage my sense of belonging. Some of them didn't care about my being Black, in the way someone might not care that a person has brown hair. Some didn't care about my being Black in the way that a person might not care about someone having a cleft lip—to them my trait was only a stigmatization to which they did not subscribe.

Then there were those who did care about my race. They had been taught to associate it with negative things and therefore it caused them a flitting up of negative emotion. But even these people cared about me more than they did about the lesson they had been taught. So, to facilitate my sense of acceptance, my experience of normality, virtually all involved went about suppressing my Blackness in their minds and hearts. The racial ingredient of my persona was blotted out. But thinking they were only blotting out a portion, a fragment of me that I could exist independently from, they committed an erasure of my entirety. For them, they had bypassed a nuisance element in my makeup, maybe even a contaminant.

None of these people wished me ill. Their motive was love. Love is seed to a strange and fractured tree of possibilities. To be fair, there were also those who had an affinity for the racial part of me. Yet, there were few among them for whom my race invoked an easy, natural, and positive appreciation that wasn't exaggerated or condescending.

My youthful tongue had not been able to articulate that for which my spirit screamed. Now, I knew that I had not been crying out for my Blackness to be ignored. I just wished that it not be treated as such a curiosity. I did not want it to be regarded as such an alien, foreboding stain on my skin that it should not be mentioned. I had stood in the intense glare of spotlight not because I was different, but because of how people reacted to my particular difference. The haunting of 400 years was evident in their eyes.

The day came when the backed-up waters overflowed my emotional dam. Having my biological family enter my life, the racial pride I had developed during college and graduate school, and my acquired retrospective of childhood, unleashed a hurricane of my latent torment. Now, beside the laid-back lap of the Pacific Ocean, my festering wound had breached its hold and my storm had come ashore.

By the time I reached my third year of graduate school I had lost my health, badly ended my longest intimate relationship, and estranged myself from family. I had reached the apogee of my orbit from them, openly scorning the idea of my belonging to the family, including our relatives. I was molten lava seething. My river had been released and I could not nearly contain it. I was depressed and full of self-pity. My body could not withstand the negativity and turmoil; my immune system dwindled into vulnerability. Then it fell apart.

For a full two years I was laid completely out with Coccidioidomycosis, or Valley Fever, a fungal disease contracted from spores in the dusty areas of the southwestern part of the country. Valley Fever is a non-contagious infection often suffered by migrant farm workers. The infection damages the lungs and normally resolves itself over a period of months; but in some cases, particularly with Black people, it becomes more severe and can kill. I felt like, with me, it almost did.

I lost 30 or 40 pounds, not of fat, but of muscle mass. At its peak, the fatigue left me too weak to pick up a fork, much less walk. Night sweats were a most uncomfortable symptom. Many nights I soaked through three or four shirts, shirts I had to wear to combat an undulating fever with chills. In the midst of this illness, I was caught in the clutch of a severe self-absorption resulting from contending with my base emotions for the first time. I shot my blame directly at the people in whose presence I had formed those emotions. This peaked to the point that I was not speaking to my family, especially Mom. I was alone, worn, and my nervous system was shot. If you had cut me in half across the waist and looked down at my cross section, I am sure that you would not have found 25 annual rings to indicate my years, but 70.

By midway through those two years of sickness, I understood that I had become so ill because the person I had been was dying, and who I would become was clawing to the surface. This was a violent, ugly, uncontainable metamorphosis. Unfortunately, I splashed the people who loved me most with the acid of my transformation. There came a dark, dark moment during that third year of school, when I realized I could possibly lose permanently everything that meant something to me—my health, my family, any chance at a healthy intimate relationship. The reckoning swept upon me like an impatient wrecking ball and smashed the mirror glass of my self-deception. I saw what stood behind: I had been dominated in my life by the putrid byproducts of my wound.

The roster was lengthy. Anger, resentment, negativity, defensiveness, fear, manipulation, self-pity, and selfishness had taken hold inside my soul and grown long, deep roots. I realized I had a choice. I could either commit myself to becoming a healthy person, or I could go throughout life unhappy and forever isolated.

The path ahead was clearly a personal one, yet it also began to reveal a purpose that returned to me the vision of my earliest days. My personal heart wasn't the only thing that needed changing. My story was being played out all around me in every kind of direct and indirect relationship between people. It was a story of denial of self, and bearing witness to it had made me sick. In particular, there was the shadow story of the other adoptions nationally I knew were being enacted.

I read an article concerning a man who, along with his wife, adopted a child internationally. In response to the interviewer's question of why this man and his wife decided not to adopt domestically but instead from another nation, the man answered that he and his wife thought it would be "neat" to create a multiethnic family . . .

Foster care is an ice cream parlor
I'll take one of those
yes, a vanilla one
none left?
okay then how about
a cream?
a chocolate swirl?
or maybe a latte
no? okay then a coffee
okay then I'll take the
dark chocolate
somehow we'll have to find
a way to leave his chocolate behind

Lady, I wouldn't place his chocolate behind
with you if you were the last thing standing in the wind.

'Neat'? I had heard of similar motivations from other White adoptive families. It reminded me of that ages-old attitude of too many Europeans and White Americans toward the rest of the world as something exotic that would be 'neat' to own. It was too close to the idea of possessing a plaything. Missy Anne danced with Kizzy in my imagination. *But this is not my family. They couldn't have adopted me because it was neat. Could they? I wasn't a collection piece, was I?* The fact alone that I had to consider and vanquish the idea eroded my peace. The familiar sensation of quicksand shifting beneath my feet made its millionth appearance.

I was repulsed by the idea of a mass devaluation of other cultures as objects for curiosity's sake, rather than as legacies to be honored, preserved, and fostered. My pledge as a seven-year-old, dropping hot tears onto a soaking pillowcase, returned. This condescending mindset existed in too many adopting families. I knew it. I could feel its energy breathing from afar. I had to stand up against it . . .

Black folk ask me
wrinkles in their face
old wounds rising in their chest
why'd they adopt you?
was it an experiment?
were they trying to save the world?
blood blisters in my breast
I am Frankenstein
I am unrest
why'd they adopt you?
stop it
why'd they adopt you?
stop it
why'd they adopt you?
because you would not
stop it

My first stand had to happen in my heart. My task was clear: I needed to face myself with an unprecedented honesty. Then, I needed to face my parents and communicate with them in a productive manner. I had to cease letting my reactions to life destroy my nervous system. If I couldn't manage to break through my thickest wall and express to my parents how I had been affected by my experience, I would be lost.

By this point, I had developed a more demanding need for my parents to show themselves to me in new ways. I wanted them to show me that they were willing to deal with the prejudices and biases of their upbringing, and not only to appease me. I wanted them to exert that effort because they were committed to it in their hearts as something that was important for them, exclusive of me.

Growth led me to a firm ground where I was ready to reclaim my life story. *I have a right to know the facts of my own life. I am not a secret.* The faint apparition that was my genesis story trailed along tightly after me, buzzing in my ear until I could stand it no longer. I had to give the apparition solid form. I finally asked the question to Mom and Dad, separately. "There is something I need to know. We've never talked about it, and it's bothering me. Why did you adopt me?"

They both answered first with pauses, as though they were caught off guard and perhaps had not thought of the explicit reason for years. From both of them, the answer came. It was one I would hear with great consistency from other White transracially adoptive families in coming years. "We just wanted to give a child a better life."

That's it? There has to be more to it than that. I was astounded. Their answer did nothing to clarify for me why they valued me as a particular person. I wanted to know what it was about *me* that meant something important to them—something important enough to want to take me into their home and raise me. And what was it about *them* that made them decide to take in a Black child in 1960s America?

I pondered their answer for months. It didn't make much sense to me. If there were special convictions they carried, or even if they didn't realize what they were getting into, I needed to know that. I needed to know something human about their thoughts and feelings at that time. This was about self-assurance. I was grasping at straws, wanting final conviction that I belonged, that my place in this family was bound by something earnest and deeply rooted. Mom and Dad's simple, altruistic answer had just the opposite effect.

We just wanted to give a child a better life. I could not accept this as the full extent of their motivation for taking on such a large responsibility. I knew that my family taking me in had been a monumental commitment. It opened them up to a world full of criticism, attention, and parenting challenges. I needed to know about the values, circumstances, and fears involved in making such a choice. I needed to understand any selfish motivations as well. I knew people *did* adopt children for their own benefit, and not just to be saviors to children.

Deep down inside, what could Mom and Dad have been thinking, feeling, worrying about when they considered adopting us? What questions did they ask each other? More nervously, I wondered what questions and concerns occupied their private space, that space they did not share even with each other. What prejudiced feelings and thoughts were remnants within, the product of their own socialization? I knew their hearts contained no hateful energy. I was concerned with the private, steadily creeping attitudes left over from their impressionable childhoods. I had to know. *Why, really, did they adopt me?*

I knew that their motivations had nothing to do with wanting to engage in some kind of convoluted social experiment, as some Black people had surmised to me. Their desire to adopt us was not about trying to decimate the Black community, or raise a counter-agent to go back into the African American community upon reaching adulthood and wreak havoc. These were presumptions I had actually heard. My best muster of understanding was that their rationale was less dramatic and more mundane than my fears were whispering to me. Unfortunately, the implications of their decision were not so mundane.

My insistently laconic moods sometimes got the better of Mom. She finally responded in exasperation. "Would you have rather us left you in foster care?" She asked this very genuinely. I had pushed her to frustrated uncertainty about whether I truly felt better off having been adopted. I cringed. Her comment left me thinking that she believed me to be unappreciative of my family. Still young and burgeoning with perspective, I could not find a way to communicate the things I struggled over without it being taken as ingratitude. *Would she ever have said that to Kristin, if Kristin had tried to tell her something in her childhood had hurt her? Would she have said, "Would you rather have not been born?"* The expectation of indebtedness is the bane of the adoptive child.

On a gray, rainy day while visiting home, I found my courage. Years had passed. The adult relationship between my parents and I was dawning. They were grayer. I was Blacker. It had come to this. "Mom and Dad, I need to talk to you." Every fear that had forced its way through me held a reunion in my chest. I was terrified, but the pressure of bottling up 20-plus years was now the stronger force. The words left my lips. Just like that, I had entered a new season. In slow motion, I found myself telling my story . . .

This is how I hurt
when you did this I
and when you did that I
and when this happened I
and you and you and you
It hurt so bad
I was so broken
I was your child
I was their token

Mom, I needed you
Dad, I was so lost
snow kept coming
I suffered ice and frost
died a thousand times
wished a million things
can't take this pressure no more
don't hardly have the wings

can't run away from you
no legs left 'pon which to run
my heart is on the table
please go soak it in the sun
please don't dismiss deny diminish
castigate rationalize explain away
not today

you thought you raised a rose
I froze became dandelion seed
billow kite for bitter breeze
I promise you this is who I am
If you brush it off
I shall never show it to you
again

My words were strangled and retched raw, like regurgitated acid. It burned coming up my throat . . . too much emotion. Dad listened, crying. I had never seen him cry before. He thought: *I wish I had been able to share myself with my Dad while he was here on this Earth. Oh, the things I wish I could have said. I am happy for you, my son.* Mom was broken hearted. Maybe we all were just as relieved as hurt. Relieved that we had reached what we all had been running from. We knew the bottle had been shaken, the carbonation had long been hollering to get out. My turtle shell was too small for me now. It cracked in the moment as I grew. My growing was quick. I surged forth molted, from my cocoon, forcing each of us into a needle storm. We three sat around a table on the porch. Outside, even God was crying, rain everywhere. Shells were breaking. Old skin tore against three chairs. New skin glistened in its shiver.

After listening to me release my festered stream, Mom said, through frustrated, confused tears, "I tried to treat all you kids the same." It was a plea, an absolute dissolution. Everything she had cared for was in the arms of her motherhood. She heard me telling her that she had failed. That was not what I was saying. But she was a mother. That was what she heard. *All those sacrifices, all those diaper changes, bottles, feedings; all the times I took their stones cast against me for loving you; all my dreams that died; all the soul I spilled and never cleaned up because I was cleaning up after all my children. How, God, can my son be telling me that I failed? Mom, didn't I do it like you did? I did it just like you did.*

I treated all my kids the same. When I heard those words a dawning light splashed all around in my mind. Her words represented the banner of parental strategy that had always waved over our house. This was the explanation, finally, that allowed me to begin to understand why my parents had so overwhelmingly not addressed in tangible, audible ways the undeniable fact that Greg and I were Black, and that we were adopted. Mom was saying that she had done her best to show that her love for us was equal to that of all her children. And she had done it by relating to us as if the facts of our adoption and race didn't exist. She had whitened them out.

I had to subdue my egoistic need for redemption before I could see the answer to my questions, and realize it had been before me all along. My resolution of my parents' motivation to adopt was simpler than I wanted it to be. It gave me breath just the same. As they had said, they only wanted to give a child a better life. And I can only imagine that amid the totality of their pure and loving intent, they could not have seen looming the full horizon of the implications they were stepping into. This is who my mother and father were—secure, directed, and devoted in their love for us children. Anything else to them was the periphery of life.

Later, as I reflected upon the way my parents had set their course as young adults, I realized that I could have not expected lengthy consideration of my adoption from a man and a woman who decided to marry after only seven dates. It was not their composition. Theirs was an innocent simplicity. They wanted more children, the consequences of that possibility were not a thing they were designed to dwell upon or hold up life for. For them, life was for moving forward.

But the remnants of their socialization would come with them. Mom tried with all her heart to understand what I was trying to communicate to her about my experience. But much of it was difficult for her to wrap herself around in an instinctual way. Even then, in my 20s, my family seemed to have a hard time saying the words 'Black' or 'African American' in reference to Greg and me or others. I received their attempts as stiff, awkward offerings. During one Christmas, Kristin gave me a collection of plastic figures representing the Christian nativity scene for a gift. The figures were Black. No one mentioned anything about the collection as I was opening it. The whole family sat there, anxiously staring at me as if they were thinking, *Okay, this is it. How is he going to react to the figures being Black?*

I didn't comment on the race of the figures, so Kristin asked, "Didn't you notice?"

"Notice what?" I said.

"They're special," she said.

They're special. This lit my flame. I responded, "What's so special about them? Do you mean that they are Black?" My angst got the best of me, "As far as I know from history and geography, what's special is the way these figures are usually portrayed as being White. These figures here, there is nothing special about them." My words were followed by the familiar awkward silence. None of them managed to utter that ominous word, 'Black', and the nervous moment eventually passed.

My resentment had once more percolated to the surface, and now there was an additional uneasy vibe put out in the air between us. At that time, they just couldn't win with me. Kristin had been trying her utmost to relate, to support, and to show her care for me by giving me that gift, which is what she and Mom had been doing since that breakthrough conversation when I finally let down the wall. Mom had been buying me little Black figures, and placing Black figures around the house, eagerly pointing them out to me whenever I was home. I think she had missed my point.

I was in my 20s now and Mom's somewhat forced and unnatural placement of Black figures around her home didn't really help things. Still, I couldn't help but be carved by her effort. Now it was healing time. I had to give my family a break. They could never carry in their emotional makeup the same meaning for some things in life that I had. I could not have expected them to have the same visceral reaction to the image of a Black man's murder at the hands of police; or to a story of a lynching; or to televised scenes of Black poverty and violence. I could not have expected them to be as troubled emotionally by the knowledge of scores of Black children being 'miseducated' and undereducated. They reacted to these stories as human to human, but my reaction was as kin to kin, brother to brother. This was not their orbit. I had to give up that expectation. And I needed to begin counting my blessings.

Several times, Black persons offered me this: "Your parents must have raised you well. They must be good people." It was a refreshing surprise and a relief to hear Black folk look across the perimeter that was my parents' race and recognize their goodness. The words left me buoyed with pleasure at the person's lack of prejudice, and needled me with a reminder that in so many ways I had been nurtured with a rare devotion. *Go down to the Potter's house and there I will give you my message.*

Mom and Dad gave themselves to the task of raising children. They dove into that pool, with virtually no guidance through the unique challenges of raising Greg and me. Love and determination gave them wings. Their cultural personalities limited how far they could fly. But I had to appreciate their giving now, and climb free from my wallow in the quicksand of what I had lacked. My family must have been wounded from hosting my hurt. They also needed fresh air, a chance to heal.

As I began to allow my family their rightful human imperfections and difference from my personality, I opened up into a determination to work with other adoptive families and children. Nearing that place from which I could relate to other adoptive families without losing myself in judgment or unrealistic expectation, I set out to make the life I had led count for something. It was time to heal through teaching. That early promise I made myself came back to me: Do anything to prevent another confused Black child from clawing away at her chest or at the mocking nighttime air. Clawing because she feels so far away and different from her White family, and because she is dying to go to a place where she belongs—wherever that may be.

I listened intently to numerous adoption stories, and the patterns of emotion and ideology were remarkably evident. I was retrieving my own story through the lives of strangers. These families were greenhouses for all the beautiful and blemished blossoms of what it means to be family. And what it means to relate as races. Clouds huddled, dark and purposeful. They decided to rain through me. I could not help but be hospitable to the stream. It came rushing . . .

The magic began as I came, embryonic into this world
prepared with my own recipe, my own stories to tell
culture kissed me quick and clean, courted me with lullabies
hot breath on my neck, seduced I began my childhood

I don't fear the bad White people, I fear the good
they are the ones who refuse to see me
all the while absolutely sure . . . they see me

and safety? The good White folk, with love and opportunities to
offer, but for whom Black folk are alien, frighten me more than any
Black ghetto ever could. You wish to place me safely?
place me in a home where even the Black of me will be free
not locked away in the pantry growing mold, a neglected ebony
that would be the death of me

this is not charity, these children are not commodity, their glow is
not ghoulish grin of jack o' lantern for our device, they are lanterns
of a possible life, cloaked in a madness not of their making
cuidado con la luz de la mariposa . . . careful with the butterfly light
your candles droop to the flame, wax runs loose alights
singed is everything . . . butterfly never now will sing

I know White mother from breast of Netherlands
who holds her Black children's essence in her hands
treats that splendid pool like butterfly, does not crush from fear
nor smother with guilt, is not stained with American racial weight
free to love Black butterfly, bears proof that threat to fragile wings
is not of genotype, for sure as night has hosted moon , and tides leap
frog and frolic in warmth of June, 'twas state of mind that spilled
splendid pool and killed Black butterfly

you say . . . *I treat all my children the same* . . . I say no you don't
and no you don't . . . for it is not the act but the impact
you plucked splinter from skin, called your pluck a remedy
but were you to pluck a rose from earth, you could not call your
pluck the same, for it would be not remedy . . . but kidnap . . . see?
White people tell me . . . *I wish I had a culture* . . . I shake my head
invisibly, for oppression has born forth White children lost
somebody tell them life *is* culture . . . each of us is its ambassador

they claim proudly . . . *I have transcended race* . . . their words are smoke
trail of deception's flash descent . . . transcend your prejudice
leave race alone, it was fine before your newborn lips ever drew
breath or suckled from human social stew, much less before you
decided to delete Divine meaning from God's variety
quit trying to snatch peaches from the apple tree
stop trying to make my elbow bend like my knee
holster your imposition impulse . . . *see me*

you snow your flakes through the breezeway that is my insecurity
which is fine when day is cold, but when warmth descends a blanket
your flakes melt away, insecurity returns to greet me
you are gone then, for the snowing of flakes is a fickle love affair
you snow now elsewhere, your weather is a foul design
the puddle left behind? All mine.

Trying to fit in as a child and young adult by suppressing most
of my true nature was ultimate self-destruction. I was a vague
apparition in a crisp, White world. My spirit seemed so distant
and foreign to this place where everybody else seemed a secure
appendage to the scene.

Now, I was disappointed in myself. I didn't feel that my
family or friends learned anything in particular about Black
people from my presence. I hadn't presented myself as
anything other than the White cultural patterns that were
modeled for me. Of my actual spirit, I hid what I could manage
to hide. I kept to myself all my attitudes about life, and the
things we learned in our schoolbooks and in class. I barely let
on about what I felt about slavery, segregation, oppression,
discrimination, or anything that called into question our
nation's racial illnesses. I made secrets out of my admiration for
certain Black national figures, and zipped my lips about my
disdain for the prejudice-stained character of certain White
national figures. I maintained a facade that stretched my soul.

The strain was more evident to me whenever I returned to
Los Alamos and perpetuated my lie to my family, the
Mortensens, and others close to me. It ate at me even when I
was away from Los Alamos. I was a fractured soul and my soul
kept letting me know about it, following me in whispers,
granting no escape. I had been dislocated, muted, and a
betrayer of all whom had come before me.

I had constantly done the mental and emotional two-step.
One step toward my true personality under the cover of my
private inner world. One step back toward the image I knew
others had of me as a Black person. That image was colored

with assumptions that I was just as 'White' in my outlook on things as they were. Shamefully, this was what I wanted them to believe, even if it was never true.

My blossoming into the living manifestation of what my spirit had been all along was a bittersweet thing, as I sensed that on some level it hurt those closest to me from my early days. At the same time, I basked in the relief that came with honestly exposing the truth of who I was.

I resolved that those who were meant to be meaningful in my life would overcome any struggles they had with my unveiling and would be happy for me because they knew I was finding peace. I knew those who loved me—the soul of me and not the perceived similarity of me—would share this happiness with me, even when part of that similarity revealed itself as an illusion.

My newfound loyalty to the person I was had nothing to do with the depth of my love for my family. Human nature probably tugged at my parents with ropes of insecurity as I went my way. But my way was made to journey through only a part of theirs, and my growth could never be a diminishing of who they were to me. The opposite was true. Through self-discovery, I gained more appreciation for what my family had been to me all along. I saw that they had been steady in their support, their forgiveness, and their embrace.

No matter how good of spirit were the many souls I met in the world, each shone light on the fact that I had been placed with a special woman and man. Mom and Dad gave all their children a precious and rare gift: the permission to be ourselves. I cherished that gift. Now, I was finally taking that permission my parents had always granted. In my taking, I knew there might be some parts painful to my parents, as there were some parts painful to me. But with each step, I gained more peace in being the adopted Black son of my White mother and father, Darlene and James Potter.

I wished to continue the growth of that peace until I was in harmony with all of what I was. That ultimate peace would be the greatest gift I could have given back to my parents and to my brothers and sisters for the riches they had bestowed upon me. I had always been, even in the midst of my most strongly pulsing pain, a very, very rich person. I saw this now. My riches had been family and friends that most would envy. I was now seeing that for the depth of what I suffered I had received blessings that were tenfold greater.

My spirituality had always been of a nature that was most similar to the Earth-bound, quiet, understated spirituality of our neighboring Pueblo, Hopi, and Diné communities. I had drawn my energy from the earth, sky, water, and air around me. Now, in this struggle, I needed more than ever the graces of something greater—I was moving to end my drowning. That reliable Wind began to speak.

My peace was to be found in my acceptance of myself, by claiming my purpose and truth, and standing for it. My salvation would be in letting go of the wound, releasing my blame from those I had targeted with its arrow, and taking responsibility for becoming the person I knew was my destination. I had been at the pitch-black bottom of my pit, and I knew it. Now came the great blessing that saved my life once more.

As I lay, pathetic in that thick, smothering despair, Divine Creation shone itself down into that hole and gave me light. *I know who I am.* My face was reflected in a wide river running backward through the lives of all those who had shaped me, fed me, fertilized me. It was time for me to claim the essence with which my Great Spirit had sent me here. Djembe drum started its talking in a booming wave that parted the indigo sky of my blindness. That Ghanaian drum, carved from one large piece of tweneboa wood and headed with goatskin, morphed into a giant echo chamber and spoke.

I had been named 'Austin' while in my mother's womb. I was 'Baby Boy' in my first hours on Earth. I was 'Baby Boy Scott' as a foster child. I would be 'John Scott' for the next 100 seasons. During much of that time, I was 'JP' to most that knew me. I believe now that my legal name was often avoided in speech because its energy was not a proper manifestation of my spirit. I had been called so many names—people were subconsciously looking for the sound that suited me. Now, on the cusp of climbing out of my self-imposed bleakness, it became clear to me that I had outgrown the skin of my parade of names. Time to leave it on the rocks.

Storyteller showed up to lead the way in her curmudgeonly manner. She was a good six feet tall now. Her shoulders had broadened. Eerie thought told me that this woman was evolving into my shape. Was I somehow sprouting a clone, or just my first fully formed version? Her voice interrupted my madness. "A person becomes an infant twice in this life," she said, "and so should twice be named. The second infancy is that during which we become adults. For most of us, this period seems to come during the mid-20s, after having sloughed off our earlier fantasies about having achieved honorable maturation. During this second infancy, when we begin to become adults, though still green ones, a person should reflect upon the appropriateness of his or her name.

"In the first infancy, we are named only because we cannot name ourselves, though parents and other family members believe it is because they are ordained with the God right to name a baby human. In this way, adults grant newborn spirits a name for safekeeping. Sometimes this name is an accurate reflection. Sometimes it speaks more to how others wish to see the newborn than to the spirit the newborn is. No one other than the person herself and God has ultimate insight into the essence of that spirit. That essence is what must finally be named.

"When true adulthood has been reached—that plateau of personhood defined by self-knowledge—we are faced with a responsibility. Knowing ourselves, we must tell the world what to call us. The elders told me, 'If you do not do so, the world will not hesitate to call you what it wishes. And you will become that name.' This name you receive for yourself in adulthood need not be new. Perhaps the birth-given name is proper and can remain.

"But child, know this. You cannot take a name. You must receive it. A name is spirit. Spirit is a name, a security blanket of inheritance. A quilt of names that will faithfully keep us warm if only we pick it up and put it on. Spirit is the conduit through which our ancestors speak to us. It is not exotic cultural imagination. Rather, we without it are a flawed imagination of what human is. But you cannot choose it. It must choose you."

In my case, the names I had carried had been receptacles of great affection, but they never struck that certain cord in my chest. Never resonated as truth. My choice was made. As it was written, "When I became a man, I put away childish things."

My spirit wandered back to the bamboo forests just off the mangrove swamps and clay banks of the Kamby Bolongo. Dwarfed in the shade of rosewood, oil palm, mahogany, and rubber trees, I was a young boy on the eve of adulthood. Djembe drum cleared its throat. An eclectic gathering of stoic warriors from the local Mandingo, Wollof, Fula, and Sarahuley people stood in a circle around me. This movement would be my initiation, my naming ceremony. I was fed by memories of Kunta's manhood ceremony, and by his taking the lash in the dirt of American soil, demanding that his name was Kunta. This was not trivial imitation of art, it was inspired vibration and it shook me. I planted my feet in the clay and stood determined that I would do this thing.

I was scared. I was in a motion I could not halt, breaking away from my lifelong spiritual bondage. I was fearful because I knew that it would hurt my family to know I was to change my name. But God's urging was stronger than my fear. I could not resist. I knew that if ever I were to embrace my family it would have to be as my true self. A taunting question had come to its answer. All this time, my detachment from Mother Mary had not been a fate preventing me from bonding fully with people. It was that my spirit would not allow me to bond through a false membrane. It would not allow me to offer up a complete intimacy under the conditions of suppression. Relief flooded me. My newborn separation did not have to dictate my orbit in the human world. The hole in my gut was a symbol of my journey and not the precursor to my path.

I remembered Storyteller's words. *I must not go looking for my name.* I would not look in books, forage through the underbrush of popular media, or seek out a name that sounded good. I knew it already existed, patient for me all these many moons. *The sky will bring it to you.* Understanding the process could be long, I was prepared for years to pass. I was a butterfly before it has become one. Waiting, bound inside the cocoon, yet rattling along with the cocoon in the springtime wind, knowing that the skin around me was never quite the name of me, and that I would eventually shed it as I emerged into the light. I waited. Two years passed.

To name yourself in adulthood is to tempt the wrath of the world. People become set in their ways of relating to others in their life, and if you should dare to change your name in any way, beyond the prescribed marriage-change allowed women, you risk a private and public lashing. I anticipated the buzzing whiplash. *How dare you disrupt my vision of you! How dare you disturb my habit! Your name is my possession.* I was prepared for the backfire. I worried about the feelings of my family, but I knew I was doing what I had to do. I could only hope they would find a way to maintain the spirit of supporting my inclinations as they, other than with race, always had.

In October of 1994, under a night crowned by the circle moon, my name came to me. I received it. The sky was black. The universe seemed to pause, inhale. Then it ushered in an electric wind, cascading down at me. It was a bison stampede. I received the Great sound, knowing what had come. It entered my chest, ran up and down my spine. The sound was *Jaiya*. I recognized this word, this energy so well I flooded with tears. This was a part of me that preceded even my birth. It was a God echo, bouncing around my inner walls. The words 'Jordan' and 'John' came in the days following, in the same way, if not quite as powerfully. Though 'Jaiya' was the name that affected me most, I remained faithful to the stampeding voice that brought the three beacons. The ordering of the words was to be 'Jordan Jaiya John'.

I had never before heard or read of the word 'Jaiya'. But the first time I spoke it, it melted into my chest and spread across me in a warm blanket. The way I felt speaking the word was like an overdue introduction. Like when I had first seen Mary's face. *Jaiya, . . . that's me.* I wasn't sure the word existed in any language, but if it did, I was not pressed to know its meaning. I was its meaning. I had lived it.

It didn't take me long to share my epiphany with Mom and Dad, yet it was one of the most difficult things I had spoken to them. I explained what this meant to me. "This is something I have to do. I know this will be hurtful to you, but I want you to know this is not about rejecting you. I just desperately need something I can feel fully attached to. I need this, and I think it will only help me be a better person in my relationship with you."

I could feel their tides recede back inside their chests. I had delivered unto them another blow. Their pauses were long, but their responses were true to form. Mom said, "If you think that's what you need then go on ahead and do what you have to do. It'll be all right, John. You don't have to put so much pressure on yourself."

Dad was honest. "It does hurt, because that's my family name. And we gave you your name with a lot of love."

"I know, Dad, but I need this."

"We'll try to understand. You know we always support you. You have to follow your own voice."

"I love you both. I feel bad about this, but you'll see it's what I need."

"We love you. We just want you to be happy."

I put down the phone, relieved. I had finally stood up for something that was true inside. They had respected it, though it pained them. I saw that I was responsible for initiating my stance in the world, and that no one else could do it for me. *We just want you to be happy.* Happy was on its way.

My name is Jordan Jaiya John. This is who I have been all along. The universe had waited patiently for me to recognize. I ruminated on the ideas of family, heritage, and the honoring of a person's predecessors, but exactly who were my predecessors? I was a grown person, still with one foot back in that elementary school classroom, ashamed and confused as I was forced to identify where my ancestors came from. Those ancestors were in a way, through familial spirit and love, the biological relatives of my adoptive family.

But my people were also that boundless stream of blood and spirit from which I was descended, and which spoke so loudly through me. I would never neglect or shy from embracing that again. That voice was my dominant one. It was imperative to my health, happiness, and peace that I follow it, just as Dad had always instructed. If my parents' adopting me was not a betrayal of their biological children, or of their own relatives, then neither was my adoption of my own rightful name a disloyalty. My Potter family connection existed in my heart more than in the name, so I did not think I had betrayed family. Had I not recognized and adopted my own name, I would have betrayed myself.

With this new spirit, I moved to Washington, DC, to be a professor at Howard University, and face a sea full of Black students who would add great rings of substance to my spiritual tree. I had moved into a Black neighborhood during the one year following graduate school when I worked in

Portland. But this would be my first long-term, complete immersion into a dominant mass of African-descended people, and I came with a longing to get wet much like so many others Howard had received on its grounds. I was led by my voice here, sensed a Higher purpose, a need for this season. *Spirit moves me closer to completing a circle.*

As when I was 17, I was again fearful that the students would 'smell' my background on me, and reject me outright. I was humbled by this moment. *My transformation brought me here.* I had been an extremely quiet, shy child, frightened by Whiteness all around, and now I was about to stand in front of hundreds of African American students who still were culturally unfamiliar to me. I would be called to use my speaking voice as an authority figure for them. I was expected to teach, guide, mentor, and elevate. I made this voyage riding on inspiration, and knew it was the proper location for this season. Clarity borne of faith carried me. I was overwhelmed at the divine opportunity. *I once sat in classrooms, mute, trying to scrape my Blackness off against the underside of desks. I'm a teacher now, of Black students. This is unbelievable.* The Great Circle was getting greedy for its completion of my life's particular variation.

I prepared myself for the rejection. Instead, from the first day of class, I was swallowed in love and affection. The kinship circle was here, too, and took me. Creation had arranged for me, after a lifetime malnourished, to receive a high-potency dose of Black nutrition all at once. For the next four years, I existed among thousands of individuals, struggling in their own ways with their identity in a racially resistant nation. Discovering this made me feel better about my own struggles, and brought sadness as well.

As I broke in my new name, I was broken into all the unique, common, mystical, mundane flavors of being human that any racial or ethnic group of people provides. I recognized *Jaiya* in the biological family I was growing into, I reconstituted *Jaiya* in the adoptive family I approached from a new ground of strength, and I recovered *Jaiya* from the tender souls of these beautiful, imperfect students, children of Africa's womb.

These students came from around the world. All I had to do was connect with them—in class, in my office, or around campus, and they would offer up to me a tour of Africa's cultures in global variety. The Great Spirit had led me to the drinking hole I required. A few of those students, and others I met, introduced me to the meanings of my names. I learned that 'Jordan', besides being the biblical river and holy land I had always been drawn to, is from the Hebrew, 'Yarden', meaning, *The Descender* or, *Descend*; and also: *To flow* or, *Flow down*. 'John' was also Hebrew, for, *Godly*; *God gave*; and *Yahweh (God) is gracious*. In that light, I recognized 'John' as the name of both 'the Baptist' prophet who had performed his greatest service in those Jordan River waters and foretold of The Messiah, and also as the apostle acclaimed as the author of the fourth Gospel and Revelation.

I was shown that 'Jaiya' is a powerful word, found in cultures spread wide over the Earth. In the Sanskrit language of India, 'Jaiya' means, *Victory*,—not as in our culture's sense of victory, but as in *Complete annihilation of the ego*, a spiritual triumph of humility and oneness. In the Yoruba culture of Nigeria, 'Jaiya' is the phonetic combination of 'Ja', meaning *break* or *tear*, and 'Iya', meaning, *mother*. I was overwhelmed when I discovered that, taken technically, this can mean, *To break or separate from mother*. I thought of Storyteller's admonishment: *Know the essence and you will have found the meaning.* Also, in Yoruba, 'Aye' means *Earth* or *Life*, and is part of the phrase, "Mo je aye:" *I'm loving life*; and the phonetic 'j'aye': *Love life*. 'Aya' means, *Afraid* or *Chest*, so 'j'aya' would mean, *To break from fear* or *Broken hearted*. The synchronicity of these meanings with my personality left me awestruck. I had spent my life controlled by a smothering fear—a fear of being myself, and it had broken my heart.

And there was another African meaning. This for the sound 'j'aye': *I came through the struggle and lived.* A young West

African woman shared with me that 'Jaiya' was part of a Muslim term in her culture: 'Nabieu Jaiya'—*Allah's Messenger.* Finally, I would discover that I had been born into this world on a Thursday. In the African tradition, there were names for such children. One of those names was 'Ya', from both the Twi people of Ghana and the Ewe of Eastern Africa. Again, I was humbled, realizing that 'Ya' was a primary sound of my name, 'Jaiya'. I was drowning in sweet revelation. *God has always known my name.*

I had been provided the meaning of my name from world ambassadors, many of whom were found in my Howard University classrooms. My life's purpose dawned as a sunburst. I was humbled by how far I had thus far fallen short of the challenge given to me by my Great Spirit and Life Above. Beyond humbled, I was at once empowered and resolved to stand for who I was. This Black child's welfare was now, in his mid-20s, rounding into full effect. And the completion of the great circle his life had been following loomed to the South.

Woods is callin' you, Man
Feel that evenin' wind dancin'
through the willow trees?
Hear them scat talkin' old men
tellin' lies 'round the fire?
I know you can, Man
You came from that
It wants you back
Woods is callin' you
Man

BACK TO BETHLEHEM

[Excerpt from a letter to Whitfield Jenkins from Mary Woods,
February 2, 1983]:

Dear Mr. Jenkins:

No doubt, this correspondence will provoke a certain amount
of shock, and even chagrin, upon your reading its contents.
However, I feel it only fair at this time to inform you of a situation
of which you are a part, but which I could not write you about
earlier; the latter being my inability to obtain your address prior to
now.

To come straight to the point—on October 26, 1967, I gave
birth to a 7 pound, 7 ounce son. You are the father of that child.

IN the spring of 1996, after having settled in on the East
Coast, I was ready for my next step. I harbored an obvious
need to meet the man who was my biological father, Whitfield
Jenkins. We had spoken and written to each other every few
months or so since I first received a letter from him, three days
before my 23rd birthday in 1990. By the time I came to

Washington, DC, I began to realize that Whitfield might be experiencing at least as much, if not more, anxiety about meeting me. I at least had the benefit of having gone through the experience with Mary. He was the newborn on this one. Whitfield and I had always talked about wishing to meet, and the years were coming and going. It occurred to me that I might have to take the lead on materializing our reunion. *So, Florida is where this will happen.*

My initiative to go to Florida was heightened by a strong conviction and a particular emotional inspiration. Back in January of 1994, while I was still in graduate school, I had received a letter from Rose Jenkins, Whitfield's youngest daughter. She was only 16 years of age at the time, and therefore single years to her seemed like gaping voids of endlessness. Unknown to the rest of her family, she had decided to dispense with the slow passage of time and orchestrate a rendezvous. Concluding her letter, she wrote:

"My dream is to one day be able to meet you because you are my brother, we have the same father. I hope that one day my dream will come to reality.

Love always,
your lil' sister, Rose D. Jenkins."

The words turned me into mush. My little sister, a person I had never met, truly wanted, and needed to know me. I was astounded and humbled. Tears washed me.

I shared Rose's letter with my close friends and made a vow to myself to somehow meet this part of my growing family. *How can I resist such an honest, loving plea? I have to do this, make my little sister happy. I don't want her waiting too much longer. She's waited long enough. We all have.* Now I was living in the DC area, a straight shot down to Ocala. *No excuses.* I took another deep breath, made the plans to fly down to Florida, and stepped into the next iteration of what was truly a dream.

On the flight down to Orlando, I was calm and assured. I had long felt a providential hand guiding this awe-inspiring reconnection with my biological roots. The cabin noise was a monotone carriage bringing me to sleep's shallow end. My half-dreams wandered through the possibilities of the trip ahead. When I stepped on the Earth again, it would be to conclude a separation of 28 years. *How is this man going to look? How awkward will the air be between us? How easily will the conversation flow?* I was approaching a great moment from 20,000 feet in the air, like Mom did back in '64 flying to New Mexico for the first time. *God, you have made me rich.* I could not have been much higher.

I stepped off that plane in Orlando on March 26, 1996. Walking up the ramp from the plane to the gate, my senses went on high alert. I could smell the well-trodden carpet. The light in the corridor was dim, yet vibrant to my eyes. I braced for the sighting. I knew that upon entering the gate area, I would scan the crowd of faces only briefly before recognizing *my father's face.* I stepped into that space.

The first image I beheld, front and center in that bustling crowd, was that of a huge Black angel, his condor wings outstretched across the entire gate area it seemed. Whitfield stood in front of me, his long arms elevated out from his sides, his huge hands opened up with fingers spread as if trying to grasp a dream. His face was lit with a smile I will not forget. My own smile melted into his. Slow motion found me stepping into his embrace. "Hey, Partner, welcome home," Whitfield spoke into my ear.

I could not speak. But I am sure he heard everything my feelings had to tell. All the while my peripheral vision caught his wife, Loretta, and my sister, Rose, letting forth tearful rivers of their disbelief. Their tears were my passport to a whole world that had always been a part of me, but which fate had orbited me past in my living. Their tears were my welcome mat, my at last release of this chapter's anxiety; a whisper from Above that all was well. Loretta and I squeezed each other tight, the sounds of overwhelmed emotion spilling out of us.

My body still in her arms, the intangible part of me levitated. *Acceptance.* Rose and I swallowed each other in arms and emotion. *I can't believe this—this is actually my blood sister.* Even my nervousness had wings to it. The four of us floated through the airport, out to the car, and headed for Ocala, 90 unbelievable minutes of conversation away.

As we entered Ocala, I was transfixed at everything outside the car window. This place was a southern portrait of the kind I had often imagined. The old, rural feel was strong. The land was thick with trees, the homes modest. Even from the car, I could see that there were two Ocalas—the one Black and the other White, two communities tethered within the same geography; a juxtaposed set of worlds about which I was eager to learn. We arrived at their house in the Black community of *Happiness Homes*, and got out of the car. Each step of this process was a ritual for me. I passed through each moment granting it the solemnity it required. I stood and exhaled. The air was humid, heavy, and smelled slightly sweet.

I saw the banner on the front window of the house: "Welcome home, Jaiya." I had no more tears left, so a sigh was all that left me. I stepped through the front door—another ritual. Inside, I was overtaken with relief and comfort. I was shy to the house itself, as though I were visiting a holy place. Loretta helped me dismiss that pretense by heading straight for the kitchen, where in minutes she had brought the house to weeping with the oily steam of frying fish. *Eat plenty. Eat plenty.* It was time to be family, plain and simple. My sister, Tijuana, the oldest of the three, came home from work, and we began our physical knowing with oversized grins and a heap of a hug. I met her husband, Reggie Woods, and their two boys, Edgar ReVay and Jordan. *This is too much.*

One of the first things Whitfield did during that visit was to take me out to the country area outside of Ocala to Bethlehem, the community where he was raised. Located within a broader area called Zuber, Bethlehem was named after the community church. We drove past horses grazing on ranches that had once been the woods Whitfield had played in as a boy. We arrived at Bethlehem, my mood reverential again. Whitfield showed me the decrepit, tiny structure he had known as his home. Though the weather-darkened boards of the shack were still firm, the remains were tattered and grown over with vines, weeds, and trees.

The shack was only a couple of hundred yards from the Bethlehem Church. We got out of the car and walked over to a graveyard located not too far in front of the church. Sun was beating down. Heat was a curtain rising up, off the ground. Seemed like the woods were talking; my reality was creeping toward suspension again. We stopped in front of a particular gravesite. I looked down and what I saw made me woozy. Whitfield spoke the fact reverentially, his grown man's voice given up slightly to the longing tone of a child. "This is the grave of my father, Boss Jenkins, your grandfather, who passed away at the age of nearly 103 in 1984."

I saw the lettering on the plastic and tin plate: Boss Jenkins, Sr., February 17, 1881 – February 7, 1984. I was more than woozy. Woos became a cruise, and I was on it sailing at 100 knots toward the clouds. In a matter of moments, I had gone from a lifetime disconnected from my biological roots to reuniting with not just one but two of the generations preceding me. I had won a grand jackpot, and had stumbled over a treasure chest of gold on the way to retrieving it.

Whitfield passed on my legacy to me, the legacy he had been holding for me for this long and now ended season. He started speaking in his way that would become familiar: "Now, let me just give you the history on this . . . My father was born 50 miles north of Ocala in Alachua, Florida, on February 17, 1881. He left home at 11 or 12 to work and support the family. This was a time when children were labor resources toward a family's survival. My father walked long distances into the woods, to where the work camps were located. He worked cutting cross-ties for the railroad.

"I remember him, past age 60, leaving home with his club axe, broad axe, and cross cut saw slung over his shoulder. They said younger men couldn't match his work pace. He soaked himself in sweat, rarely took a break. The sun never found him lazy, not when it rose, not when it set." I recalled my sledge hammering folk hero of years past. *John Henry, I've found you again.*

Whitfield continued, "He worked hard, drank hard, and was always ready to sweat again on Monday morning. He was a tough, hard man, who didn't go to the doctor for sickness or injury. He and his like rather relied upon sassafras tea, an herb and root concoction boiled in a Maxwell House quart coffee can and drank bitter without any sweetener. That was their medicinal cure-all. Didn't have time or money for anything other. I was given the stuff often. I'll never forget the taste. Folks used to chew the root for toothaches. Sassafras was the old way. Don't know whether it came from their Indian roots or African roots but it sure enough came from their roots.

"My Daddy, he was still cutting cross ties when my youngest brother Charlie came along in '45. He was 65 years old then, and still doing hard labor for $2 a day. He would take baby Charlie with him out into the woods, sit him under a sweet gum bush with his formula and diapers and go and cut those cross ties, checking on Charlie when he could. That's why the two of them were so close. Folks always said of Daddy, 'He took care of his boys.' He had to. My mother, Rosa Lee, had been sick for a good while with breast cancer, and finally passed in '45 just after Charlie was born. Daddy had lost his sweet Rose, but no way was he not going to raise her five boys to men.

"All five of us were delivered by midwives at home. There was Ezell in '34, BJ in '39, me in '40, Daniel in '42, and then Charlie. They say my mother was a smart woman, with academic inclinations. She was a rare woman to finish high school, which was the eighth grade in those times. I understand there were plans at one time for her to work as a teacher. But times were hard and survival was the priority. What my parents did with meager earnings was incredible.

"Out of those two dollars a day, Daddy managed to support his family and purchase this 40-acre farm, even coming out of the lean times of the Depression. He bought it in '42, plowed and worked the ground with his horse. Grew vegetables and sold them at the market. Raised hogs to feed us from. I think of heroes, I think of my father." *My grandfather.*

I was standing on 24 acres of land our family still owned, in the middle of a patch of a history that meant everything to me. That history swirled around me. When it came to a standstill, I was newly oriented into my universe. My grandfather had been born in 1881, a time still caught in the slowly receding shadows of active slavery. It does something to a young man, in 1996, to stand so close, only two generations separated from a slave reality so many people portray as having happened hundreds of years and dozens of generations ago.

That close brush lit me with ancestral passion. Long smoldering ashes woke. My lungs filled with determination to finish my grandfather's business of achieving full dignity for an African people here in America, even as my eyes spilled over with humility. Standing upon the ground of this man's resting place, regret took hold. I ached to have met him; heard his voice one time; felt the lines, rises, and falls of his face; to have felt his breath on me; caught the vibration of his laugh. I yearned to smell the leftover scent of his passage through the 1880s. Feel the leather of his skin, and look him in the eyes so our souls could have their say. I remembered sitting on Grandpa Potter's lap, euphoric, and wanted that same memory with my flesh and blood. I imagined Boss Jenkins placing his weathered hand on my shoulder and whispering to me in a gravelly voice, "Son, hard times are part of the living. You just keep on swinging your axe. You've got a lot of us behind you, and a whole lot to live for."

I soon noticed how the rest of the family playfully tuned Whitfield out when they could see he was about to go into one of his philosophical flows. But this was all new to me. I ate it up like a first meal after a desert crossing. Pieces were aligning in the vast hold that was my identity. Light was breaching into occluded places where moss-coated roots still survived, despite such a long drought. To me, this was no tired family history. It was my brand new reflection in the mirror.

Whitfield quickly recounted for me, as he had done previously in letters, his feelings about the circumstances of my life. In his typical understatement of emotions, he said, "Jaiya, it was hard for me to discover your circumstances and not have had the opportunity to take on the responsibility that was mine. The consolation I have is there is a God who will limit our suffering. I ask your understanding and forgiveness for the pain and frustrations I have been responsible for in your life."

The tone of his voice told me that he was struggling with that particular regret. "It's hard not to think back and wonder, 'what if,' but I know life has its own plan for us. It's obvious your parents did a great job with you. And I know that Mary acted on your behalf with love in what must have been a difficult situation. I have nothing but the highest admiration for her courage, convictions, caring, and stamina. And I can see that your parents raised you in an outstanding manner. I can find solace in all of that."

My ongoing need was to convince him, and Mary, that I held no resentment toward them. That I had not spent my childhood pining for my biological parents, and that I would not trade the life I had been given for any other. I wanted him to know I held him in a light without shame. Gaining familiarity with his sense of principle, I knew guilt came to him on the pages of that first letter he received from Mary. I hoped that his knowing me would relieve him of that heaviness.

I slept that first night in the house of my father, my family, with a joy and sense of familiarity that dropped me to comatose depths. Just as I had slept at Mary's home that first time I saw her, my body was now surrendering all its tension to a harmonious energy it recognized as its root. I slept every other night spent in that home with the same deep, womb-like peace. Each morning, it took extended time to climb the ladder back up to the living, waking world. A fact that quickly became a source of amusement on my family's part. "You know Jaiya sleeps half the day away when he comes down here," Rose would say, taking her affectionate jab at me. *If only they knew me like my family knew me growing up.* If only they knew the holding power of a 30-year reunion sleep.

I was a newborn baby the entire few days I was in Ocala— eyes wide open and searching. Scanning and absorbing. My senses were on alert, picking up the smallest object. I was so intense in taking it all in that I noticed even the cracks within the cracks of sidewalks. And oh how I tuned into the physical traits of my family. I had accumulated enough jokes through the years about my size 16 shoes to fill a volume of books. One of the first things I took note of was a sight that made my self-esteem purr like a tomcat after his first meal in weeks. I thought: *These people have some big feet. Praise the Lord.*

I learned that Tijuana, Ali, Whitfield, and Loretta had all attended Florida A&M University, about 180 miles to the northwest in Tallahassee. I thought back to the spring of my senior year in high school when I struggled with whether to go to college at Lewis & Clark or FAMU. Now, I could only shake my head in awe. Had I chosen FAMU, I surely would have crossed paths with my own sister without realizing it. *I would have walked the halls my father walked.*

In that youthful moment of high school, I had been drawn like a homing pigeon to the very same FAMU campus and to this greater northern Florida area where my ancestors on both sides of my family spent their seasons. Boss Jenkins, my grandfather, had been calling to me in 1985. He had crossed the Great River only a year before, but even after he became an ancestor, perhaps he needed to see his grandson come and stand beside his son. Maybe he needed to see the mending of the circle that had been breached back in 1967. All of those roots had been pulling at me in '85, like a sacred ground beckoning to a stalk gone astray. My wings still clipped, I had not been ready then to heed that call.

I was ready now. I adjusted to the sounds and rhythms of the house just by breathing easy and opening up into my own natural movement. I synchronized myself with the environment piece by piece. That northern Florida accent and cadence were new sounds playing wicked riffs in my ear. Especially the time-honed banter between Tijuana and Loretta. It had the rapid-fire quality of Mom's conversations with Grandma Danz, Donna, and Sue. Man, those two could flow. Their words played off each other like inhale off exhale. Intonations, pitch, rise, and fall. It was a music lesson masterful. Each day I translated it quicker, harmonized to it better. It went from rat-a-tat patois to smooth saxophone. It became familiar and ingrained.

I jumped into my role as uncle to Tijuana and Reggie's boys, Edgar ReVay and the baby, Jordan. They jumped into my lap just as quickly. This was another way for me to connect with my sister, through her children. ReVay was depth and emotion. Jordan was motion and commotion. He reminded me of my brother Rudy at the same age. When ReVay said, "Uncle Jaiya . . ." for the first time, I was a mess, though I hid it. Their father, Reggie, was good people, that's all—real, sincere, down to earth. And was that brother talkative! We struck up easy conversation over football, basketball, fishing, women, and life. Like an older brother, he soon fell into sharing his insights and lessons learned. I sopped it up. *Reggie Woods. Mary Woods. Something about the woods and me.*

Tijuana, like Loretta, was a strong, confident, intelligent woman. She fell close to her mother's tree. They were both whirlwinds of seemingly boundless energy, true heads of the household, running things. Loretta continued my reunion fantasy by embracing me as a son from the beginning. Loretta was a nationally recognized principal of Fessenden Elementary School and seemed to have more energy than a post-nap preschooler. She was a force of nature, and the love she had poured for all those years into her children, she chose to direct into me as well. She immediately doused my fear of how she would receive me. There were no 'steps' between us. We joined as kin. She became Mother Loretta, Mo' Lo'. Tears found their way through me. I loved her quickly and completely. *God, you have given me three mothers. For such richness, you must have a great task to ask of me.*

Immediately I saw that all of the Jenkins females were powerful, dominant women. Rose was the youngest but in no way the meekest. Her singing voice was like the good end of the garden's soil: rich, thick, swollen with life. She carried an intense sensitivity and perceptiveness. Rose had radar in her head and heart—she picked up everything in the people around her. Nothing got past her. She also was wonderfully blunt and honest. But if you cut past that, you found a compassionate, tender heart.

My fourth night in Ocala, we all went to Rose's debutante cotillion. Watching her in her special moment was an experience like being in a fairy tale. Rose was glowing and beautiful in her white dress; and the castle ball-like formality of the night was almost too much to take. She and two friends sang *Count on Me.* I was a puddle yet again. I took pictures left and right, brimmed over with pride, love, and wonder. *This is my own blood sister, Black and beautiful and a part of me.*

The whole time, I felt the persistent gaze of elder eyes on me from my backside. That was the evening that I met Papa Jack and his wife, Peachie. They were like kin or godparents to the family. Meeting them that night was a jump into the deep end of a pool of affection. Papa Jack was overcome at this reunion moment—more, it seemed, than any of us. I felt him soaking me up from his seat behind me during the cotillion. He rushed up to me afterward and introduced himself with a grin for the ages splashed over his cherubic face. Tears adorned his eyes and his smile just wouldn't let go. All he could say was, "Look at you! The spittin' image! Boy, Whit, you can't get away with this one. The spittin' image!"

With those words and that affection, I fell in love. I adopted Papa Jack and Peachie right there on the spot, and told them so, too. They felt just like the elderly Black couple I had never realized I yearned to have as grandparents. Not until that night, when Papa Jack and Peachie's loving Blackness eclipsed the light of my drifting days.

Before I went back to DC, my brother, Sultan Ali Jenkins, came home from school at FAMU. I was sitting on a stool at the counter between the kitchen and the living room. Ali came around the corner, and I stood to greet him. He must have had his growth spurt early, midway, and late, because my man was huge. An offensive lineman finishing out his senior academic year at FAMU, Ali was big-tall, big-boned, big this-away, and big that-away. I loved every inch of him. I had been worried about how he would receive me, but in my enthusiasm, I just wanted to smother him in a bear hug—if my arms were long enough to get around him. We hugged, anxious, hopeful, and overcome. Pride was first to my heart. Pride for a younger brother who was both a stranger and lifelong shadow unseen.

Relativity is powerful like the ocean, and just as deep. Surrounded by the skin tone of White and Hispanic people, I had always thought of myself as dark brown. Until I got out into the world and realized I was light-skinned compared to other African Americans. It took years for my identity to shift from that narrow measurement I took thousands of times in Los Alamos, to the more accurate and broad comparison I understood out among the truer variations of human tone. Being in Ocala cemented that awareness. I had to laugh, looking at each of my Jenkins family kin and realizing I was easily the lightest in complexion. I had gone from dark in a light-skinned family, to being light in a dark-skinned family. God had humor. Then He took me to church.

I sat in a pew in Greater Hopewell Missionary Baptist Church, and in a singular moment, realized I was the lightest-skinned person in the congregation. And although it was as if God were saying, *You are destined to always stand out*, it was also supremely satisfying to be immersed in so much dark skin. The symbol of my previous, shamed self-consciousness was here, all around me. Those who wore that skin wore it without the slightest second-guessing, ambivalence, or rejection. Here in this church, in this intimate space, the air hummed with the energy of mundane self-acceptance of dark skin as simply the way things were supposed to be. I remembered my days in the pews back in the Immaculate Heart of Mary Parish. There, holiness eluded me. Here, I felt the rush of energy that told me I was qualified to receive a Higher grace.

As those relationships developed, I learned things about Whitfield and the others that brought me comforting peace like extra strength cocoa butter on sunburned skin. The peculiarities of biological family connection were still new to me. When I found out that Whitfield also had long admired Muhammad Ali, I melted. When he told me that he had sparred with Ali down in Miami Beach, shortly before Ali (then Cassius Clay) fought Sonny Liston in '64, it blew my mind. Whitfield had even named his son, my brother Sultan, after Ali, as a middle name. I was astounded that a man I had clung to from afar for so long, a man whom I had fantasized was my biological father, had in fact danced in the ring, traded blows and sweat with my actual biological father. Growing up I had no clear concept of what I was missing, except that I was apart in some way from myself. Now that obscurity was coalescing into clarity. *This is what I was missing.*

No matter how great an athlete Whitfield had been, it was the way he have gave his life to the causes of his Black community that grounded my roots. I recalled Storyteller's words: *Your roots are up in the air, like a baobab tree. You can live long like that, but that ain't no way to fly a kite.* Now, I was seeing where my passion for human and civil rights came from—not only from Mary's spiritual impulse, but also here, from Whitfield's unyielding devotion. I learned quickly of his legacy of sacrifice

for his community. The résumé was evidence of a warrior
spirit:

- Three terms over 12 years as a governor-appointed commissioner on
  the Florida Commission of Human Relations
- Two years as peer-elected Chair of that commission
- Eleven years, President of the Marion County Branch of the NAACP
- Fourteen years, Third Vice-President of the Florida State
  Conference—NAACP
- Current First Vice-President, Florida State Conference—NAACP.
- Three terms over 12 years as Chair of the Ocala Housing Authority
- Current Chair, Ocala Lease Housing, a nonprofit developer of housing
  for low-income residents

Pride flushed through me. *Here is a true soldier . . . and he is
my blood father. I am passion's seed and was adopted and raised by
passion. This is who I am.* Most of all, I admired not Whitfield's
titles and accomplishments, but the spirit with which he had
endured the experiences. He remained most faithful to the men
and women living in modest homes like the one he knew as a
child in Bethlehem. He warred for those people. Not for the
ones who wore suits as symbols of superiority or who swung
their status around like wrecking balls. Whitfield stood with the
common man because that was who his father was. Like Dad,
forever faithful to the teachings of Grandpa Potter, Whitfield
would never betray his father.

My whole being filled up like a previously parched riverbed
as I began to discover the many ways, in personality and
mannerism, I was truly connected to these people, my family.
Little things like the way Whitfield and I get in and out of a car
the same way—head first getting in, butt first coming out. The
first time Rose saw me getting in the car to drive, she shouted
out, "Ma, look at Jaiya!" She and Loretta whooped and hollered
in disbelief over the similarity. I pulled at straws to build my
castle of connection. When I found out Whitfield's navicular
bone had been shattered from the bullet he took in Danang, I

was pleased to note the parallel with the fact that I had broken the navicular bone in my foot.

My brother Ali and I were of a completely different skin shade. But our mannerisms were eerily similar, as were those of Whitfield and me. I soon realized why, the first few times I visited Ocala, people on the streets were looking at me as though they had seen a ghost. Ali and I, to a notable degree, walked, moved, and made facial expressions that were reminiscent of each other. Each time someone pointed those similarities out, I became that little child, washed in a prideful wave of belonging. To be recognized in that way was like sweet water down my throat on a sweltering day. Ali's baby pictures, hanging in the living room, revealed a striking resemblance to my own. *Mom, you would not believe this. You might even think these are pictures of me.*

My bones recognized Ocala and Bethlehem as home from the beginning. I slept so deeply there, allowing the old community to visit with me in my dreams. Something in me roused itself in Ocala. This was not my imagination speaking— it was my heritage waking, my ancestral inheritance clamoring. I eventually attended the first two Adams family reunions, the family of Whitfield's mother, Rosa Lee. The first reunion was held, hot and sticky, out in the country woods outside Ocala. I was awed like a small child at Disneyland. I didn't know hardly a soul, but was being greeted by people by the dozens as kin. Young adults came up on me with, "Hey, cousin." Older women sugared me with: "Sweetheart, would you help me with this," and, "Whitfield's son? Oh my, look at you." My family membership was assumed—no confusion, no crazy facial expressions. My face held calm, but inside, I grinned hard at departed Alex Haley's spirit, recalling his own African reunion. *I feel you now, brother, I feel you now.*

The woods. I had been called here, to the cradle, where the heat and humidity fell heavy from the trees. I had the sense that everything growing in this place had been growing since the last century. This was a time machine. I learned more about the full-blooded American Indian roots of Whitfield's family only three generations preceding myself. I was surrounded with countless cousins, uncles, aunts, nieces, and nephews, and the masses of loved ones considered kin. Whether we spoke or not, didn't matter. That I was there, with them, was enough. Most of them could not appreciate this gathering in the way that I could. I was starving. I gathered up pieces of my family heritage like a greedy scavenger just before winter. It was a good harvest.

I soaked up the elderly ones. They were receding from this world only because they were outgrowing it. They were graduating. I soaked them up, because Storyteller was whispering things to me incessantly in my ear: *You know why the heads of some elders bobble back and forth uncontrollably? It is because their body and nerves have synchronized in double time with the beat of their heart. They are in harmony. This is taken as an ailment. In fact, it is a divine maturation. They've heard Glory's song.*

Ocala was truly the Deep South, only two hours or so away from the border of Georgia, and growing to know its subtleties was an experience. I could feel a distinct vibe between White and Black people unlike that in the Southwest, West Coast, and East Coast I had known. There was a clear distance between the groups, but in a peculiar way, less tension in the racial interaction. The coexistence somehow felt more natural, more honest about its friction and divide. This was no racial utopia, but at least the people were familiar with each other. I did not see an alien reflected in the pupils of the White locals, just a person who resided on the other side of their color line.

Ocala was like bathing in the Jordan River. It took me home in a powerful updraft of self-retrieval. I found myself in those obsidian evenings under the large evergreen oak tree at cousin L.C.'s, communing with a group of men two generations older—men whose cadence told of their timeworn, ritual gathering in this place. They spoke of mundane things with an understated brilliance of wisdom I knew could easily be lost to an ear that heard them as simple country Black men.

Their tongues spoke rhythm, foolishness, and neglected dignity unbridled: "What you do is . . ." and "I'm gonna tell you how it is . . ." and they did. Told it how it is.

I was silent again, this time for a good reason. They, I, we were a circle, left alone, simply 'to be', with no contortion, acquiescence, or mask of grin and deference. We were Black males undone. Not that tempered light that lurked through mainstream days. We were imperfection without chaperone, grilling barbecue in the smokehouse, choking on the thick smoke, drinking gin from paper cups, passing conversation from one mouth to the next with the trusting surety of a veteran relay team. There, I found the substance that eluded me earlier in my days. It was my sweet inebriation.

"Jaiya? Rise and shine! You ready to do some fishing?" Mother Loretta pulling me, tortured, from my early morning sleep, just like Mom did all those times before. Except Loretta is kinder— no yanking the sheets clean off me, no setting the dog on me, no fable about doughnuts waiting on the table. Mo' Lo' needn't have been so resourceful as Mom had to be, dealing with a child who tried his best to sleep half the day away. Not now, not here. I feel my past all around me, taunting me to prove myself on the waters. I rise quickly, excited by the prospect of the catch. Rose is calling us crazy as we head out in Reggie's pickup, boat tied to the back, heading for the bait shop.

Rose and Tijuana will taunt us mercilessly if we return home empty handed—I'm determined to show them I know something about fishing. The moment takes me, and I'm back with Dad and Grandpa Potter, roused from sleep in a dawn still unborn, frigid black sky greeting us as we dare to coax trout from a New Mexico water hole. I'm back . . . with my cousin Dale, on a small boat under a prima donna sun, pulling 48 catfish from a rock quarry in Illinois—a once in a lifetime bounty I still am not sure was not a dream.

Now we're on the Bayou, or on Lake Harris, or Lake Weir. I'm in the boat with Reggie, Loretta, and one of their fishing partners, Bronson or Chap, and Loretta's already boasting and competing, like we're playing spades or bid whist. It's that healthy, bonding flair of Black intimacy, found on ball courts and at the card tables, and it's flowing now. The strongest gender in this boat is clear, and it's not male. *Look'it this woman.* Scent cloud of the schools of fish coming off the surface. Even here, there is a racial phenomenon. As it is my nature, my spirit tunes to it, studying. I had seen the arenas of sports and entertainment loosen the shackles restraining White and Black from engaging each other as human. Now I see it happening again, and the stimuli are lapping waters, boats, and the meditative goal of making skeptical, lazy fish take the lure. Across boats separated by a few feet of water, Black and White speak to each other, like humans:

"Morning."

"Morning."

"What you working with today?"

"Worms. You pulling anything?"

"Got a few blue gill, some shell cracker. I left some for you. Fid'na try that hole over there."

"Good luck."

"You too. Enjoy the day."

It is a ritual, this conversation. It is contained within its boundaries but sincere with its affection. The true impulse of a person is revealed when the overwhelming beauty of nature cleaves social detritus from hearts like fish from the bone, and lifelong racial lessons are for the most part left behind on the shore. This is the impulse to commune with living things, even with those in the 'other' category.

Temple, church, holy place—that's what this is. Baking under Florida's morning sun on placid, quiet lake water, perched in a boat pulling mullet from their bed; or seducing catfish from the pier—good living. But it is more. It is how I pay homage to the simple Black lives lived before me. My imitation of past lives cast in the under-glow of a society that called them savage. The lake waters are my shrines. I go there to sit a spell with lonely spirits that are my family. And to let my skin get black in the same sun that shone, right here, on my grandfather 120 years ago.

The relationships continued to fill me up. Going with Ali around the corner to talk late night with Loretta's sister, Big Ma, and her husband, Big Daddy, was an act Ali had performed hundreds of times over. For me, meeting kin folk was spectacular, fireworks to an infant. I didn't take that for granted. Growing into the Jenkins part of my family filled me up more than they would ever understand. I had never sought out a romantic ideal in them. In fact, I wanted to know their bruises and blemishes, just as my family and I had shared ours back on the volcano's belly. I sought the texture of their imperfection. As I shared in their joys and tears, struggles and fears, the more I was made whole by an attachment deferred.

The Jenkins family shone light on the Whiteness I had known, just as the Potter family shone light on this Blackness of which I was now a physical part. The two families were divergent in one way that served as a classic portrayal of White and Black mindsets. My adoptive family did not often speak on race—to them, it was a subject. A subject that was largely external to them. It floated out there in the air as dust they could only see when the light through the window was right. They could choose to speak on that subject if they wished, or if circumstances forced them to do so.

To the Jenkins', though, race was not a subject. It was their life. They were subject *to* it. They talked about it as freely as they spoke of the weather, without discomfort, shame, or fear. It was old and worn to them, even for Rose, the youngest. When you have truly, consciously reckoned with a thing your whole life, it tends to lose its power to discomfort you. It becomes the weather. And just like the weather, it is there to greet you every single day.

Wounds were closing and my spirit was rearing up rapidly—fueled by knowing my biological family. I had filled in trenches and canyons in my being as I opened myself to my root. This was new earth within me. I could stand on it and use it as a foundation for improving my relationship with my adoptive family. As with Mary, Allan, and Arnold, knowing the Jenkins' allowed me to strengthen my attachment to Mom and Dad, and my adoptive siblings, even Greg. My adoptive family seemed to notice from afar that my reunion with my biological family was a good thing. They could tell that it was not driving me further from them, but was instead allowing me to heal and develop in a way that caused me to drift toward them.

Privately, I sat on those stools in the Jenkins' living room in wonder. We studied the differences and similarities in each other. They were fascinated at the opportunity to witness the manifestation of a blood relation forged in Whiteness. I was eager to absorb the subtle, layered traits of their Blackness, to hold it up against my own. Much of what they saw as different in me from them, they attributed to my having grown up around White people. *If only they knew.* They could not know how similar they were to my family in New Mexico—the contrast of skin, hair, and facial features was a thin mask overlaying a substantial commonality. And where the two families diverged was not always in the way they would assume.

I sensed my Black family viewed me in part through the prism of their understanding of White culture. It was a perception of Whiteness that, relative to my intimate one, seemed one-dimensional. I had been reared in that sea and knew well the extreme variety that was there. My differences from the Jenkins family were much more a product of my personality than of White cultural influence. From my unique vantage, I marveled at the cosmopolitan swirl of family, race, and personality I was privy to now.

I had lived and loved as family and friend in both the homes of White and Black human beings. Life chose me, among others, to be an intimate student of these two enduring

U.S. American antagonists. I had been stretched by the task, but light had also dawned in my mind; light so brilliant and freeing that my only response was devotion. Devotion to this relationship we struggle so mightily with—Black and White. Truth was a giant totem before me. So many White people greatly suffered from a prejudice of superiority that had left them blind to human beauty and validity in so many people of this world. Too many Black people suffered from a prejudice of wounds that had crusted our hearts over with stifling protective layers. A crust that had clogged the passageways for our inherent spiritual love—honor for others, for each other, and for ourselves.

Black and White, we were tragic souls in a land of richness and poverty unable to extend fully out to one another because we could not first extend completely into ourselves. The failure to love in one direction ultimately had ceased the flow of love in all directions. We were, as my mentor Tom Pettigrew had always exclaimed, victims of the tyranny of prejudicial actions, ideas, and crimes against the spirit. Our inclination, our gravitational pull was to love, even across boundaries, but social pressure kept us confined within the powerful arms of conformity.

I saw it in pristine vision now: my purpose. James and Darlene Potter were in me. I was Dad's son, with his same irreverence for conformity. There was no shame for me now in standing apart from the crowd; making choices and taking paths in my life that were directed by my drum. My father spoke his passions through subatomics and physical laws. I would speak out on the ways in which we humans coexist with each other—the substance of spiritual laws. And like my father, I would not be silenced. My individuality left others confused and unsettled—I was not living my life in the image they construed for me.

I was Mom's child, with her willingness to sacrifice comfort in order to nurture and protect what she believed in. Looking ahead, I knew much of the world would scathe at me for what I stood for, like it had at Mom for the children she chose to stand by. She gave me her grit, toughness, determination. *We stand by for the long haul.* Mom's life enabled me. I had precedence.

My adoptive fate—this man and this woman, this family— was of a Higher wisdom. I had been an acutely sensitive Black child, placed in a White family, in an excessively White community. My life had been a vivid acid-test. I was the litmus paper dipped in the mercurial substance of human spiritual health. I had come up stained in colors that told two stories: one of love and possibilities, the other of fear and retreat. I had gone down to the Potter's house and received my message: *As the clay may be shaped, so shall I shape you to do my bidding, as I have shaped you all. In this house, you shall be forged, and neither the sting of it, nor the song of it, shall be the lesser contribution. For it is by My left hand and My right hand; by the sugar and by the salt; by the day and by the night, that you shall take your form.*

Those who rage
but hold their tongue
and bow before their torment
are meant
for torture's steady rot
and the shame of true imposter

shine brightly
every ounce your given light
horde not a bit that
heavenly gleam
happiness is honesty unleashed
and nakedness is pure
as holy water turned to steam

HEALING IN THE SAND

THIS dream is true. I swear it so.

Storyteller appears. She is now exactly my height. Cowrie shells
hang from her ears, glinting in the sunlight. Lowering herself
into a cross-legged squat on a tree stump, she begins to shoo
away dragonflies with Indian paintbrush stalks, while chewing
on honeysuckle blossoms. She opens her mouth abruptly,
launches into a mid-conversation tone, as though we have been
talking for hours. Wearily, she says, "My child, I do not think
you have heard the greatest adoption story ever told."

"Why do you say that?" I ask.

"You walk with the weight of an isolated man. You are not
anchored to the legacy from which you are wrought. Sit here
next to an old lady and give me company. I shall give you your
anchor." She begins. Her voice changes quality. It is erudite
and efficient—seemingly inhabited by a spirit unknown to me:

"There came to be, upon a patch of reeds beside a river in the north of Africa, a baby, contained in a thatched floating bundle. A young woman discovered the baby. He was brought to live with another woman. This baby became a boy, raised alongside another boy, as brothers.

"As they aged into the confused land between childhood and what men were told they should be, cracks emerged like fine snow crystals on the embroidery that joined them. In physical body, the boys diverged. The heir grew muscled, firm in the face, the crown of his head closer to the sun. The other stretched into a wiry slenderness, and the muscles beneath the skin of his face became slackened beyond their years.

"The slender one was struggling with the steadily churning sound of a river somewhere beneath him. The water flow sounded itself wherever the boy stood. Each passing season showed him more so that he was the only one in his family, in his community, that could hear this sound; and that he was the only one affected by its vibrations. He knew the core of this river shadow had to do with the fact that he was a Hebrew, while all those around him, including his lifelong brother, were Egyptian. It was obvious to everyone due to his physical appearance. It was an increasingly dominant truth to him because of the private river beneath him. He heard the words calling to him. *I have brought you to this house so that you may receive My message. I have made you for this.* A voice was growing, spoken only to him, and the voice was a canyon widening by the day, with himself on one side, the people of his life on the other.

"His struggle became tangible the first time he chastised his friend: 'Ramses, how can you be at peace with the enslavement of Hebrews by Egyptians?' Ramses was not only shocked, but also offended that his dear brother would voice such a thing. The conversation that followed revealed truths that had resided since the slender one was a baby, being pulled from the riverside, and in fact, for generations long before.

"'Moses, people are not responsible for their own station in life. That is God's doing, such as how you were brought to my family. I have always seen you as different from other Hebrews. You know that.'

"'I am not comforted by the fact of your seeing me as different from other Hebrews. I *am* Hebrew, Ramses, and I cannot help but be disturbed that you have even a small amount of inferior regard for a people that are a part of me. It makes me feel apart from you and all of this family and community.'

"'Would you had rather we left you by the riverside?'

"'Ramses, when you have sought solace upon my shoulder for the pains of your life, even those pains that I have caused you, have I not sat steadfast in empathy, listening, supporting and always respecting that which has stricken your heart or fouled your mind? But when I speak to you of my greatest turmoil, why is it that your only resort is to accuse me of a lack of gratitude? Why are you not able to face the truth of what I am saying and grant me the right to my own heart's grievance?'

"Moses continued. 'Is that all I am to you, the symbol of your own charity? You performed no charity. Rather charity was done for you. Whose night owns this bitter wind? Not yours but God's. The circumstances of our lives are not made only by men, as our swollen self-regard would have us believe. A child owes gratitude only for the nature of a relationship, not for the act that brought the child into the home.'

"Ramses was lost. He repeated his mistake. 'Moses, we brought you in and gave you a better life. Where is all this anger coming from?'

"'Gave me a better life than what? Than I would have had among my people? Than I would have had by the river's edge? You do not know my fate. It is not your place to judge whether I would have had a lesser life. All that matters between us is the humanity we provide one another in the life we do share.'

"'Moses, you have always been sensitive. I believe the problem lies within you. If only you would move past this Hebrew contemplation of yours and just focus on being human.'

'"But Ramses, it is exactly because I am determined to be human that I take umbrage with your lack of humanity in regarding not only me, but also Hebrews as a people.'

'"You are well provided for, educated, healthy, and held in high regard. What do you have to be upset about?'

'"Should I bind closed my mouth with river reed lest I disturb your ill-conceived tolerance of my true nature? The Egyptian part of your own humanity has always been embraced, Ramses. You do not nearly understand how little peace you would have without that.'

'"Moses, I have loved you like a brother, and my family has loved you like all its children. We have sacrificed for you, fed you, and raised you. Is this not love?'

'"Let us speak of love, Ramses. While you and others celebrated in your minds your goodness by means of loving me, there I lay at night, smote by your incomplete love for me. Your love never reached me in the place where I was most vulnerable and needful. Your love never reached me in the place where I am Hebrew. All around me, I have seen Hebrews in bondage. I have stewed and torn at the unspoken yet awful dripping conversation of Egyptian disregard for Hebrews. All the while, there I stood as the unseen centerpiece to that conversation. It is like spending a lifetime in the middle of a feast where everyone is toasting their superiority over people like you, and then you are expected to raise your glass the highest and toast the loudest, or be called a traitor. What madness is this?

'"Love?' Moses was in full steam now. 'What work have you done to achieve that total love for me? I have seen not the sweat upon your back or brow. I have seen not the tears to fall or the pure, whole-body cry of reckoning with the terrible truth of your place in my people's long torment. I am sorry, Ramses. You and your family have not loved me in essence. You have only loved the image of me you wished to be true.

'"Ramses, I fear the day will come when you and I will face a great and costly sundown. You will ask me to choose between you and your family and those who I am descended from. And all along, I will have only wanted both parts of me to be a thing in which I could find honor. On that day, you will demand that I betray everything my soul shouts to me, in order that you may maintain your incomplete love of me. And Ramses, I am telling you now. I may have spent my life muted and submissive to your Egyptian pulse, but on that day, I will stand not on the side of the Hebrew or the Egyptian, but unrepentant under the burning sun of God's demand that we grant one another a total love.

"Moses persisted, 'Ramses, hear me, for I was born in body in the days before I was plucked from the riverside, but in spirit am I born only now: I would walk through the breast of the sea before I betray for another day this that I believe in. Love is easy. We love each other in portions and degrees. Total love, a name for honor, is a greater thing. I know you love me with all of your heart. But all of your heart reaches only a portion of me. I will know that you love me fully when you show me that you love my people.'"

I will know you love me when you show me that you love my people. Those last words of Moses, as recounted by Storyteller, are a fading echo that brings me back to present time awareness. I am sitting beside her on a lump of volcanic upheaval. Shards of yellow sunlight play as piano keystrokes on our backs as the pine tree canopy moves like a dance partner to the wind.

"Yessir, Pharaoh loved him some Moses. But love is more than roses," she grumbles. Before I can take a grown breath, Storyteller moves quickly as a hummingbird, reaching into her pouch, pulling forth a handful of corn pollen. She murmurs, "This stuff was gathered by a virgin, you know. Most powerful healing medicine there is," wiping it with three fingers on my forehead, cheeks, and lips.

I smell only the beginning of the corn pollen's scent and then I am gone. Down a spiral in my mind, a swirling dark blue and black chute into another dimension. When I next see light, it is refracted and wobbly. I am underwater in a river. I surface for air and from surface level see a Forest Service officer walking up to a Spokane Indian. The young Indian is crouched down in the river, his face close to the water surface.

"What are you doing crouched down there in that salmon spawning bed?" the officer demands, accusingly.

"I am whispering to the salmon of their journey ahead." the Indian answers. He is sure of voice and perturbed at being questioned about the obvious. "Their road has been made perilous by your kind."

"What do you mean, 'my kind'? We work hard to make sure these salmon are fished only by those with the proper license."

"*That* is what I mean by 'your kind'," the young Indian replies. He is already fatigued of this nonsense.

"But how can you question our commitment to the welfare of these salmon?" The officer is indignant and confounded.

"I have known of your strange ways since I was on my grandmother's knee. She told all of us little ones, 'Those who do not value the spawning bed do not truly value the salmon spawned from that bed. Do not look toward that part of the stream from where the salmon are being pulled for your answers. Look with your strongest eye toward that part of the stream where the journey begins. There you will find solutions and there you will find those whose concern has roots into the center of the Earth.'

"Now, please go," says the young Spokane. "Your noise about licenses and commitment is drowning out the whispering I must do here."

I cannot hear the officer's reply to the young Spokane, for I am at that moment pulled back underwater by a hand clenching my ankle. I lose time as I drift in the blue blackness. Then I am back on the basalt boulder next to the old lady with a child's hands. She is munching acorns, complaining about their taste. "You are older than I am, you know," she says.

"What do you mean?"

"You were made as a funnel. All of the world's emotion comes through you—like saltwater through a seaside cave. But you have not learned how to carry it or how to heal. Not in the old way. This has aged you. You must learn the old way."

"What way is that?"

"The way of the sand."

"What must I do?"

"Over there, on the ground, in that patch of sunlight. Get on your knees. Now, take that stick and draw a large circle around yourself. Good, now inside the circle, draw the world of today. The world that offends your soul."

I am unsure of the task and my skill for it. "I don't know about this," I say.

"Give me an animal," she says.

"What?"

"Give me an animal. Name me an animal."

"Eagle," I say, humoring her bizarreness.

"Good choice." She makes me an eagle. I fly.

Cold ossifies and becomes my skeleton. In that chilled state I descend from a cloud and behold the nightmare of my imagination. I am overhead the Atlantic Ocean, and it is molasses in motion. I sweep down closer, and the molasses takes on a grainy quality. I am reminded of a vision of millions of buffalo carpeting the prairie in the time before the great slaughters. I am close enough now to see that the waves have faces. *There are Africans in the water.* I am witnessing 150 million Africans swimming the Atlantic. Three hundred years are condensed into this one moment. They swim, saltwater stinging their wounds, giant plankton pushing its way down into their throats. They are a poor imitation of whales, they have no baleen; they are choking. Panic grips me as I recognize . . . *all the faces are mine.*

These Africans are not swimming so much toward Africa as they are toward a spirit destination. They seek reunion with their dignity. Their progress is painfully slow. The waves sink and surge. The Africans pitch and yaw in that awful carriage. Then I can see beneath the water's surface. *There* is the obstruction. There are bones in the water. Bones of those who swam before them, but could not make the distance.

I reach down to help . . . at least one of those swimming. My fingertips almost touch the back of one, when I am caught in an updraft. I am flying high into the azure sky again. I arrive at my grandfather's grave in Bethlehem. As I realize the meaning of the inscription on his marker, a light dawns. The inscription reads: "Boss Jenkins, Sr., February 17, 1881 to February 7, 1984. It occurs to me: *It has been said that the maximum conceivable span of a human lifetime is roughly 135 years. Contrary to popular history's tongue, slavery still smoldered at the dawn of 1900, one hundred years ago.*

I understand in this moment a truth of our nation's social survival and my own childhood. We must recognize that slavery, as a phenomenon of human degradation, occurred not hundreds of years ago as is popularly contended, but rather one conceivable human lifetime ago. My Black childhood in White hands was one human lifetime removed from slavery. Its long shadow extended not only over us, but well past and ahead of us in time. My own grandfather was born to former slaves, in 1881. When he came into the world, Harriet Tubman was spry and yet 24 years from joining the ancestors.

My father's father was born to former slaves. I hover over this gravesite, dawn of truth exploding in my mind. We are a society very much still in the shadow of that monstrosity that fused the nervous system of our racial relations. We are barely born out of that season. Cure is a scoundrel coyote, prancing back and forth on the horizon, valleys away. In this form, I have the eagle's vision. I see everything. The whole panorama of our society is played out before me.

My gaze catches a particular scene in motion. A disturbed teeming anthill of disarray unfolds beneath my flight. I see myself standing on a blackened trading block, a ghastly grin across my face. Invisible fingers are creating that grin, pulling back my lips to reveal the story my gums would tell. I am being judged for my fitness to be placed in a family. I am Barter's bastard child. I see myself marching in a parade of thousands of children. We are led by people who swear to themselves and others that they have no prejudicial, biased, or blinded attitudes. We children teeter toward an abyss laid with good intentions. I am dizzied by my view, sickened in flight. Adoptive parents, blistering with fear, are running away from their own children. Not away from the children's physical bodies but from their spirits, from their *Truth*.

A downdraft interrupts my horror vision and carries me to a riverside. Storyteller is wading in the water. I hear an osprey crying. "That's not a bird," she contradicts. "That's Kokopeli playing his flute. It's healing time. Over there, go to that fallen tree and kneel in the sand," she says.

"Wait," I say. "What have you done to me? You just sent me through my worst nightmare."

"Don't ask a question if you are going to answer it yourself."

"You call this healing?"

"You must see a wound, and know it like a longtime lover, before you can tear it from your being. It must first flood you. It has to hurt. That is the glory of pain. Something you all have become too soft to commonly endure. That you have made it back here is a good sign. Now, go and kneel."

That woman will be the end of me.

Storyteller thinks to herself: *I am your beginning.*

"Now, draw your circle, as you attempted before. Let your hand be guided by inspiration. This time render the world as you envision it in its divine form. Envision perfect harmony and balance."

I sit, staring at a billion sand particles. This is beyond me. Storyteller grumbles and comes from the water, hiking the soaking bottom of her dress up over her feet. Usually barefoot, I notice she wears moccasins, though she has been in the water. Reading my mind, she explains, "Sand gets hot during these things."

"What things?"

"The Tibetans call it mandala. My people call it sand painting. It is a prayer for healing. For the past hour, while you were an eagle, you were in a meditative state, cleansing yourself, preparing for the Great prayer. Now it is time for your mouth to shut and your soul to open. Draw."

She sprinkles corn pollen onto the crown of my head. I smell roasting piñon nuts, though no such trees grow here. I disassociate from my body. I watch from a few feet above as my hand draws intricate lines and symbols in the sand. The tide is rising but each time it rushes up, it seems to shy away just before it reaches my circle.

I finish. Amazingly, both circles I have drawn this day are there in the sand. The first circle, of my wounds, is somehow drawn as a center circle, with this new circle a concentric ring around the first. My artistry makes me proud until I remember I was not the artist.

"Are you through strutting your plumage, peacock?" Storyteller digs at me. "Now listen, to complete this prayer, this experience, you must get dirty. Lie down on top of the circles and roll around."

Confused, but wise enough not to question at this point, I do as she says. The sand scalds my skin. I do not remember having stripped off my clothing, but I am naked. Storyteller's witness to this is no more discomforting to me than if I were nine months of age, and she were my mother, pulling me from my bath. *I am sinking in the sand.* My memory retrieves a bird's eye view of Greg, Kristin, and me, on our backs making snow angels at Urban Park back in Los Alamos. I am rolling, fading, sinking. . . .

Fever takes me to delirium. I race across time in a direction I cannot discern. The travel and the pace of it lag me yet I retrieve my energy soon after I arrive. The first thing I see is a small bird on a small branch of a tall tree. The bird, the branches, the plum-shaped seeds hanging down—all are painted in sunlight from the East. It is sunrise. A river runs. Trees with stilts for legs grow out from along the banks. In the hollows inside those stilts, turtles float in the water's edge, watching me.

I do not know what form I have taken, but my vision is sharp as it was before. The landscape opens wide in front of me, stretching boundlessly. Mesas stand as castles everywhere. A rainbow bleeds all its color into the bottom stripe—a surreal crest on a utopian day. I see the things that I have dreamed of and they are real.

Water, great and wide, serves as teacher to us all. Its placid surface, navy blue and velvet, puckers to the air, kissing it with ripples that grow pregnant, ripening into expanding circles. The ripples follow each other like toddlers after their mothers, chasing the larger ripples ahead as they run toward shore. Sky kisses back, bestowing raindrops that disappear into the water surface, joining that largeness and causing their own ripples. This wide water is Life, desperately trying to teach us about the laws of spirit: There is abundance and integrity in the circles. Nature, She is redundant. She always returns to what works.

The circle . . . this shape, flow, force is recognized as a God-Thing, with designs and fertility beyond our comprehension. Child welfare as a system honors the Africans in the water, who are now children. They still carry my face. In the swells of a sea now much more placid, those faces are smiling, their feet no longer entangled with the bones below. The placement of all children into foster and adoptive homes follows a guiding principle that honors familial and cultural roots. *Now, finally . . . I am my brother's keeper.*

This is a model of *concentric placement.* There is a circle of life, through which a child and all living things come to this world. That circle has purpose. The closer to the circle center a child is—womb, woman, family, community—the higher the concentration of those ingredients crucial to healthy development. Ingredients designed and endowed by Creation, life, and the generations. Honoring the power of these concentric circles allows children the *best opportunity* to develop a holistic sense of identity, and thereby a healthy spirit. This holism is composed of meaningful and positive connections and attachments to the child's heritage, unique nature, and life purpose. The approach minimizes the detachment, alienation, and isolation with which all children struggle.

I see all of this before me and weep. The child I once was has now spoken and has been heard. My old skin is now no more than a flimsy sheath left on a rock far behind. Still feverish, I drift through dimensions and come to the fall of 1998. This is not a dream. I am back in my waking mind, where reality is brisk and raw. My daughter has been born. My adoptive and biological families have come to take part in the naming ceremony. Virtually all the pieces of my soul have converged at this, the moment of my greatest gift, this birth of new life.

I am flooded with grace. The two worlds that had always drifted in separate orbits now occupy the same space. I am standing at the center, fearful, overcome, swallowed up in the blessing. My White adoptive family, with its Midwest and Southwest peculiarities, is finally encountering my biological African American family, flavored with its southern ways. *Did I really ask for this much?* I did. My heart is more than in my throat; it is bursting from my breast.

I stand in the middle of the two families. I am frightened to death with a need that I cannot bear to have go unfulfilled. I am shaking. If these two families do not honor each other, but instead are so much as tinged with my lifelong haunt that is racial illness, then I will be lost. I will not believe in either of their loves. I will be an orphan again, a child of prejudice. I am shaking as I watch their eyes meet. I see their flesh touch and their spirits react. This is my Moment of Truth because . . . *I will know you love me when I see that you love my people.*

They love my people.

Tears fall so hard on the inside I drown from within. I keep the waterfall private because I cannot explain the release of three decades of tension. More air is released in the room as all my family, adoptive and biological, have the opportunity to confront their fears and curiosities by meeting each other. Faces and races become people and pulses. Ideas become human. Anxieties flee away into securities of the flesh.

Mom and Mother Loretta fall into an old ceremony together: preparing the feast. *Eat plenty. Eat plenty.* Fish fries. Women things happen between them. Dad and 'Pop' Whitfield find their hold in philosophy, meaning-of-life things. They talk of their new, shared granddaughter. Man things take place. And in that space, in my small home smoky with tears of skillet oil, a new family is made. It is all things Southern, Midwestern, and Southwestern. It is athletic and scientific. It is both pumpkin and sweet potato pie. I witness. My spirit soars high. At that very moment, out in New Mexico, a drought takes hold that will give birth to a forest fire that will consume the house in which my soul grew fractures.

The Diné have a saying: "T'aa akó t'éhí," or, T'aa akó dí," which means: *That's the last word; It is done; finished.* As the two circles of my family stand together, gathered around my daughter, my heart is clear: *It has come to this. It took Its sweet time over three decades, but Circle has completed Its course.* My gratitude is a prayer. I punctuate my *Amen* with the Diné word painting sacred lines inside my soul's cavern where I once hid away: *T'aa akó t'éhí . . . completion has come to me this day.*

Djembe drum calls us for the naming ceremony. Transported, we are beside the Kamby Bolongo (*Rio Grande*), its talking current our escort to the ancestor world. The circle moon above us is an ivory stone lighting the sky into an indigo lake. For the first time, the indigo feels good as it blankets me. I am hot and moving toward a breach. As I bring forth the newborn girl child, my own skin has a placental sheen. My mom and dad, and mother and father, and from afar, my mother, watch the rest of me come wet and naked into this world. I hold my daughter high above my head, cradled in my hands, closer to the astral ivory stone. My words to her are a prayer:

"Behold, the only thing greater than yourself . . ."
That you shall never feel my pain
"Behold, the only thing greater than yourself . . ."
That your own pain shall bless you as mine has me
"Behold, the only thing greater than yourself . . ."
My God: I thank you for this life.

She is, *I am,* born.

This book is a prayer I send to the sky: For all the children whose nights
are long and fears a sorrow song, may your voices be heard.

AFTERTHOUGHT

HERE has been written a prayer: that the reader will have
come here with a newborn's openness, to hear of a story and
be touched in the place that makes change. This was the book I
least wished to write. Yet I was hounded for years by a
responsibility to the children of foster care and adoption, and
to our imperfect humanity as we strive to achieve harmony
amongst our souls.

My childhood was far from a tragedy. It was sublime and
seeping: erosion in a flower garden, browning of the leaf. It
was a good life. It was a life embroidered with pain. The first
truth does not eradicate the second. The second truth does not
diminish the first. Both stand on their own as stories to be told.
Woven together they become more than stories. They become
a celebration. I have sought to obey the saxophonist in the
alleyway—not grinning in the place where I grieve, not
shaming in the place where I celebrate.

Representing thoughts and emotions through italicized
words was an important aspect of this storytelling. So much of
my experience was not contained in words spoken, but in
hidden, suppressed energy. Those forces reached me just as
surely as if they had been spoken. Their silent quality also made
it all the more difficult for me to express to others just what I
was experiencing, because there was little tangible evidence of
it. Especially difficult was explaining it to those who were not
motivated to tune into my unique experiential frequency.

My silent, invisible reality was not much different than
what African Americans have always grappled with and
attempted, with great frustration, to articulate. It was for me

like moving through an invisible medium of barely audible whispers, haunting echoes of hostility, and shifty fumes dismissed by others as illusion. This reality was a swim through the sepsis of racial aversion. A contaminated emotional water table, latent and deep, but doing damage as sure as it is there, dwelling. If it had a scent, it would be sulfuric. If it had a physical form, it would be hollowed out and expansive, like New Mexico's Carlsbad Caverns, laced with oozing stalactites and stalagmites, unfettered in their colonies beyond the reach of sunlight. It is not easy to communicate this reality, much less live it. And those who would adopt Black children, those families of any race, must be willing to walk through those very same caverns their adopted children will unavoidably traverse.

Today, many adoptive families share their children's adoption stories from the outset of the relationship, in celebration and honoring of that truth. In my case, much of the details of my life, recounted here, were not available or revealed to me until I was writing this book. Three decades is a long time to wait to be introduced to yourself. One of the ancestors' most urgent lessons to us is clear to me now more than ever: *Know your story.* There is limitless power in the story. That is why it is the first thing taken from a people or person in an attempt to control identity.

In truth, it was not until the last few weeks before finishing the manuscript that my story started speaking to me without shyness. It began to speak up soon after a phone conversation with Mom, in which I felt for the first time ever the energy of encouragement from her in support of my voicing this long muted part of me. In the conversation, we traveled together back in time, mother and child, to those distant but like-yesterday moments when she soothed and stroked me with the lyrics of her love. A love posed upon a beautiful voice musically painting folk songs all over my skin like the mineral oil I had been massaged with as a baby.

In retrieving our memories of lyrics to those songs, something shifted in my chest. The veil of anxiety and fear that obstructed my reaching into the private treasure chest where my story resided dissolved an amount. Enough for me to feel for the first time as though I had Mom's permission to *speak on the things you are, my son, speak on the things you are.* That is when I began to cry and laugh in red rivers and blue waves of poetry. For all of life is but a poem. What marvel-inspiring forces of nature mothers truly are; somehow everything always comes back to and down to them.

The universe walks in circles and so do we. Life demands repeat performances and duplicated circumstance. As I give birth to this story I am 33 years of age, the same age Mary was when she gave birth to me and then endured our separation. As I bear forth this bawling infant, this story, Mom and Dad, due to the wildfire, temporarily live in the same apartment that they resided in back in July of 1968, when I first came into their home.

Through a larger mischief consistent as the tides, we are, all of us, very much like the trees, gathering rings of interconnection inside ourselves as we accumulate our seasons. And in the end, all stories are one. With this story, I seek to honor this life with which my Great Spirit God has enriched me, and in doing so, to honor my family and all the beautiful ones who have left their imprint inside of me.

An irreverent man of wiry build, who shot jumpers and sarcasm with equal enthusiasm from the roost of his outdoor basketball court, once told me, "First-time writers tend to be self-indulgent." Well, Old Man Vince, this book has been ultimate self-indulgence. But just as you may say, "At least I took the shot," I now may say, "At least I told the story."

Great God is my Storyteller and Story tells that this is done.

T'aa akó t'éhí.

Jaiya John

Jaiya John lives in Silver Spring, Maryland. He is blessed with the beauty of his daughter, Jordan, and serves his life's mission as a teacher through writing, speaking, and mentoring. He is the founder and executive director of *Soul Water Rising*, a human relations mission, and a former professor of social psychology at Howard University in Washington, DC. **Web site: www.jaiyajohn.com**

Niambi Jaha and **Eric Gann** created the cover design for this book. Ms. Jaha, a fine artist who lives in Chicago, also served as the publishing midwife for the book. She is the founder of *Project Butterfly*, an institution supporting young women and girls of African descent through the transitions of life. **www.projectbutterfly.com**

The Medicine Wheel depicted inside this book is a powerful and common spiritual artifact and symbol in various American Indian cultures—portending healing and good fortune. It is made round to represent the Circle of Life. The cross in the center represents the four winds, four seasons, four directions, and four grandfathers (teachers). The centerpiece represents Sipapu—*The Place of Emergence*, or the creation of the world or universe. Traditionally eagle feathers were used, but being sacred are not sold commercially. This artifact is *strong medicine*.

WWW.SOULWATERRISING.COM
WWW.JAIYAJOHN.COM

Printed in the United States
67665LVS00002B/121-123